Woodshop
Dust Control

Woodshop Dust Control

SANDOR NAGYSZALANCZY

The Taunton Press

Cover photo: William Duckworth

Taunton
BOOKS & VIDEOS

for fellow enthusiasts

First printing: 1996
Second printing: 1998
Printed in the United States of America

A FINE WOODWORKING Book

FINE WOODWORKING® is a trademark of the Taunton Press, Inc.,
registered in the U.S. Patent and Trademark Office.

The Taunton Press, 63 South Main Street, Box 5506, Newtown,
CT 06470-5506
e-mail: tp@taunton.com

Library of Congress Cataloging-in-Publication Data

Nagyszalanczy, Sandor.
    Woodshop dust control / Sandor Nagyszalanczy.
        p.   cm.
    "A Fine Woodworking book"—T.p. verso.
    Includes index.
    ISBN 1-56158-116-X
    1. Woodwork.   2. Dust control.   3. Wood waste.   I. Title.
TT180.N27   1996
684'.08—dc20   96-10487
                                                          CIP

About Your Safety

Working wood is inherently dangerous. Using hand or power tools improperly or
ignoring standard safety practices can lead to permanent injury or even death. Don't
try to perform operations you learn about here (or elsewhere) unless you're certain
they are safe for you. If something about an operation doesn't feel right, don't do it.
Look for another way. We want you to enjoy the craft, so please keep safety foremost
in your mind whenever you're in the shop.

This book is dedicated to the memory of my teacher and mentor Gregory Bateson, who taught me the ways of inquiry that daily give me the courage to untangle the tangled web of technical information and transform it into plain ideas that make sense.

ACKNOWLEDGMENTS

First, a special thanks goes to Curt Corum at Air Handling Systems and to Peter Fedrigon and Robert Witter at Oneida Air Systems for all their kind and tireless help in educating me about the technical aspects of dust collection systems.

Thanks also to the following manufacturers and their representatives for assistance and support: Jon Behrle at Woodcraft, Chris Carlson at the S-B Powertool Company, David Draves at Trend-lines, Michael Eads at Racal, Liz Finnigan at Freeman/McCue, Irvin Hauser at Dust Boy, Todd Langston at Porter-Cable, Ed Levy at Penn State Industries, Mike McQuinn at Ryobi, Quintin Rottering at Beam Industries, Mark Schiefer at Delta, Jamison Scott at Air Handling Systems, Raymond F. St. Louis of R.F. St. Louis Associates, Chen Sun at Sunhill, and Robert Terry at Teckaid.

For the technical support they offered, I'd like to thank woodturner Stephen Blenk, Karen Grober, Warren Hudson of CS&S Filtration, John McConegly (General Manager of JDS), air-handling consultant Jeff Millstein, Chris Minick, Haskell Mullins and Brian Pridgeon of 3M, Rick Peckham (air-filtration specialist for Airguard Industries), Thomas Retford of Cincinnati Fan, and Paul Wrobleski (president of P&S Filtration).

I'd also like to thank friends and those woodworkers whose shops I visited who helped with photos for the book, including Jeff Applebee at MacKenzie-Childs, Andrew Church, Kristin Decker, Lloyd Diamantis, Michael Fisher at Toys of Yore, Cliff Friedlander, Ann MacGregor Gibb, Roger Heitzman, Eric Himlan, Klaus Meyer at G. Stickley, Steve Robins (for his insights and celestial observations), and Jeff Watson.

Finally, I'd like to thank my father, Lorant Nagyszalanczy, for his patiently crafted drawings that so well illustrate the concepts presented in this book.

CONTENTS

CHAPTER 9
Collection Hoods and Other Devices

INTRODUCTION

Some years ago I visited traditionally trained Japanese carpenter Makoto Imai at a tea house he was building in Marin, California. He seemed to spend an inordinate amount of time sharpening and setting the blade on his wood-bodied, pull-style hand plane. But when he guided the tool along a 10-ft. long beam of Port Orford cedar, that immaculate blade produced a shaving as wide as the blade and as long as the beam. The shaving danced off the edge like a scroll of poetry unrolled by the muse of fine craftsmanship.

I kept that shaving, and often wish that every shaving and chip that I produce in my shop could be as lovely and inspiring. But no matter how nice the furniture I've built over the years might be, the shavings, chips and dust that result from my efforts are only debris. It's stuff that piles up and makes a mess of my floors and benchtops and occasionally clogs my nostrils and chokes my lungs.

I think most woodworkers agree that sawdust is one of the banes of the woodshop: an unfortunate and messy by-product that we can hardly avoid (even Imai has to sweep up the floor in his shop). Sawdust and chips are time-consuming to collect and a nuisance to get rid of. And unlike the small piles of neat shavings that Imai produces when he planes a beam, woodworking machines churn out great heaps of chips and shavings, as well as throw a ton of fine wood dust into the air. And as medical studies continue to reveal, fine dust isn't only a nuisance, it can pose a significant health hazard. Does any woodworker really need more convincing that woodshop dust must be controlled?

One way to handle the problem of wood dust is to forsake modern cellulose-munching machines and become a traditional hand-tool user. But I, for one, have been unable to wean myself from modern mechanical conveniences. Instead, I have tried to do what most other woodworkers do: control and abate the dust and chips created in my shop so they aren't such a big problem. The hard part is knowing which devices and methods to choose from the extensive assortment available for dealing with woodshop sawdust.

Some devices, such as shop vacuums and central collection systems, are designed to capture dust at its source—at a woodworking machine, a sanding table or a work station where portable power tools are used. These devices provide the most direct and efficient means of dust control, since the majority of chips and dust are captured and collected before they can escape. Heavy chips that end up on the floor can be vacuumed or swept up, but the fine dust that ends up wafting about the shop can remain respirable for hours. Airborne dust can be abated by several different secondary control methods, including ventilation and air filtration, or by wearable protection devices such as disposable masks, replaceable-cartridge respirators and powered air-purifying respirators.

Unfortunately, buying the right respirator to protect your lungs or picking a collector powerful enough to handle your shop's sawdust output isn't as straightforward as the process of buying a hand plane or a table saw. It's not unusual to be confronted by a confusing maze of facts and figures when shopping for dust control and collection equipment. Wading through technical data about particle size, filtration efficiency, airflow and ductwork sizing, and cfm and static pressure ratings is usually more befuddling than helpful. A troubling result is that many woodworkers end up with dust control equipment that provides only a poor or partial solution to their dust problems.

It is my goal in this book to acquaint the reader with a complete range of modern dust control devices and methods to suit just about any small-shop situation and style of woodworking. I'll present the technical information that you'll need to choose and use these methods and devices in layman's terms that you won't need an engineering degree to understand. And I'll suggest some ways to help you achieve effective dust control without breaking your budget.

The chapters of this book are arranged to progress from simple and inexpensive dust control measures, such as wearing respirators and ventilating dust from the shop, to more complex and expensive means of dust abatement, including shop vacuums and portable collectors on up to full central collection systems. Because installing a complete central system is an involved undertaking, the last four chapters are devoted to covering all the steps, from choosing a collector and designing ductwork to fine-tuning the system for best performance. Whichever dust control measures you choose, you'll end up with a cleaner shop that's more pleasant to work in, with air that's safe to breathe. Once you've adopted your own system for tackling dust, I'm sure you'll never allow a little thing like sawdust to get in the way of your enjoyment of woodworking again.

CHAPTER 1

The Problem of Dust in the Woodshop

As a by-product of the woodworking process, sawdust is created at practically every phase of a project: when the lumber is dressed (with thickness planers and jointers), when parts are cut out and machined (with power and hand saws, routers, shapers and drills) and when parts are shaped and smoothed (with stationary sanders and hand and power finish sanders). Different types of operations create different-sized chips, from large shavings to fine dust. This assortment of wood debris can present a variety of problems for the woodworker, from being a mere nuisance and a hassle to get rid of, to being a safety hazard and posing a serious risk to good respiratory health. In this chapter, I'll examine these problems, and then explore solutions in subsequent chapters.

Different forms of dust

It's important to differentiate the various kinds of dust created in the woodshop because each type of dust is best contained and controlled by a different set of strategies. Further, you'll need to consider the amount of different-sized debris you create when selecting and sizing your dust collection system's filtration. Let's start by looking at each kind of wood debris (see the photo on the facing page), how it's created and what kinds of problems it presents to woodworkers. Sizes

Different kinds of woodworking tools create different kinds of wood debris, including large shavings from a hand plane, chips and sawdust generated by bladed and bitted tools, and fine wood powder created by sanding operations.

obviously aren't absolute—a single tool and operation can produce a wide range of sizes of dust particles and wood debris; I've separated them out here only for the sake of discussion.

Large shavings

The largest shavings typically found in the woodshop are produced by cutterhead tools, including thickness planers, jointers and shapers (fitted with long or large-diameter cutters), and hand tools such as chisels, carving and turning tools, and hand planes. These tools typically shear wood from the surface or edge of a board, removing fibers in thin sheets, as shown in the drawing at right.

Hand operations such as planing a surface with a well-tuned hand plane can remove wide, continuous sheets of wood—not unlike unrolling a roll of paper towels. Shavings produced by a machine's rapidly spinning cutterhead are shorter, since the cutterhead travels through an arc, with each blade stroke removing a short shaving as it passes through its cut. Thickness planing or jointing long-grained softwoods (such as pine and hemlock) at slower feed rates produces longer, larger shavings, while planing short-grained hardwoods (such as mahogany and ebony) at higher feed rates produces shorter, smaller shavings and chips. Shaping operations with large cutters can also produce large shavings and chips, as well as small chunks of wood that are occasionally torn from a shaped edge or surface.

Because of their size and volume, large shavings accumulate very quickly and occupy a lot of space. If your shop is small and you don't get rid of large shavings regularly, you'll end up with pulpy mountains that can trip you underfoot and make getting around the shop hazardous. Stationary machines with dust chutes or catch bins can fill up so quickly that shavings clog the tool's cutterhead. The catch bin on my old Davis and Wells 6-in. jointer works fine during the occasional

Large Shavings

Large chips and shavings are created when bundles or sheets of fibers are sheared from surface or edge of wood.

Cutting action of plane blade

← Grain direction →

edge dressing, but can quickly get stuffed when I'm doing any significant amount of edge trimming, say when preparing a gang of boards for gluing up into panels for cabinet doors.

It's astonishing how quickly you can generate an extra-large-plastic-trash-bag's worth of shavings when thicknessing a stack of boards on a thickness planer (see the photo below). The shavings seem to pile up faster than snow during a winter storm in Buffalo. One of the most common problems that results from not collecting large shavings from a thickness planer is that the shavings end up on top of the board just ahead of the outfeed roller. The roller then presses these shavings into the top surface of the board as it is expelled from the planer. You end up with shavings that must be scraped off the surface of the freshly planed board or, worse, a series of shallow depressions where shavings have been embedded into the surface. This problem is particularly vexing when taking deep cuts on very hard woods; the thick chips can leave indentations that are nearly $1/16$ in. deep!

Large shavings can also present significant problems when shaping with large cutters working with the grain of the wood, during tasks such as raising panels or shaping railings and large moldings. If the shavings aren't collected, they accumulate around the cutter and tend

Without dust collection, the large shavings generated by even a small thickness planer can grow into mountains of debris that require cleaning up after each planing session.

to obscure the operator's view of the cutterhead and workpiece, which is clearly very dangerous, especially since there's a natural tendency to sweep shavings out of the way with your hand.

Turning wood on a lathe can also produce sizable shavings that can become a nuisance. With a properly sharpened tool taking a shear cut, continuous shavings can stream off the edge of the tool like ribbon unwinding from a spool. When turning green wood, these long, fibrous shavings can quickly obscure the edge of the tool and entangle the tool and/or the turner, posing a hazard as well as a nuisance.

Because of their relatively large size and weight, shavings are the most difficult of all wood waste to collect, even with a small central dust collection system. It takes more capture velocity (the speed of the collector's air suction) and a higher volume of airflow to capture and transport large shavings than to collect smaller chips and sawdust. A powerful, well-designed central collection system provides the best means for successfully collecting shavings from woodworking machines. Shop vacuums with small-capacity canisters can quickly become overloaded, and long, stringy shavings easily clog the small-diameter (1-in. to 1½-in. dia.) hoses found on many models these days.

Chips and sawdust

Chips and sawdust are produced by a very wide range of cutting tools, including power and hand saws, boring tools (such as drills and countersinks) and small- to medium-sized shaper and router bits. Depending on the type of blade, bit or cutter and a number of other variables, debris can range in size from shredded-cheese-sized chips to fine-grained sawdust. Generally, large chips and coarse sawdust are produced by cuts taken with the grain, as when ripping stock or dadoing on the table saw (see the top drawing at right). Smaller chips and finer sawdust are created by cuts taken across the grain, as when crosscutting (see the bottom drawing at right), or by cuts into end grain, as when cutting tenon cheeks on the table saw, plunge-cutting a mortise with a router or boring dowel holes in a face-frame rail (see the drawing on p. 8). Other factors that influence the coarseness or fineness of chips produced include:

- The design of the tool: the number of knives/teeth and their design, relief angles and gullet sizes, as well as the diameter of a cutter and its rim speed. Router bits or small shaper cutters with more flutes/knives tend to produce finer shavings. Rip blades with chisel-like low-angle teeth and large gullets produce longer shavings than cut-off blades with ATB (alternating top bevel) teeth. Larger-diameter, faster-spinning blades and bits generally take more cuts per inch, and hence produce finer chips.

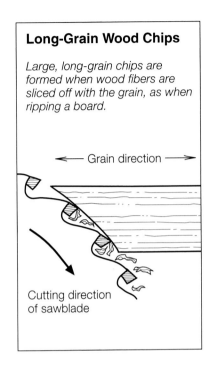

Long-Grain Wood Chips

Large, long-grain chips are formed when wood fibers are sliced off with the grain, as when ripping a board.

← Grain direction →

Cutting direction of sawblade

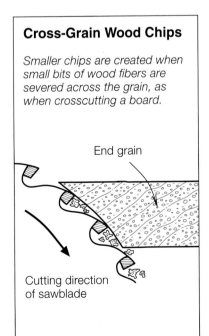

Cross-Grain Wood Chips

Smaller chips are created when small bits of wood fibers are severed across the grain, as when crosscutting a board.

End grain

Cutting direction of sawblade

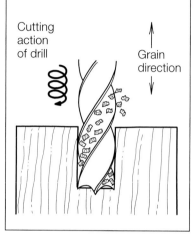
- The type of material and its strength and density: Cutting dense hardwood produces smaller chips than cutting softwood. Plywood tends to produce smaller chips (since cutting in any direction cuts through layers both across and with the grain). Cutting and machining particleboard, hardboard (such as Masonite) and fiberboard (such as MDF, or medium-density fiberboard) produces fine dust, which also includes dust from the adhesives used to manufacture these products.

- The condition of the blade or cutter, including sharpness, balance and degree of runout. A dull sawblade tends to make finer dust than a sharp one, and a poorly balanced cutter or blade with lots of run-out takes a slightly wider cut, thus producing slightly more sawdust.

- The nature of the process, such as regular cutting with a shaper or router bit vs. climb cutting (feeding the stock with the direction of bit rotation, instead of against it). For example, climb cutting creates chips that are shorter and blunter, which are thrown out differently by the tool. Also, higher feed speeds tend to produce smaller chips.

Although they are less bulky than large shavings, chips and sawdust can also pile up with surprising rapidity. Often-used machines, such as table saws, that aren't served by a dust collection system can quickly accumulate enough sawdust to clog the working parts to the point where you can't tilt or lower the blade easily (tilt stops for square and 45° cuts are probably thrown off as well). If you own a table saw with an enclosed base (such as a Delta Unisaw or a Powermatic model 66 saw) that isn't connected to a collection system, you've undoubtedly had frequent occasion to open the trap door on the base and scoop out copious quantities of sawdust (see the photo on the facing page). Shaper and router tables can also generate mountains of chips and sawdust, even when using relatively small bits and cutters.

In addition to clogging a machine or power tool's internal works, accumulating sawdust can also lead to ruined workpieces. Small chips that keep the end of a board from bearing flush against an end stop or fence will result in parts that are cut too short or too narrow. When working freehand with a portable power tool such as a saber saw, free-flying sawdust tends to obscure the line of cut, often resulting in a miscut.

An important reason for sucking away chips and sawdust during the cutting process, as opposed to just sweeping them up afterwards, is that it actually reduces the dulling of cutting edges and teeth. Chips that aren't evacuated from the area of the blade/cutter often bounce around and are recut many times before they're ejected. This repeated cutting causes more heat buildup in the cutter and dulls teeth quicker, since they're doing more work than they need to.

It's astonishing how quickly sawdust and chips can accumulate under closed-base machines, such as this table saw. If not cleaned out regularly, chips can quickly foul the tool's works.

On a less technical level, sawdust also has a tendency to stick to the bottom of your work shoes (it seems to have a special affinity for the tread pattern on sneakers). You end up tracking it around the shop and, if you work at or near home, into your house as well.

Fine wood powder

Although small amounts of fine wood powder are produced during most wood-machining operations, powder is primarily created when you sand wood. Whether you deposit a thin layer of powder on the bench or create an ominous cloud of woody effluent is greatly influenced by your means of sanding. Random-orbit sanders (electric or pneumatic) are hard to beat for their ability to smooth a surface quickly

Power sanders, such as this random-orbit sander, can make quick work of smoothing rough lumber, but create clouds of extra-fine wood powder in the process. This fine wood powder is easily airborne, where it becomes both a nuisance and a health hazard.

and efficiently, but they are notorious for throwing out great billowing clouds of dust in every direction. Even if you simply sand by hand with a piece of sandpaper wrapped around a wood block, you still end up creating a noticeable amount of very fine dust.

Fine wood dust is composed of particles that are really broken pieces of wood fiber abraded from the side, face or end grain of a board (see the drawing below). Think of each particle as a tiny chip that's been scraped off by an abrasive particle (glued to a paper or cloth backing) as it scours the surface of the workpiece. Generally speaking, the finer-grit sandpaper you use, the finer the abrasive particles and the finer the size of the dust particles produced.

Sanding dust initially poses a problem to the abrasive used to create it: Fine wood dust created by power sanding equipment, such as drum sanders and stationary belt, wide-belt, disc or oscillating spindle sanders, tends to become embedded in the surface of the abrasive where it clogs the abrasive particles and decreases their efficiency. This problem is especially marked with resinous woods such as pine and oily woods like teak. As more dust becomes embedded, more heat is produced during sanding, which causes glazing that can shorten the life of an abrasive disc, drum or belt or ruin it very rapidly. Since a replacement belt for a wide-belt sander (such as a Timesaver) can easily cost over $100, surface clogging can be a big problem indeed.

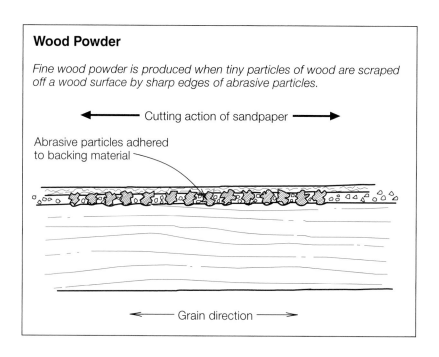

Wood Powder

Fine wood powder is produced when tiny particles of wood are scraped off a wood surface by sharp edges of abrasive particles.

← Cutting action of sandpaper →

Abrasive particles adhered to backing material

← Grain direction →

Most other problems caused by dust are the result of the particles' smallness: Very fine dust is measured in microns (one micron equals one *thousandth* of a millimeter). Large dust particles, 100 microns and bigger, tend to fall to the floor quickly. In contrast, wood powder can be so fine that particles are easily suspended in the air where they waft around for a long time (a 5-micron particle stays aloft for 30 minutes or longer, depending on the amount of air movement in the shop). The lightness of the particles explains why you can run a power sander over a large panel, blow or brush the top clean, and then come back half an hour later and find a thin layer of fine powder recoating everything. If you don't keep the floors and benches tidy, just picking up a board or walking around the shop can raise a dusty cloud. Even the act of tidying up with a broom and dustpan can stir the dust up. This fine dust also makes it difficult to do any kind of finishing in the same space that you make sawdust; particles continue to settle as the finish dries and you end up with a nubbly surface.

Fine dust easily floats under doorways and through ventilation ducts, to infiltrate spaces adjacent to your workshop, such as your office, finishing booth or, if your shop is attached to your house, your living room. This dust also clings tenaciously to your clothing and travels indoors whenever you run in for a cold drink in the middle of a work session.

The good news is that it is much easier to capture and collect fine wood dust than it is to corral larger chips and shavings. The air volume and velocity produced by most shop vacuums is sufficient to collect the dust produced by portable power tools that have ports for connecting a dust bag or vacuum hose. Dust production during hand-sanding operations can be mitigated by the use of shop ventilation or an air-filtration device (see Chapter 4). And capturing the dust produced by a large drum or stroke sander with a central collection system isn't much of a problem, provided that the hood that directs the flow of air to capture the dust particles is well designed (see pp. 169-172).

The bad news is that the fine dust that isn't captured can present the most serious hazard to the woodworker: an assault on respiratory health. Ironically, it's the smaller dust particles—10 microns and less—that can create respiratory problems that range from mildly annoying to life-threatening, as we'll see in the next section.

Revealed by the beam of a bright flashlight shining in a dark shop, fine dust particles glow like a shaft of illuminated fog, a phenomenon known as the Tyndall effect.

Sawdust and respiratory health

Most woodworkers who have installed dust collection in their shops, be it a small shop vacuum or a large central collection system, rest easy thinking that they've got sawdust beat. But usually there's still an invisible culprit lurking in the shop: the wood powder with particles so small that it can pass right through the filters on some vacuums and the fabric used in some central collection bags. Like demon seeds ready to unleash contagion, these diminutive dust particles are so light that they can travel around on the air itself, held aloft by static electricity or circulating air currents. You can barely see them under ordinary lighting, but they're there, remaining airborne for hours after the last board has been sanded. If you have any doubts, shut the lights off in your shop some evening after a sanding session, and then shine the concentrated beam of a flashlight across the shop; the light will reveal a swirling swarm of talcum-powder-like dust (see the photo above). The phenomenon is known as the Tyndall effect; you've seen it in the movie theater when dust or smoke passes in front of the projection beam. What's more insidious, the smallest of these particles are invisible to the eye yet are the most harmful to your lungs.

How small are the fine dust particles that can harm us? Particles between 10 and 20 microns (we can't even see individual particles smaller than 100 microns; that's one-tenth of a millimeter) tend to become trapped in the outer passages of your respiratory system (resulting in the grotty goo that you see on a clean hanky when you blow your nose after a sanding session). Minute wood-powder particles—particularly those between 0.3 microns and 10 microns—easily penetrate deep into the farthest reaches of your lungs, even into the tiny air sacs called alveoli. Really tiny particles (under 0.3 microns) are small enough to be expelled by exhalation.

How fine dust hurts your lungs

Because we breathe in a certain amount of dust in our everyday lives, our bodies have built-in protection mechanisms, as depicted in the drawing below. These respiratory defenses include nasal hairs, which

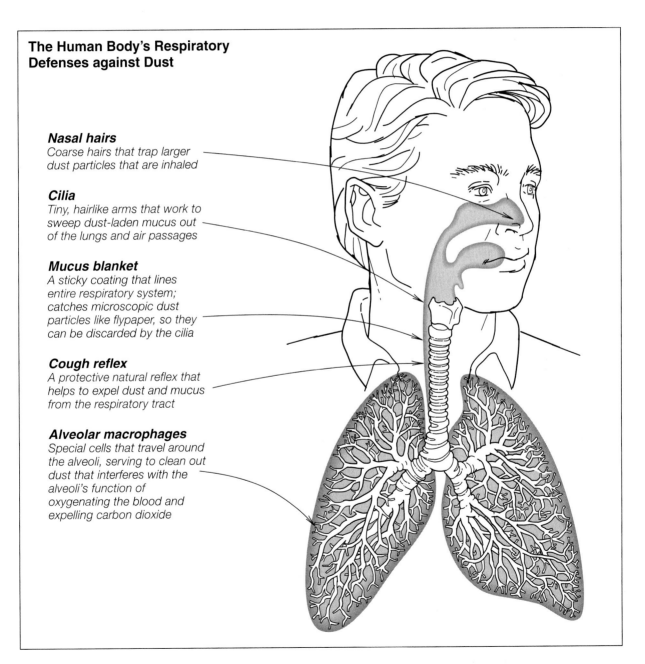

The Human Body's Respiratory Defenses against Dust

Nasal hairs
Coarse hairs that trap larger dust particles that are inhaled

Cilia
Tiny, hairlike arms that work to sweep dust-laden mucus out of the lungs and air passages

Mucus blanket
A sticky coating that lines entire respiratory system; catches microscopic dust particles like flypaper, so they can be discarded by the cilia

Cough reflex
A protective natural reflex that helps to expel dust and mucus from the respiratory tract

Alveolar macrophages
Special cells that travel around the alveoli, serving to clean out dust that interferes with the alveoli's function of oxygenating the blood and expelling carbon dioxide

snag large particles as you inhale; the mucus, a sticky blanket that lines your respiratory tract and acts like flypaper to capture errant dust particles; and the cilia, which are tiny hairs that line your respiratory tract. Like the tentacles of a sea anemone, the cilia work to transport dust particles trapped in the mucus (using a beating motion that takes place about 10 times each second) and move them toward the back of your throat where they can be swallowed or coughed up. The cough reflex is a protective reaction that works to expel the mucus and dust that can build up in the respiratory system. Finally, there are the alveolar macrophages, which serve to clean out dust that gets into your lungs' alveolar sacs.

Minute dust particles harm us by interfering with the lungs' functions in a variety of ways. As large quantities of dust particles become lodged in the lungs, they tend to foul the dust-ejection systems described in the paragraph above. First, large amounts of dust clog the natural cleaning action of the lungs' cilia, which leads to irritation. As the cilia become more clogged, their effectiveness is reduced, so the lungs lose capacity to eject dust. Eventually, chronic exposure can lead to permanent damage of the lungs' tissues, which can result in the buildup of scar tissue.

By restricting the absorption of oxygen into the blood, chronic exposure to fine dust can lead to shortness of breath and dizziness. Further, the effects of dust can weaken the body's natural defense mechanisms, making you more susceptible to bacterial and viral infections and illnesses. The results of long periods of exposure to fine wood powder are very similar to cold and flu symptoms and typically include coughing, sneezing, bronchial inflammation, shortness of breath and a runny nose as a result of increases in discharge of saliva and phlegm from the respiratory passages. The kind of lung problems that sometimes develop in woodworkers from chronic inhalation of wood dust are similar to those developed by longtime smokers: chronic bronchitis and emphysema. Worse, chronic exposure to wood dust may even cause lung cancer (the International Agency for Research on Cancer has classified wood dust as a Group 1 carcinogen).

Another kind of health problem that can be directly linked to exposure to fine wood powder is nose cancer ("nasal adenocarcinoma" in medical vernacular). Woodworkers are about 1,000 times more likely to develop nose cancer than non-woodworkers (although only one out of every 1,500 active woodworkers will ever have to deal with this horror). As with the respiratory problems described in the previous paragraph, nasal cancer tends to develop over many years, sometimes with decades between initial exposure and the outbreak of symptoms.

Other dangers carried in wood dust

In addition to the harmful effects of the dust particles themselves, woodworkers can also be negatively affected by certain soluble chemical components carried in or along with wood dust. These chemicals include a whole gamut of resins and extractives, commonly found in (but not limited to) exotic species of hardwoods. Extractives serve a living tree by repelling insect attacks and retarding the decay of the tree's non-living heartwood. Wood dust carrying extractives can exacerbate the effects of the fine dust particles themselves or cause allergic reactions in woodworkers who are sensitive to the extractives' chemical makeup (sometimes after only limited contact). These chemicals include natural compounds with frightening-sounding names, such as alkaloids, glycosides, saponins and quinones. Wood species with extractives that are more prone to cause allergic reactions include redwood, mahogany, boxwood, Western red cedar, yew, satinwood, teak, ebony and wenge. Western red cedar is one of the most infamous of these species, because it contains an allergen called plicatic acid that causes a condition commonly know as "red-cedar asthma."

Another possible source of allergic reactions from wood dust are the spores of fungus that can be contained in the dust. Certain funguses cause decorative staining in woods, known as spalting (see the photo below). Even fungus occurring in the bark of a tree can cause allergic reactions. A condition known as "maple bark disease" is ostensibly caused by the fungal spores found in maple bark, which are released when the wood is cut or when maple burls are turned on the lathe.

Decorative wood popular for turnings, such as the spalted olive turning at left, or as lumber for furniture, such as the spalted maple board at right, can cause severe reactions in persons allergic to the fungus that causes the spalting.

As well as the potentially harmful effects of the natural compounds found in wood, there's also the danger of being exposed to the dust from adhesives used in woodworking. These include glues used to manufacture wood-based materials, such as particleboard and plywood, and glues used to make parts or assemble projects. Some of these adhesives, such as polyurethane glue, contain compounds such as isocyanates, which can cause severe reactions in some people. Working with recycled wood (from old houses and barns) can also present health problems. Surfaces may have once been coated with lead-based paints or treated with wood preservatives, which typically contain toxic substances, such as pentachlorophenol and copper naphthenate (known commercially as "copper green"). Pressure-treated lumber has also been impregnated with these kinds of preservatives. When you cut, plane, shape or sand such wood, you create dust that can carry these substances into your lungs, where they are subsequently absorbed into your bloodstream.

Severe symptoms from exposure to the chemicals in wood dust may include skin rashes, headaches, facial swelling, wheezing and coughing, and conjunctivitis (irritation of the eyes). Fine dust from tropical woods, such as Indonesian teak, cocobolo and rengas (Borneo rosewood), can cause irritation to the skin. Ingestion can also be a factor, since particles trapped in the mouth and nose usually end up getting swallowed, where toxins are absorbed by the digestive tract. Even touching these woods can cause skin rashes in some people.

Just as with the respiratory problems from fine dust particles themselves, what makes the breathing of other chemicals carried by wood dust such an insidious problem is that symptoms don't always manifest themselves quickly. Unless you develop an allergic reaction that suddenly alerts you to a wood-dust-related health problem, symptoms might take years—or even decades—to appear. I read one story about a longtime woodworker who was commissioned to build a couple of dozen redwood cabinets. One afternoon, he noticed he was having difficulty breathing (his bronchial tubes became inflamed by the volatile oils in redwood dust, causing constriction in his air passageways). By the time he got home, his breathing was so labored that he had to go to the local emergency room, where a doctor diagnosed a condition known as occupational asthma. Treatment required him to take a bronchial dilation medication, and, because his air passageways were sensitized and prone to overreact to *any* kind of dust, he had to stay away from dusty environments (such as woodshops) and continue taking medication for several years.

As with most serious health problems, it's always more difficult to overcome a problem once the body has experienced chronic damage. This is yet another good reason to evaluate your dust control needs carefully, so that you're not trading your future good health for the enjoyment (and income, if woodworking is your vocation) you get from a lifetime of woodworking.

How much dust is too much?

How much wood dust can you breathe and still be safe? To protect people who work in the wood-products industry (as well as in dozens of other industries), the Occupational Safety and Health Administration (OSHA) has developed a set of guidelines for wood-dust and worker-respiratory safety. While the regulations imposed by OSHA are designed for woodworking businesses with one or more employees, the guidelines provide a good introduction to understanding how little fine dust it takes (over time) to cause respiratory problems.

To meet current OSHA regulations (in effect since September 1992), a shop's dust control measures can allow no more than an average of 5 milligrams (1 gram equals 1000 milligrams) of dust particles 10 microns or smaller per cubic meter of air over an 8-hour period (known as a "time weighted average" or TWA). For an average small shop (say, a 24-ft.-square garage with 9-ft. ceilings, equal to 147 cubic meters), the OSHA standard would allow a maximum of 735 milligrams (about a half-teaspoon) of wood dust over an 8-hour period. This means that in a single work day, the average amount of fine dust allowed by OSHA in a cubic foot of space equals only a little more than one-tenth of a milligram—about the weight of a flea! Allergy-prone dusts, such as Western red cedar, must be kept down below half that amount: 2.5 mg/cu. meter over an 8-hour period. While these amounts are averages over time, OSHA also specifies a ceiling for dust concentration for any longer than 15 minutes. The ceiling for wood dust, known as the "short-term exposure limit" or STEL, is 10 milligrams per cubic meter. At the time of this writing, OSHA was about to instigate new air quality standards; for information about the latest OSHA standards, contact your state office, listed under "Industrial Relations" in the State Government section of your local phone book.

What's more, OSHA standards are not the strictest. Other studies I've seen state that the maximum level of respirable particles should not exceed an average of *2* milligrams per cubic meter of shop space over an 8-hour period. In a garage-size shop, this translates into less than 300 milligrams (a quarter-teaspoon) of dust per 8 hours. While these amounts may sound minuscule, daily exposure over many years clearly has no small impact on respiratory health.

How can you tell if your shop has too much fine dust floating around in it? Unfortunately, you probably can't. To quantify accurately how much airborne fine dust there is in your shop requires a direct sampling measurement, which is done by taking a sample of dusty air and then processing a predetermined volume through a special device that tells how much dust there is in it. You can hire an industrial ventilation specialist to come into your shop, evaluate your dust problems and make recommendations as to remedies for them. However, hiring a specialist is an expensive proposition usually necessary only for professional businesses, and one that most hobbyist and part-time woodworkers don't really need to undertake.

But, on a practical level, if you're doing any power sanding without some form of collection at the source and spew out great clouds of visible dust, you can bet that you're churning out unhealthy levels of invisible, respirable dust as well. Regardless of what tools you use, if you find yourself picking gobs of dust out of your nose at the end of an average day of woodworking, you can be quite sure that you're being exposed to too much dust.

For most of us, the best way to ensure that the air quality in our shops is not deleterious to our health is to act preemptively: Control fine dust before its adverse effects become a problem. The means to put the kibosh on dust involve implementing control measures such as collecting at the source, using air-filtration devices and wearing personal protection devices such as respirators, all of which are discussed extensively in later chapters of this book. Controlling fine dust is especially important if power sanding is something you do often, because no other form of dust production equals the output of power sanders.

Fire and explosion hazards

Beyond the risks of long-term exposure to wood dust, the greatest immediate hazard of having wood chips and dust around the shop is the risk of fire: Just think of what you typically employ to touch off a blaze in your fireplace or barbecue—it's probably fine wood kindling. Any wood debris, from shavings to chips and sawdust, can be ignited with remarkably little effort. A tiny spark generated from the operation of a machine's on/off switch, from an electrical cord being pulled out of its socket, or from the process of grinding a sharp edge on a turning chisel (see the photo on the facing page) can be all it takes to turn your cozy shop into an inferno.

Smoking in the shop is clearly a grave hazard; I heard one story (which fortunately didn't end tragically) of a tobacco-toking boss who had his workers frantically shovel a mountain of planer shavings into the

Grinding an edge on a tool, such as this turning chisel, can generate a shower of sparks that can quickly ignite any fine wood powder that's collected around the base of the grinder and cause a shop fire.

street after he'd accidentally dropped the glowing end of his cigar into the pile. Similarly, tossing an oil-finish-impregnated or solvent-soaked rag on a sawdust-strewn floor or chip-filled waste is asking for trouble. Even if your shop is usually clean and tidy, it can't hurt to keep a fire extinguisher on hand to prevent a small fire from becoming an all-consuming blaze.

Although it might not seem obvious, fine wood dust can also pose a very high fire risk in the shop (as well as an explosion hazard, as discussed below). There are many documented cases of shop fires caused when fine dust deposited in a thick layer atop overhead light fixtures was ignited by the heat of the lamps; with fluorescent lights, the heat of the ballast can be enough to cause a fire.

Believe it or not, chips and shavings from working unseasoned wood, such as from turning green wood, can also pose a fire hazard. Damp shavings left in a pile produce organic heat, like a compost pile, and can even generate enough heat to combust spontaneously. Just to be safe, remove damp shavings from the work area or keep them in a fire-safe container.

Cleanliness is the best way to prevent a fire in a workshop. Even if your shop has a central collection system, make sure to get out the shop vacuum and clean any piles of chips that build up around benches and machine tools (even well-designed central collection systems aren't 100% efficient; some chips end up around the bases of the machines). If your shop has overhead lights, get up on a ladder once every few months and vacuum off the top surfaces of hanging fluorescent fixtures or the reflectors on incandescent lights. The wand attachment that comes with most shop vacuums is a great tool for this job. To ensure fire safety prior to disposal, store dust and chips in a metal or fire-resistant container. A regular 33-gal. galvanized metal trash can with a tight-fitting lid works just fine.

Avoiding the big bang

It's ironic, but the same dust collection system that can help you keep sawdust off the floor to reduce the possibility of fire can be responsible for a rare, yet devastating kind of danger: an explosion caused by the ignition of fine wood dust by a static electric charge. When even modest concentrations of fine wood dust are mixed with air (the lower explosive limits are 10 to 300 grams of dust per cubic meter of air), an errant spark can cause an explosion with tremendous force (see the photo at left). In a woodshop, the most common place where dust concentration can reach explosion potential is in the collection system itself: inside the ductwork, the blower or, most often, the dust filter bag or canister. If a spark from a static electric charge ignites a cloud of fine dust, it can cause an explosion strong enough to blow the dust collector apart. But what's worse is that the burning dust and gases that are expelled by the shock wave can produce additional dust clouds (especially if the shop is dusty), which can also ignite, creating a chain of explosions that might even level a large shop. Although such woodshop explosions are a relatively rare occurrence, I've read a few grisly

A small pinch of fine wood dust sifted over a blowtorch flame combusts with surprising volatility, demonstrating how readily fine dust in a collection system can burst into flames. (Please don't try this at home!)

accounts about woodworkers who were thrown through walls and were badly burned—enough to make it clear that it's worth taking every reasonable precaution to prevent explosions.

The best way to prevent fine dust explosion is to keep your shop clean, eliminate any open flames in the shop (such as from a furnace, water heater or cigarette), choose a central collector with a nonsparking fan wheel and make sure your dust system is properly grounded (see pp. 154-156). Grounding allows static charges to dissipate harmlessly, rather than building up and releasing in a sudden burst, which can trigger combustion. Proper grounding is easiest if you're installing metal ductwork. It's also possible to provide grounding in a plastic-pipe system, but ignition from static charge is that much more likely.

One more thing. Although it's probably not a big issue in most shops, you should be aware that working with aluminum can present a really serious danger, even if your wood-dust system is perfectly safe. Any reactive metal dust, such as from grinding or sanding aluminum, is much more susceptible to fire and explosion than regular wood dust. If you commonly work with aluminum in your shop, be sure to read the National Fire Protection Association's regulations regarding the collection of reactive dusts (available from NFPA, Battery March Park, Quincy, Mass.; 1-800-344-3555).

Disposing of sawdust

My friend Roger Heitzman, a custom furniture maker in Scotts Valley, California, used to say that he gauged the success of his woodworking business by the size of the pile of chips and shavings (he called it "Mount Sawdust") that accumulated behind his rural shop. Before going into a lot of detail in subsequent chapters about the various methods of collecting dust and chips, a word is in order about what to do with these generally unwanted woodshop by-products.

Many large cabinet and furniture manufacturing plants that generate mountains of sawdust have installed equipment that turns their waste into energy. Some factories use special furnaces that burn sawdust and chips directly, producing energy for powering plant equipment or for space heating. Others feed collected dust into a special industrial machine called a "bricketer," which compresses and fuses chips and shavings into little round briquettes that can then be burned in a furnace. Unfortunately, such machines are big and expensive, making them highly impractical for all but the largest woodshops.

If you have a small shop in an urban area and don't produce much more than a bag or two of sawdust a week, you can probably get away with disposing of sawdust with your regular household garbage. Many municipalities require that sawdust be deposited in sealed bags before being placed in refuse cans. This requirement is to keep clouds of dust from being raised when cans are emptied into collection trucks. Plastic trash bags (4-mil-thick lawn-sized) work well. If your sawdust output is small and you're against using plastic bags, you can fill regular paper grocery bags, and then seal them with masking tape.

Some sanitation districts also specify that refuse left for curb-side pickup should not include construction debris. This restriction will probably be a problem only if you're running a commercial woodshop and the sawdust and cutoffs in your trash outweigh the regular household garbage. If the city or county refuses to collect your debris, you might have to contract with a private disposal company. Alternatively, you might consider burning your wood debris, though stricter air-quality standards in and around many suburban areas prohibit outdoor burning and incineration.

If you live outside of a sanitation district, you're probably already hauling your sawdust to the local landfill along with your other trash. To reduce fire hazard, keep sawdust that's awaiting a trip to the dump in metal containers (stored away from buildings). If you must pile your sawdust, locate the piles well away from buildings and dry vegetation, and keep them covered.

Other creative ideas for getting rid of sawdust? If you have any friends who are into ceramics, it's possible they'll gladly haul away some of your sawdust to use in raku-style firing of pottery. If there's a large pet store, horse farm or animal feed and farm supply in your area, the owners might be happy to pick up your sawdust and shavings, depending on the wood species, to use for animal bedding (they might even pay you for it!).

Using sawdust for compost and mulch

If you have a big yard and want to turn your woodshop disposal problem into a garden-soil improvement program, then composting is the answer. Composted sawdust and wood chips can be used to build up the humus content in soil. The catch is that it takes some time and work to transform sawdust into useful compost; you can't just shovel it into the garden because fresh sawdust will rob the soil of nitrogen. You'll need to mix the sawdust with organic matter, such as grass clippings, garden debris and food waste, to help the sawdust break down. You can compost the sawdust of just about any kind of wood species, although you might want to limit the quantity of extractive-laden exotic species dust you mix in.

To transform sawdust and shavings into soil-enriching humus, woodworker Andrew Church built a two-compartment compost bin behind his shop. Here, he digs garden-ready sawdust (which has been mixed with garden clippings and 'aged' for more than 8 months) from the bottom of the decomposition bin, then transfers it to the 'ready-to-use' bin behind him.

A compost bin, such as the one shown in the photo above, will help keep the material contained during the 8 to 12 months it will take for the material to be ready to use. For even richer compost, mix three parts of sawdust to one part of thoroughly decomposed poultry or animal manure (parts measured by volume, not weight). You can add some calcium cyanamide or sulfate of ammonia to help speed up the breakdown of the sawdust (add 1 lb. for every 20 lb. of sawdust).

When you're ready to mix the composted sawdust into your garden, apply about 10 lb. to 15 lb. to every square yard of ground. Dig in the new material thoroughly, which will also help aerate the soil. Although the compost definitely improves the quality of the soil, it doesn't really enrich it—composted sawdust has few nutrients, so it doesn't take the place of regular fertilizer.

A more direct use for large chips and shavings is as a mulch around the bases of fruit trees and bushes. Applying a thick ring of chips around the base of each plant helps to keep the area around the roots moist, so plants need watering less frequently, especially in hot weather. You can dig in the chips at the end of the season; the material will eventually break down into humus.

CHAPTER 2

Strategies for Controlling Dust

If the health hazards of breathing wood dust threaten to scare the enjoyment out of your woodworking, now is a good time to get serious about dust control in your shop. It should already be clear that collecting dust, in the form of shavings, chips and sawdust, isn't enough to keep your shop completely clean; you must deal with the fine dust floating around the shop as well to keep the air safe to breathe. But this doesn't mean you have to wear a spacesuit in the shop to stay healthy during a lifetime of woodworking. There is a wide variety of filtration and collection methods to corral dust and keep your shop's air clean.

The devices and strategies you use to deal with dust will depend on the size of your shop and the kind of woodworking you do. To help you gain a better perspective of your dust control needs, I've compiled a quick overview of the major forms of collection and control in the first part of this chapter. The advantages and disadvantages of each are summarized in the chart on the facing page. In subsequent chapters, I'll delve deeper into each type of dust control and collection method, presenting you with a more complete picture of how to choose the right equipment and install and/or use it in your shop.

Implementing complete and effective dust collection doesn't necessarily mean that you have to run right out and buy a lot of equipment: At the end of this chapter, there are some alternative strategies you can employ for reducing the production of dust in your shop as well as basic means of reducing your exposure to dust in the long run.

A SUMMARY OF DUST CONTROL AND COLLECTION METHODS		
Method	Advantages	Disadvantages
Personal respiratory protection (disposable mask or reusable respirator; powered air-purifying respirator)	Disposable masks and respirators are inexpensive and readily available; can provide good respiratory protection in lieu of primary dust collection.	Disposables that don't seal well to face can compromise respiratory health; reusable cartridge-style respirators are uncomfortable to wear for long periods; powered-air respirators are expensive.
Shop ventilation	Easy, inexpensive way to exhaust fine-dust-laden air from shop at minimal cost.	Limited protection from fine dust; most useful in temperate climates; unfiltered fan can pollute local environment.
Air-filtration devices	Remove fine dust particles effectively without exhausting shop air; simple units can be shop-built; unobtrusive; easy to install in most shops.	Initially expensive to buy; some units are noisy; filters need occasional cleaning and replacement. Doesn't totally replace primary collection.
Shop vacuums	Compact, portable and relatively inexpensive; good for primary collection from portable power tools.	Limited effectiveness in collection from most stationary machines; limited chip-holding capacity; most units are noisy.
Portable collectors	Less expensive and more versatile than installing a central collection system; can be used to collect from most stationary machines.	Not strong enough to use with long lengths of hose or ductwork; can be expensive; can take up room on the shop floor.
Central dust collectors	Powerful; convenient way to collect from most stationary machines in the shop.	Expensive to buy; require additional purchase and installation of ductwork; need space inside or outside shop for installation; some units are noisy.

A disposable face mask provides inexpensive respiratory protection from the long-term effects of fine dust created in great quantities during jobs such as belt sanding.

Masks and respirators

It's ironic that although wearable personal protection devices are the last line of defense against respirable wood dust (which is best collected at the source), their low cost and ease of use make them the first choice for many woodworkers. Respirators offer inexpensive protection for hobbyists who need only occasional protection or for small-shop woodworkers who have not yet installed some kind of dust collection system.

Respirators are worn around the nose and mouth and prevent dust from entering your respiratory tract, which is especially important when generating fine dust during sanding (see the photo above). Disposable masks are a popular choice for daily shop duty, because they are inexpensive and comfortable to wear. Reusable cartridge-style respirators can be fitted with a wide assortment of replaceable filter elements, making them more versatile than disposables.

For woodworkers who find it difficult to wear respirators yet demand thorough protection against dust (perhaps because of allergies or existing respiratory problems), powered air-purifying respirators are a good choice. Powered air-purifying respirators (commonly known as air helmets or dust helmets) supply fresh, clean air to the wearer via a small filter and fan device. The positive airflow makes them effective even for bearded woodworkers, who are difficult to protect with other kinds of respirators.

Shop ventilation

If you use a shop vacuum to collect chips in your small woodshop and your fine-dust production is limited, you can keep your shop and lungs cleaner by exhausting the dust-laden air outside the shop with a fan. Very small single-garage-sized shops can often get by with an inexpensive box-style household fan (see the top photo at right). Larger spaces can be evacuated by bigger squirrel-cage-style blowers (see the photo on p. 60). Incoming fresh air enters through an inlet port—an open window or a cutout in a wall or door. Filters fitted on the intake and/or exhaust ends keep new shop air clean and prevent exhausted air from polluting your yard or neighborhood. This kind of ventilation system can not only reduce your exposure to fine wood dust, but can also serve to exhaust vapors from water-based glues and finishes, and other nonflammable vapors or mists.

Since simple shop ventilation means drawing in fresh air from outside, it's a method that has real limitations, especially if you're working during a bitterly cold Alaskan winter or a horribly humid Floridian summer. If you live in such areas, you'll want to reserve this method for the more temperate seasons.

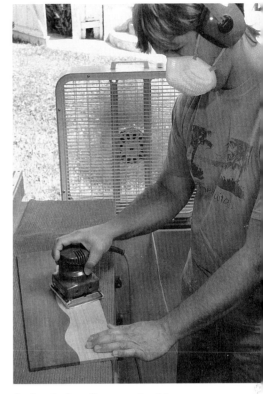

A simple box fan perched in a doorway can provide enough ventilation to remove the lion's share of fine sanding dust from the air in a woodshop.

Air-filtration devices

While ventilation replaces dusty air with clean air from outside, devices called air-filtration systems (or air cleaners) recirculate the air inside your shop, drawing in and trapping airborne wood dust before it can settle on benchtops or threaten your respiratory health. Designed to be suspended from the ceiling or a wall, these devices basically consist of a simple fan with two or more filters housed inside a cabinet (see the bottom photo at right). The fan draws shop air through the filters, where the fine powder is collected. By circulating the air through the filters many times an hour, a significant part of the floating, invisible wood dust can be removed, making it possible to draw a clean breath in the shop even after sanding.

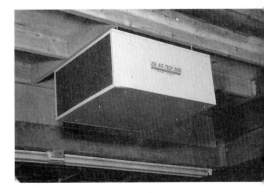

Suspended from the ceiling joists in the shop, an air-filtration device uses a fan and a series of filters to remove fine dust particles from the shop's air before they settle.

Portable shop vacuums

For flexibility in small-scale dust collection in a shop of any size, nothing beats a simple portable shop vacuum. Available in a wide range of sizes (both in terms of power and collection capacity), these versatile vacs can be temporarily connected to whichever small machine in the shop is currently in use (see the photo at left), or dedicated to collect dust and chips from just one or two machines. However, for most full-size woodworking machines, even a large unit might not be up to complete chip removal. Also, be prepared to empty the canister every few minutes unless you add an extra preseparator can to catch the bulk of the shavings ahead of the vacuum (see pp. 110-111).

The greatest virtue of shop vacuums is their portability: They unhook readily and can be pulled around the shop for sucking up chips below the workbench or during your regular shop clean-up regimen. Shop vacuums also make great collectors for chips and dust generated by portable power tools. You can fit an electronic sensor switch to turn the vac on or off automatically along with the tool, or buy a model that comes with a sensor switch already built in.

If you're sharing your workshop with the family automobile or your shop is tiny (I've seen bedroom closets far bigger than my first workshop), you can't go wrong in buying a good shop vacuum. Even if your next shop will be as large as a dirigible factory, you'll still end up using your portable vac for all manner of shop cleanup. And you can always take it with you to the job site, for tidying up after cabinet installations or trim work (your client or spouse will thank you).

The versatile, portable shop vacuum is ideal for small-shop cleanup tasks and dust collection from tools and machines that don't generate tremendous amounts of chips, such as a router used in a router table.

Portable and central dust collectors

Essentially built like a very large, powerful vacuum with ductwork connected to different shop machinery, a central dust collection system provides the heavy artillery needed to keep a busy woodshop from overflowing with shavings and chips. A central collection system is a virtual necessity in shops that have the standard complement of powered machinery: thickness planer, table saw, jointer, shaper (and/or router table), cutoff saw, stationary belt and/or disc sander, and so on. Unless you like to clean up around each tool after each work session, a central collector provides just about the only convenient way to stay one step ahead of the mountains of chips and sawdust you're likely to generate during an average day's work. All your dust and shavings end up in one place, where they're convenient to dispose of.

The size of the central collection system you need depends on the size of your shop, the number of stationary machines you want to connect, the volume of sawdust your shop generates and the number of people operating machines at one time. At the lower end of the scale are portable collectors with induction-motor-powered blowers, such as the Shopsmith DC 3300 shown below in the photo at left. The limited power and capacity of these units is enough to handle the major sawdust-producing tools in a small workshop, as long as you keep all hoses short and collect from only one tool (or possibly two) at a time. In a small hobby shop, a portable collector can be centrally mounted, with a system of ductwork and blast gates connecting a number of small machines to the unit.

Further up the ladder of power and performance for larger shops are full-blown (pardon the pun) central dust collection systems, such as the Jet collector shown below in the photo at right. These systems

Portable collectors, such as the Shopsmith DC 3300 shown here, are a step up from shop vacuums, both in terms of power and capacity.

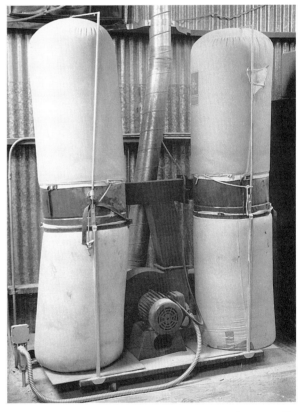

A central dust collection system hooked up to all the machines in the woodshop conveys chips and sawdust to collection bags or canisters for convenient disposal.

feature large-capacity fans and permanently mounted rigid ductwork that can serve practically any number of machines (as well as inlets for floor sweeps, clean-up hoses and, possibly, hose connections for handling portable power tools). Most central collection systems have large-capacity canisters or bags for gathering and disposing of large shavings and sawdust and sizable filter bags that thoroughly strain the finer dust out of the sucked-up air before exhausting it. If you live in a temperate area, you may avoid some fine-dust-particle problems by locating your collector to exhaust air outdoors; in a cold clime, you'll need to return the filtered air to your shop, to save on heating the fresh air that the collection system draws in.

If you run a production cabinet shop or produce architectural mill-work and do a lot of thickness planing, sawing and shaping, you'll want to consider installing a collector that employs a cyclonic separator, or "cyclone" for short (see the photos on p. 109). For non-industrial applications, these units are the smaller brothers of the cyclones you've probably seen atop large saw mills and high school wood-shops. Their job is to separate out bigger chips, shavings and dust from the air used to transport them to the collector. This debris is deposited in a large drum or bin where it's easy to empty; only the really fine dust makes it to the filters, so they aren't impacted by larger particles and they don't need to be cleaned as frequently.

Combining dust control measures

Ideally, a central collection system, portable collector or shop vacuum will capture all the dust and chips you produce at their source (a machine, portable power tool or work area); this process is known as primary collection. In reality, some dust always finds a way of escaping and ending up on the floor or, in the case of fine wood powder, in the air. Thus even with the best systems, it's desirable to have some way of capturing this elusive shop dust. Vacuuming floors and benchtops will take care of chips and shavings, but fine airborne dust is better dealt with by some form of secondary collection, such as ventilation or air-filtration devices. And although they don't capture fleeing dust, masks and respirators can augment primary collection by preventing airborne particles from getting into your lungs. The particular blend of primary and secondary collection/control strategies you choose and implement will depend on the kind of woodworking you do.

If you're building miniature furniture in a portable-shed-sized shop, the amount of dust you create is probably minute as well; you probably need to wear a dust mask only during sanding. I once visited a large shop that produced period-style furniture using primarily traditional hand tools where the only form of dust control was a large push broom used to sweep up shavings—more than adequate in that particular situation. At the other extreme, shops that do a lot of abrasive work—shaping parts using belt and disc sanders, grinders and such—produce volumes of dust that require serious abatement measures. These typically include a well-designed collection system and air-filtration devices. If you have allergies or have experienced adverse reactions to wood dust, you may find yourself needing to wear a respirator in addition to other measures of dust collection/control implemented in your shop.

Shops where several people are working at one time will need different dust control strategies than one-person operations. For example, central collection systems in multiple-worker shops—where several machines may be operating at once—are far more complicated to design than smaller systems that need serve only one machine at a time. And the larger amounts of fine dust created by more frequent machine operations may require a high-volume air-filtration system or extensive use of masks or respirators.

Alternative means of controlling dust

For most problems you're likely to encounter in the woodshop, there's some handy device you can buy through a catalog or at the hardware store that will solve it. But if dust is the problem, there are quite a few simple alternatives to going out and buying a bigger shop vacuum or fitting a more expensive collection system. These include keeping the shop clean, generating less dust and limiting your exposure to dust.

Good housekeeping
Keeping the shop clean is the first and foremost way that you can control the accumulation of dust and debris in the woodshop. Not only is it harder to work efficiently in a space that's filled with sawdust and debris, but just walking around can raise a hazy cloud of fine dust that subsequently lights on tools and work in progress. If your shop adjoins your home, fine dust will quickly find its way inside your living spaces, and a furnace in a basement shop can pick up fine dust and blow it all over the house. As we've seen, dust will also pollute the air with breathable fine powder that's deleterious to respiratory health.

When its time for your daily cleaning regime, leave the broom hanging on its hook. You'll surely churn up as much fine dust as shavings and sawdust are captured by whisking a broom around the floor. Cleaning up floors is a job much better left to a portable shop vacuum, or a hose from a central dust collection system. If you have a large floor space to clean up every day, you'll save time by building your own floor-

To make cleaning up a large shop floor a breeze, you can build a floor-vacuuming pickup from plastic pipe and fittings. A flexible hose from a shop vacuum plugs into a connector on the end of the pickup.

vacuuming pickup. I built a floor pickup, shown in the photo above, from a few lengths of 2-in. ABS plastic pipe and a few pipe fittings (my design was inspired by Matt Burak, who uses a similar device to clean up his Vermont woodshop). A pair of shopmade wheels (which I cut from some Masonite with a circle cutter) helps the pickup glide easily along the floor (see the drawing on the facing page). Slots sawn or routed into the bottom of the pickup allow dust to be vacuumed without sucking up larger scraps that can clog the hose.

For collecting large shavings (from hand planing, cutting dovetails, etc.), some woodworkers like to use a small foxtail brush to sweep the shavings from benchtops and machine tables onto the floor where they can be vacuumed up. A large plastic shovel, such as a grain scoop

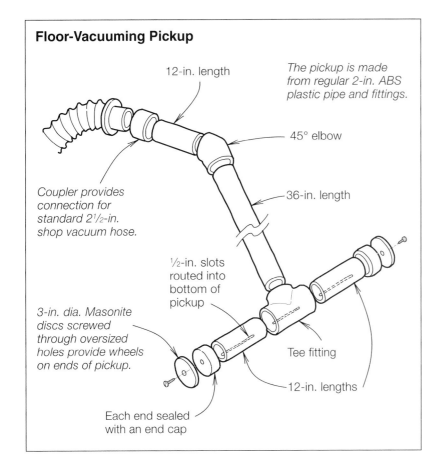

Floor-Vacuuming Pickup

12-in. length

The pickup is made from regular 2-in. ABS plastic pipe and fittings.

45° elbow

36-in. length

Coupler provides connection for standard 2½-in. shop vacuum hose.

½-in. slots routed into bottom of pickup

3-in. dia. Masonite discs screwed through oversized holes provide wheels on ends of pickup.

Tee fitting

12-in. lengths

Each end sealed with an end cap

Rather than raising clouds of dust with a pushbroom, you can shovel up mounds of shavings in a hurry using a lightweight plastic grain scoop.

(available from feed and farm supply stores) or a snow shovel, is a terrific tool for scooping up large quantities of shavings off the floor—and it raises far less dust than sweeping (see the photo at right).

Since dust clings easily to hair, clothing and the soles of shoes, you need to clean yourself off at the end of every work session to get rid of the dust before it ends up on your living-room couch. A blow gun on a compressed-air line can quickly remove dust and debris from your person, but, unless you blow off outside, it does tend to pump fine dust into the air and spread it all over the shop. Make sure to wear a mask so you don't end up breathing the dust when you blow off. I prefer to give myself a quick cleansing at the end of the day with a vacuum hose fitted with a brush attachment. I'm often plagued by small chips that get trapped in my hair and end up in my eyes when I remove my goggles, so I run the vacuum brush through my hair as well (it's actually kind of pleasant—like a vacuum scalp massage).

If your shop is at home and you often find yourself making trips inside the house, a good alternative to cleaning up before each jaunt is to wear coveralls in the shop. A quick peel and you're clean as a whistle—and no one can accuse you of depositing that thick film of dust on the family piano. I had problems tracking in dust and chips on the bottoms of my shoes (especially when it rained), so I made my own work-shoe scrubber, which is modeled after shoe-cleaning devices I've seen in trendy catalog supplies. The device consists of three hardwood-backed stiff-bristle scrub brushes (from the housewares section of a department or hardware store) mounted to a plywood base, as shown in the drawing below. I keep my scrubber by the back door and take a second to brush each shoe through it before each trip into the house.

Generating less dust

In a culture that seems attracted to minimalism in its art, architecture and fashion, it's surprising that few woodworkers have implemented this alternative form of dust control: generating less dust in the first place. Creating less dust means having less dust to control, collect and dispose of. Here are a couple of ways to reduce sawdust production without having to change the way you work significantly.

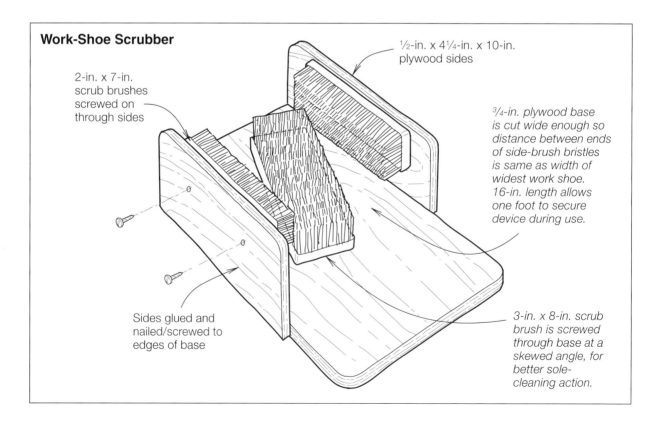

Work-Shoe Scrubber

2-in. x 7-in. scrub brushes screwed on through sides

½-in. x 4¼-in. x 10-in. plywood sides

¾-in. plywood base is cut wide enough so distance between ends of side-brush bristles is same as width of widest work shoe. 16-in. length allows one foot to secure device during use.

Sides glued and nailed/screwed to edges of base

3-in. x 8-in. scrub brush is screwed through base at a skewed angle, for better sole-cleaning action.

An easy way to pare down chip production is to fit your circular saws (table saw, radial-arm saw, etc.) with thin-kerf blades. Modern blades, such as Freud's LU87 and LU88 and Forrest's excellent "Woodworker II," are as stable and smooth cutting as their standard-thickness counterparts. By reducing the kerf on a 10-in. dia. blade to between 0.086 in. and 0.096 in. (as compared to 0.126 in.–about ⅛ in.–for a standard blade), the amount of wood rendered as sawdust is reduced by up to 25%. If you plan to do any heavy ripping or precise crosscutting of thick hardwoods, it's a good idea to use these blades with a stabilizer–a precisely ground steel plate that bears against the sawblade on the saw arbor, reducing vibration and stiffening the body of the blade.

Because the thickness planer is the major chip producer in most shops, one way to reduce shavings is to purchase lumber already surfaced "S2S" (surfaced both sides). Also, many larger lumberyards are more than happy to custom surface and dress lumber to your specifications for a price that usually isn't unreasonable, considering the cost of buying a planer.

Now for some ideas for ways to reduce dust by working a little differently: On days when you've been grinding the gears on all the big machines in the shop and your ears are ringing, taking a little break from the power stuff and making a little sawdust the old-fashioned way can be really refreshing. In some cases, you'll accomplish your task just as quickly and not owe the power company a cent for the job. For example, if you're handy with a handsaw, mallet and chisel, it usually makes more sense to bang out those few odd tenons and mortises by hand than to take the time to set up and adjust the fences and stops on the table saw and hollow-chisel mortiser. You'll be making big chips and shavings that are easy to brush off the bench and scoop up, and generating very little fine dust in the bargain. The next time you need to clean up an area of torn grain on the face of a cabinet-door panel, don't reach for a belt sander, but pull out a well-tuned cabinet scraper instead (see the top photo at right). You might work up a sweat, but you won't kick up a cloud—and you'll get the job done as well or better than that dust-spewing belted brute of a sander.

Another way to make less dust is to change the kinds of power tools or machines you do use. Many of the newer power sanders feature built-in dust collection that's much more efficient than similar models of just a few years ago. For example, the new Bosch 3727 DVS random-orbit sander (shown in the bottom photo at right) has a sealed collar around the perforated sanding disc that makes collection much more efficient. The unit also sports a disposable paper dust bag, which traps more fine dust than most cloth-bagged units do. The paper bag also makes the disposal of fine dust easier and much cleaner than with cloth bags.

A well-tuned cabinet scraper provides a clean and quiet alternative to using a dust-churning power sander to smooth an area of torn grain on the surface of a fancy-grained board.

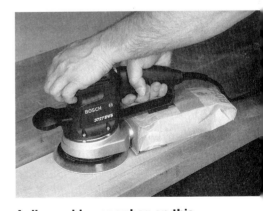

A disposable paper bag on this random-orbit sander does a better job of filtering out fine dust than most cloth bags do. It also makes the collected fine dust easier to throw away.

If you do a lot of thickness planing and are intent on making less dust, change to a wood surfacer in lieu of a standard planer. A wood surfacer, such as the Makita LP1812C, is a machine that power-feeds a board over a heavy stationary blade, removing a thin, continuous, wide shaving (instead of clouds of chips and dust), leaving a smooth surface on every pass. These big shavings are beautiful; if you plane even-grained softwoods, such as Port Orford cedar, you'll want to write letters on these scroll-like shavings. If you're not a writer, the shavings are very easy to scoop up and dispose of.

Limiting your exposure to dust

You can reduce the amount of time that you breathe dust in the shop by spending less time working in a shop that has a lot of airborne dust wafting around in it. If you're a full-time professional or happen to do a lot of power sanding, here are two strategies for limiting your exposure to fine wood dust:

First, set up your machine tools and power-sanding bench in a different room than your workbench, assembly and glue-up areas. That way, you'll have a clean place to retreat to, where you don't have to keep wearing a respirator to keep from eating the cloud of dust you've just created. If your current shop is one big open space, you don't have to build a permanent wall to create separate machine and bench rooms: A floor-to-ceiling divider built by stretching sheets of thin (4 mil to 6 mil) clear polyethylene plastic over a lightweight framework of 1x2s can do the trick nicely (see the top photo on the facing page). You can incorporate doors and passthroughs wherever needed. By using clear plastic, light will travel from existing windows and light fixtures into your new, clean room.

Second, if you live in a temperate area, you might consider doing what I did before I set up a good dust collection system in my shop: Set up your workbench outside the dusty confines of the shop whenever the weather permits (see the bottom photo on the facing page). Working outside is especially desirable when power sanding or using a portable tool that spews tons of small chips, such as a router. You'll not only breathe more easily—unless you live in a smog zone, such as central L.A.—but you'll get a tan as well (just don't forget to wear sunscreen).

You can create a clean workroom, separated from a sawdust-choked machine room, by building a room divider from transparent polyethylene sheeting stretched over a lightweight wooden framework.

One way to avoid eating dust inside the shop is to move operations that create lots of chips, such as shaping the edges of plywood parts with a router, outdoors and set up a workbench on the patio or driveway.

CHAPTER 3

Respiratory Protection Devices

If you are a hobbyist or weekend woodworker and don't have the time or budget to implement other forms of dust collection or control, masks and respirators can provide a quick, inexpensive way to counter the short-term discomforts that come from breathing dust, as well as the long-term consequences that can rob you of good health. Even if you've outfitted your shop with complete central dust collection, no primary collection system is 100% efficient: Some fine dust particles still end up escaping and wafting about the shop. Ventilation and air-filtration devices (see Chapter 4) can take care of most of this free-roaming dust, but even then, during periods of heavy sanding, you're likely to be exposed to a certain amount of fine, respirable dust. Your last line of defense against these lung-damaging particles is to wear personal protection in the form of a disposable mask, a reusable respirator or a powered air-purifying respirator (dust helmet).

When chosen and worn correctly, most masks and respirators will provide adequate respiratory protection to most individuals. But not all respirators are right for all persons. The type of device you choose will depend on a number of factors, including cost, desired level of comfort, workstyle and (believe it or not) whether or not you have facial hair. The advantages and disadvantages of each type of device are summarized in the chart on the facing page. The filters in wearable devices also differ in the kind of respiratory protection they are designed to provide. That is why you must also acquaint yourself with the filtration ratings and specifications for different types of filtering

PERSONAL RESPIRATORY PROTECTION DEVICES		
Device	Advantages	Disadvantages
Disposable mask	Cheap; readily available; more comfortable for longer wear than reusable respirator; no need to maintain or clean.	Doesn't seal well on bearded faces; less effective than half-mask type respirator; difficult to talk on phone.
Reusable respirator	Better face seal than most disposable masks; versatile—replaceable-cartridge respirators can be used for protection from dust or organic vapors.	Can be fatiguing to wear for extended periods; doesn't seal well on bearded faces; cartridges are expensive; facepieces should be cleaned after each use; must remove for conversation or to talk on phone.
Powered air-purifying respirator (dust helmet)	Combines eye, head and respiratory protection in one device; provides a positive seal around face for bearded woodworkers; eliminates fogging problems for eyeglass wearers.	Expensive ($250 to $750); cumbersome to wear, especially belt-pack models; difficult to converse; must be removed to talk on phone.

elements before buying and using them. In this chapter we'll look at each type of device, arranged from least to most expensive, as well as explore different types of filters appropriate for woodworking.

Disposable masks

The easiest way to provide adequate protection for your lungs from fine wood dust is to wear a disposable mask (officially known as a "disposable respirator" or "filtering facepiece"). Readily available at hardware and paint stores, home centers and even some drugstores, disposable masks are the cheapest form of dust protection you can buy. They protect your lungs by filtering the air you breathe through either your nose or mouth (this arrangement is known as a "half-mask," as compared to a "full mask," which covers your nose, mouth and eyes). The entire surface of a disposable mask is a filter made up of a matrix of nonwoven fibers that trap and retain dust particles. When the mask becomes dirty, you simply throw it away and fit a new one.

There are several styles and models of disposable masks that are safe and appropriate for use in most woodshops. I'll examine each one carefully, so you can better determine which suits you the best. But first, a little warning is in order: *Do not use* so-called "comfort masks,"

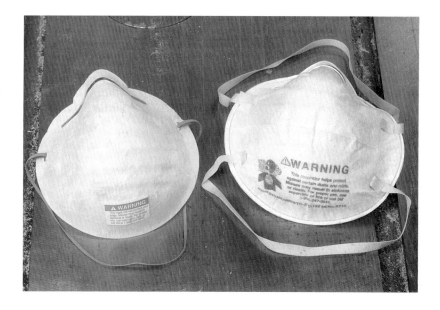

Distinguishing an inexpensive mask good only for nuisance levels of wood dust from one rated for more serious protection against particulates is as simple as counting straps: Disposable masks rated for protection against dust and mists, such as 3M's model 8560 (right), have two straps, as opposed to the single strap on the 3M comfort mask (left).

all too commonly seen in woodworking shops, such as 3M's model 8500 (shown at left in the photo above). These masks have one-layer shells, sport only a single strap and are often labeled: "Warning, this mask will not protect your lungs...." They are recommended only for protection against "nuisance levels" of dust, which is the amount of dust you might be exposed to if you spent only about 15 minutes in a dusty shop. In the electronics and food-processing industries, comfort masks are typically worn to prevent workers from contaminating the products they are processing. Their thin filter media (typically limited to handling dust 10 microns and larger) and single strap just don't offer enough protection for any kind of sustained woodworking operations.

The most basic mask recommended for woodworking has two straps and an adjustable nosepiece, both of which help to seal the mask to the wearer's face more positively. Popular models include the 3M 8710 and 8560 (shown at right in the photo above) and the Moldex 2200. These masks are molded from three layers: a paperlike cover layer that prefilters coarse particles, a center layer that's a blend of natural and/or synthetic fibers that are electrocharged so they will attract and trap small dust and mist particles, and an inner layer that's soft against the face (see the drawing on the facing page). Woodworking dust masks are available at hardware stores, packaged a few at a time in shrink wrap, but it's much cheaper to buy them in boxes of 10 or 20 from a mail-order supplier (see Sources of Supply on pp. 194-195). To keep masks clean and prevent crushing (which ruins their

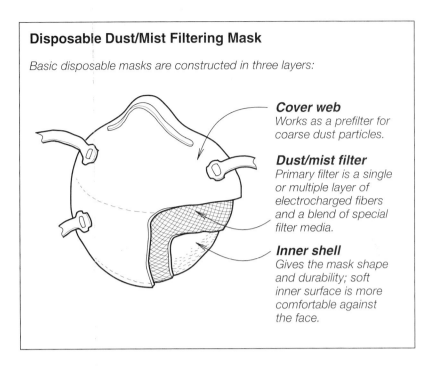

Disposable Dust/Mist Filtering Mask

Basic disposable masks are constructed in three layers:

Cover web
Works as a prefilter for coarse dust particles.

Dust/mist filter
Primary filter is a single or multiple layer of electrocharged fibers and a blend of special filter media.

Inner shell
Gives the mask shape and durability; soft inner surface is more comfortable against the face.

ability to seal to your face) between uses, you can buy an inexpensive plastic mask case (see Sources of Supply), such as the one shown in the photo below.

Alternative models of the basic two-strap disposable mask feature an exhalation valve in the center, such as the 3M 6979 (see the top left photo on p. 42). The inclusion of this simple one-way valve (which closes during inhalation to prevent dust from being drawn in) allows you to exhale more easily and makes the mask less fatiguing to wear for extended periods. You'll especially appreciate this feature if

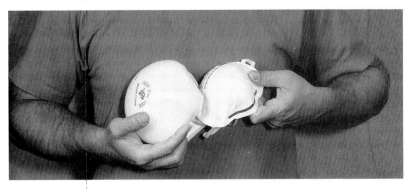

Protect molded disposable masks against crushing by storing them between uses in a protective plastic case.

The exhalation valve in the center of the disposable 3M 6979 mask shown here allows hot breath to be exhausted more readily, which makes the mask more comfortable to wear and less likely to fog safety glasses.

you're working on a hot day. Further, by allowing your moist breath to pass through more easily, these masks prevent a buildup of moisture on the inside of the mask (which feels clammy on your face). And, more important, the valve reduces the tendency for this moisture to creep up under your protective glasses or goggles and fog them up.

Clothlike disposables

Another kind of disposable mask that's become more popular among woodworkers in the past few years is a two-strap design made of a clothlike material. Models include the Arbortech Pro-Mask 2 and the Delta 1plus (see the photo below). Although these masks are more expensive than the more common molded disposables, they have several advantages: They are softer and more comfortable to wear than many molded disposables, they offer a very low breathing resistance (making them less fatiguing to wear), and they fold flat easily, so they are less cumbersome if worn around the neck between uses. A flat-folded cloth disposable can also be carried around in your shop apron or shirt pocket without compromising the mask's fit. This can be a real advantage if you put on and take off your mask many times a day, because any disposable mask loses its ability to seal if it is crushed out of shape.

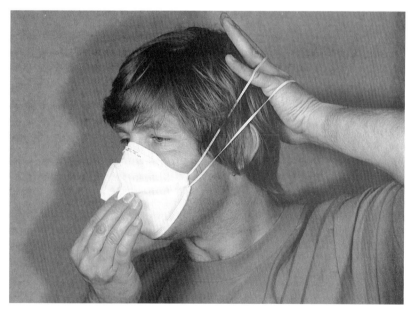

Some woodworkers prefer the comfort and flat-folding ability of clothlike disposables, such as the Delta 1plus shown here. Note that it's easier to don any type of two-strap disposable mask by holding the straps with one hand while you slide them over the back of your head.

Once the fibers of any disposable mask have become clogged, it's time to throw the mask away and don a fresh one. How can you tell when a mask is used up? A layer of dust on the outside of the mask shows that many large, visible dust particles have been filtered out, but the filter may still be able to remove fine respirable particles. Ironically, the fine-particle-filtering ability of a mask actually improves as the filter material fills up, as shown in the drawing below. This is true of all dust-filter media, including cartridge filters and filter-bag materials.

The most telling clue that a disposable mask is spent is that breathing through it becomes more difficult. Breathing becomes difficult because dust particles have clogged most of the small air passages remaining in the filter material. You can extend a mask's useful life a little by blowing or vacuuming it clean—the bigger wood dust particles are removed, but the fine particles that do the most to impede airflow stay trapped in the filter fibers.

Alternatively, you can simply throw away inexpensive disposable masks after each period of use, such as after each full day of work or after a session of heavy sanding. You should also throw away any disposable that's been crushed or distorted, or that has a nosepiece that's broken or twisted. Such a mask's ability to seal to your face has probably been compromised.

How a Disposable Mask's Filtration Improves with Use

A relatively new mask

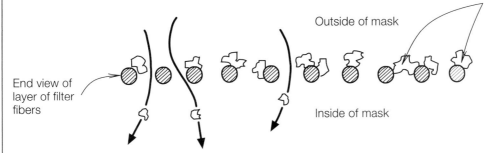

Outside of mask

Large dust particles are blocked by filter or attracted to and trapped by electro-charged fibers.

End view of layer of filter fibers

Inside of mask

Very small particles can pass through gaps between fibers.

A partially used mask

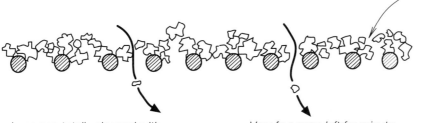

Accumulation of large and small particles reduces size of gaps between filter fibers.

As filter becomes totally clogged with dust, air doesn't pass through easily, a sign that it's time for a new mask.

Very few gaps left for minute particles to pass through.

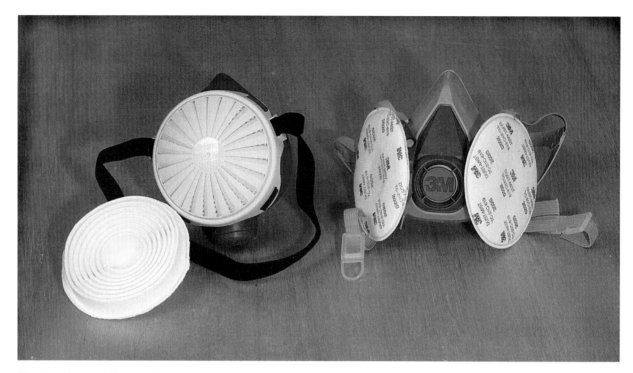

The two types of reusable respirators shown here are the replaceable-filter facepiece (left) with a large-pleated paper filter element and bottom-mounted exhalation valve, and the replaceable-cartridge facepiece (right) with dual cartridges mounted on either side of a central exhalation valve.

Reusable respirators

An alternative to disposable masks are reusable respirators, such as the ones shown in the photo above. These half-masks have two components: a disposable filter(s) or cartridge(s) that cleans the incoming air, and a reusable facepiece that provides a mount for the filters, controls the flow of air to them and ensures an airtight seal around your face. This arrangement allows you to throw away only the filters after they are clogged with dust and reuse the facepiece indefinitely. In use, inhaled air is pulled through the filters mounted on the sides or front of the facepiece. Exhaled breath then passes out of a simple flap-style one-way valve, usually on the underside of the facepiece. Another one-way valve is usually fitted just behind each filter, to prevent moist air from passing back into the filter element, which could reduce its effective life.

Respirators designed primarily for woodworking (or welding) have replaceable filter elements that are housed in a compartment, usually on the front of the facepiece. The filters in some respirators are pleated to enlarge the surface area of the filter and reduce breathing resistance (see the respirator at left in the photo above). Replaceable-cartridge respirators typically have a pair of disposable, screw-in cartridges mounted on the lower sides of the mask (see the respirator at right in the same photo). Screw-in cartridges not only make it easy to replace filters, but also allow you to change the kind of respiratory protection that the respirator can provide. There are literally dozens of different kinds of filters that are effective against dusts, mists, vapors, gases, chemicals and various combinations of these materials (see pp. 48-49). The availability of different kinds of filters makes these respirators very versatile, since you could conceivably just buy one facepiece and fit separate cartridges for dust and organic vapors, enabling you to use the respirator as both a dust mask and a spray-finishing mask.

The facepiece on most respirators is contour-molded from neoprene rubber or silicone. Silicone masks, while more expensive, are softer than neoprene and therefore more comfortable to wear (some people are also allergic to synthetic rubber). The softer silicone also tends to mold more easily to the face, producing a better seal in the process. Some respirator models have a double sealing lip around their edge to achieve a better seal on sunken-cheeked or angular faces. Like disposable masks, reusable respirators don't seal well on bearded wearers (see p. 50).

Twin adjustable straps attached to the body of the respirator make it easy for the wearer to achieve a tight fit. A yoke or cradle-style top strap, as shown in the photo below, does a particularly good job of

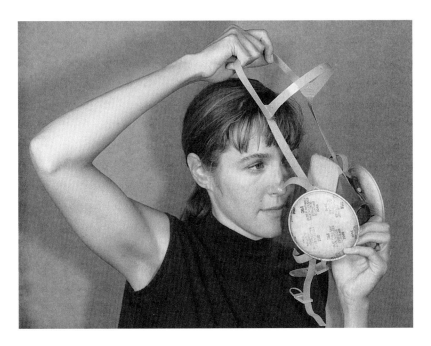

The yoke or cradle-style top straps used on many reusable respirators distribute the pressure of the strap more evenly across the back of the head. This makes the mask much more comfortable to wear for extended periods.

Washing a rubber or neoprene facepiece with a mild detergent between uses helps keep it sanitary, as well as ensuring that the valves work correctly and that the facepiece continues to seal effectively.

pulling the mask up tightly to the face without putting undue pressure on the back of the head. The result is less pressure on the scalp, and less fatigue during long periods of wear. However, some woodworkers do find that the added weight of the respirator and cartridge makes it much less comfortable to wear than a disposable mask.

Respirator maintenance

When the filters or cartridges on a respirator are used up, simply remove them from the facepiece and replace them with fresh elements. You can tell that the filter elements are used up when breathing through them becomes more difficult. As with disposable masks, you can extend the useful life of a filter element or cartridge slightly by vacuuming or blowing it clean. The facepiece itself can be reused many times, and most manufacturers offer replacement straps, valves and other parts for their models, so you can keep a well-maintained respirator in service for years.

Because the condensed moisture from your breath tends to collect inside the facepiece, you should wash it regularly with a mild detergent. First, remove the filter elements and straps. Then, take apart the intake and exhaust valves and wash them separately (see the photo above). Be careful with the thin round rubber flaps that serve as intake valves; pull them from their mounting studs gently to avoid ripping them.

After washing the facepiece, it's a good idea to sanitize it with a disinfectant. This extra step is mandatory if the respirator is shared with coworkers. You can buy solutions of commercial respirator disinfectant (typically quaternary ammonium; see Sources of Supply on pp. 194-195), or you can make your own by mixing about 2 tablespoons of household bleach into a gallon of warm water. Soak the facepiece in this solution for two or three minutes, then towel it dry.

When reassembling a replaceable-cartridge respirator, make sure to press in the rubber gaskets (supplied with the mask) before installing the cartridges. Once fully assembled, store the respirator in a plastic bag to keep it clean and dry until the next use. If you have organic-vapor cartridges (used when working with finishing materials; see p. 48), store them in a plastic bag as well: The activated charcoal in these cartridges continues to work—and wear out—even when they are not in use.

Choosing the right filtration

Disposable masks and filter elements for reusable respirators are available in an extensive and confusing array. Fortunately, the government offers us help in the form of NIOSH (National Institute for Occupational Safety and Health) certification numbers. These numbers, which are usually stamped directly on the mask or filter element (see the photo below), ensure that a particular respirator has passed a rig-

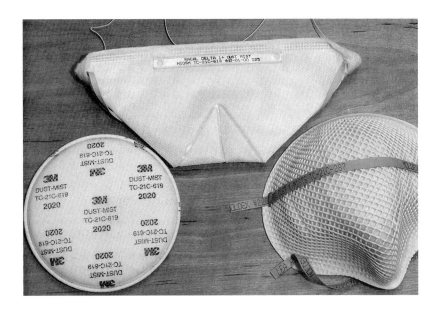

To make it easier to identify the type of respiratory protection provided by a disposable mask or replaceable filter element, manufacturers print the rating number right on the nosepiece or strap or on the element itself. TC-21C is the number to look for on masks and elements used to filter particulates, including wood dust.

orous testing program and is approved for protecting the wearer against the specified types of airborne contaminants (see also the sidebar below).

TC-21C-rated filter elements

For standard dust protection in the woodshop, the NIOSH specification number you'll want to look for is "TC-21C" followed by a three-digit number that specifies the particular model of respirator. TC-21C means that a disposable mask or filter element provides good protection against most woodworking dusts and waterborne mists. Some TC-21C filters will also protect your lungs against fumes, which are very fine particles generated during operations where metal is heated to the boiling point (such as during welding or soldering). TC-21C filters do not remove organic vapors.

According to NIOSH, a TC-21C-rated mask will stop 98% of respirable particles down to 1 micron in diameter. That's good enough to eliminate serious risks for most people from exposure to the relatively modest dust concentrations found in a typical woodshop. The NIOSH rating is, of course, a general recommendation subject to different factors, such as the presence of air contaminants other than wood dust.

New filter specifications

At the time I was writing this book, NIOSH was in the process of establishing new standards for particulate filters (other filters, such as for organic vapors, and filters for powered air-purifying respirators are not included). The new certification requirements (designated 42 CFR Part 84) that became effective in July 1995 eliminate classification of filters by hazard type (dust, fumes, mists, etc.).

Instead, all particulate filters will belong to one of three series: P-Series, R-series and N-series. P-series filters will be for use in areas free of oil aerosols. R-series and N-series filters will both be for filtering all particulates including oil aerosols; the difference between them is that R-series filters may be restricted in the length of time they may be used. Further, each series of filter will be available in three levels of efficiency: 95%, 99% and 99.97% efficient. Therefore, R99 indicates an R-series filter that's 99% efficient (one exception, though: 99.97%

efficient filters will be called 100 series, such as an N100 or P100).

The new standards will be phased in over several years, so it's hard to tell you what filters will be offered for woodworking applications, or how long it will be before you start seeing the new filters in stores and mail-order catalogs. For more information, your best bet would be to contact the companies that make and sell respirators and filters. They have technical consultants who are more than happy to discuss your needs and make recommendations.

High-efficiency filters Another kind of TC-21C-rated filter designed to handle toxic dusts (such as asbestos), mists and fumes is an HEPA (high-efficiency particulate absolute) filter. It's easy to identify an HEPA filter element by the purple/magenta stripe running around the body of cartridge-type elements (some manufacturers color the entire element magenta). HEPA elements are often combined with other filters to make multi-purpose filters, such as an HEPA/organic-vapor element. You can also buy HEPA-rated disposable masks, including the Uvex HEPA-tech and Racal's Delta 3 (see Sources of Supply on pp. 194-195). HEPA filters are extremely efficient—typically removing 99.97% of particles down to 0.3 microns in diameter—but they are also many times more expensive than regular dust/mist filters. As such, they are overkill for the wood-dust-filtering needs of the average woodworker.

Organic-vapor cartridges

Another NIOSH specification number that you are likely to find on some filter elements is TC-23C. Cartridges with this specification that are color-coded black will provide protection against organic vapors, which are produced when solvents evaporate from glues, paints and finishing materials (even the majority of water-based finishes contain low levels of solvents). Other color codes designate filters approved for protection against other gases and/or vapors, such as ammonia (green) and mercury vapor (orange). Organic-vapor cartridges contain tiny granules of activated charcoal that actually absorb vapors as these gases pass through them.

While it's good to know what kind of cartridge to choose for protection while painting or clear-finishing wood, there's another reason to know about organic-vapor cartridges. You might be tempted to choose a TC-23C cartridge reasoning that it will do an even better job of filtering out fine dust than a TC-21C dust/mist filter. Unfortunately, that just isn't the case. Fine wood dust particles tend to pass through organic-vapor cartridges. In fact, you must fit an appropriate TC-21C prefilter over a TC-23C filter in order to protect yourself against mist droplets when you are spraying a finish. Conversely, solvents evaporating from nitrocellulose lacquer or varnish will pass through a dust/mist filter. The bottom line is that you must select the right filter element for the job at hand—your lungs depend on it!

If you are at all uncertain about what kind of mask or filters you need (or you are responsible for the health and safety of your employees), do not hesitate to consult an industrial hygienist or other safety professional. These professionals are best equipped to help you evaluate your precise needs when it comes to respiratory protection devices.

On a practical note, when purchasing replacement filters or cartridges for a respirator, be aware that even units that look the same may have different size threads or bayonet-style mounting flanges that aren't compatible with your particular mask. In fact, most filters and cartridges aren't interchangeable between different brands (or, sometimes, even different models of the same brand), which means your best bet is to buy replacements from the same company that manufactured your mask.

Fitting a mask correctly

Regardless of the effectiveness of its filtering medium, no mask or respirator will work effectively if it doesn't seal tightly against your face. A poor seal simply lets dust-laden air sneak in past the filters to be inhaled directly. The fit of a mask can be compromised by several circumstances, the most common of which is facial hair. Beards, sideburns and even a thick 5 o'clock shadow can easily compromise the mask-to-face seal of any facepiece-type respirator. Some woodworkers have tried to get around this problem by covering their beards with a thick layer of petroleum jelly (such as Vaseline), reasoning that the jelly will act as a viscous sealant around the edge of the mask. Unfortunately, this approach is not effective (and I can't imagine anyone working comfortably with their face coated with goo). Other factors that can ruin a good mask-to-face seal include high cheekbones, missing dentures, severe acne and facial scars.

Molded disposable masks tend to be particularly bad at sealing to the face. I read one study (done by the Center for Disease Control) that said that it's possible for an incorrectly fitted disposable mask to leak around the edges and let in up to 20% unfiltered air. The bridge of the nose seems especially prone to fit problems. The adjustable nosepieces on some models do a better job of sealing than others. I especially like the ones with small foam cushions, such as 3M's 8715, shown in the photo at left. A foam nosepiece also helps cure problems with nose pinching (making the mask more comfortable) and prevents expelled breath from fogging your glasses. At least one manufacturer (Uvex) offers disposables with a foam sealing flange around the entire edge of the mask (available from Lab Safety) for a more comfortable fit as well as a more positive seal. Moldex even offers disposable masks with what they call an "alternative" contour, designed to fit thinner faces (also available from Lab Safety; see Sources of Supply on pp. 194-195).

If you buy a respirator from a well-stocked supplier, you can usually choose between small, medium and large sizes; medium will fit about 90% of the population. Even some brands of disposable mask come in more than one size. Since most masks are molded to suit a theoretical

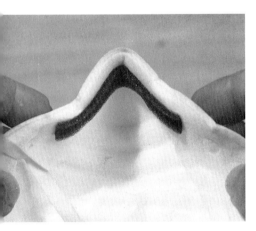

A foam inner seal around the nosepiece of a disposable mask helps prevent leaks around the wearer's nose, while affording a more comfortable fit.

"average" face, one brand might fit you better than another, so you might want to try using several models and brands before choosing a mask for everyday use.

Checking the fit

How do you know if your mask fits you correctly? There are several ways of checking. With a reusable respirator, do the "negative-pressure-fit check" by removing the cartridges or filter elements and covering the intake ports with your flat palms (see the photo below). Inhale lightly and hold your breath for 10 seconds; you should feel the mask suck in closer to your face. If the mask loses vacuum and moves away from your face before you exhale, the seal is probably compromised. Adjust the tightness and/or location of the straps and try again. If the test still fails with the straps tight, the exhalation valve might be leaking (this simple round flap inside the valve is cheap and easy to replace).

Next, try the "positive-pressure-fit check" by covering the mask's exhalation valve and blowing gently. The mask should retain pressure for at least 10 seconds. If it doesn't, adjust the straps and try again. If this test fails, check the inhalation valves for leakage and replace them as necessary. If all the valves in the mask are in good shape and either

The negative-pressure-fit test, performed by covering a respirator's air intakes and inhaling for 10 seconds, can reveal leaks in the facepiece's seal against your face, which compromise respiratory protection.

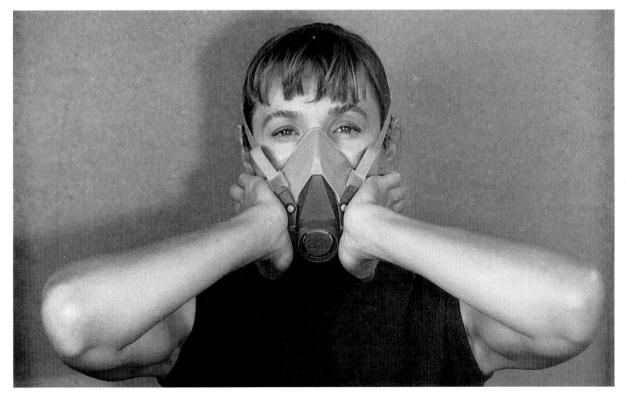

or both tests fail, try tightening both straps and wiggling the mask so that it settles into a different position on your face. Don't tighten the straps to the point that the mask is cutting into your face, creating deep red welts (the facepiece can really dig in around the nosepiece). If all else fails, get yourself another size or brand and model of respirator; subtle differences in size or manufacture will make one mask fit you better than another.

Qualitative fit testing The best assurance you can have that a reusable or disposable respirator fits properly is to perform a more formal, qualitative fit test (required by OSHA for testing respirator fit for woodshop employees). This procedure requires a special test kit (see Sources of Supply on pp. 194-195), which includes a Tyvek hood with a clear window, two types of testing solution and a pair of squeeze-bulb atomizers (called "nebulizers").

First, a sensitivity test solution is sprayed into the hood (fit over the person's head, sans mask) using the first nebulizer, to check whether the wearer can detect the sweet taste of the test solution. For the actual fit test, the person dons a T-21C-rated disposable mask or reusable respirator and a second, more concentrated test solution is sprayed into the hood with the second nebulizer (see the photo below). The wearer is then asked to perform a series of tasks, including normal and deep breathing, head nodding and talking—all intended to check how well the mask continues to seal to the face under working conditions.

A qualitative fit test provides a good way to check that a respirator fits tightly to the wearer's face and doesn't let dusty air sneak in past the filters. The test requires the user to wear the respirator inside a hood where an aromatic test solution is blown inside with an atomizer. If the wearer detects the sweet taste, the fit of the respirator isn't adequate.

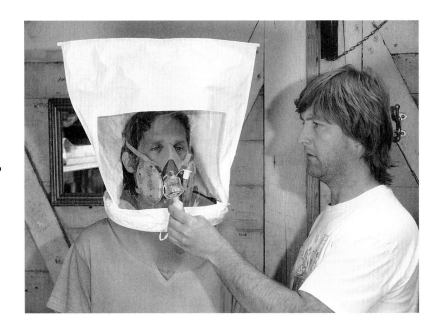

If the wearer cannot detect the sweet taste of the test solution, the test is successful and good respirator fit has been demonstrated. If the test fails, it can be repeated after readjusting the respirator. Two failures indicate that it's necessary to switch to another type and/or brand of respirator.

How often should you wear your mask?

Unless your shop has a central dust collection system and air-filtration devices that are extremely efficient, you'll probably still need to wear a mask or respirator during peak periods of dust production. Try to wear your respirator whenever you're using machines that create fine dust (or dust and chips) and always when using tools that lack effective built-in dust collection, such as many older portable power sanders. Failure to wear your respirator during brief machining operations, or removing it when talking on the phone or drinking your morning coffee, can increase your daily exposure to dust by a surprising amount. I've got an extra-long cord on my phone's handset, so I can take calls outside when I'm in the middle of dusty operations. You'll also do best to avoid unnecessary conversations with co-workers in the woodshop, since you're both likely to take off your respirators.

If you do occasionally raise great clouds of fine dust (say, from power sanding with inefficient collection) and your shop is not equipped with primary collection or some form of secondary collection, such as ventilation or an air-filtration device, it's prudent to continue wearing your respirator after sanding is complete until you leave the shop. If this describes your situation, do your heaviest sanding at the end of the workday and clean up the settled dust before you begin work in the shop again the following day.

If you can't stand wearing a reusable respirator for long periods of time (and you don't want to install a collection system), try switching to a more comfortable disposable mask, such as one of the cloth-style models, or a molded mask with an exhalation valve (see pp. 41-42). You'll probably find lighter-weight disposables less cumbersome and more comfortable to wear (when I wear mine for extended periods, I often forget I have it on at all).

Powered air-purifying respirators

Powered air-purifying respirators are an interesting alternative to disposable masks and reusable respirators. These personal protection devices are known in the manufacturing industries as "PAPRs" for short; among woodworkers, they are more commonly referred to as air or dust helmets. Unlike half-masks that cover only the mouth and nose, powered air-purifying respirators envelope practically your entire face and head and provide a steady stream of cool, clean filtered air to breathe. While they are expensive (ranging in price from around $250 to $750), PAPRs can provide a level of comfort and breathing protection often difficult to achieve with standard masks and respirators.

A PAPR is made up of a hard-hat or fabric cap that encloses the crown of the head with a visor and a clear shield that cover the entire face of the user. Most helmeted models have a flip-up face shield that can be fitted with replaceable overlays—a clear piece of plastic that adheres to the outside of the face shield to protect it against scratches that would quickly ruin the shield. An elastic-drawn, disposable seal (typically made of Tyvek fabric) fills the gap between the bottom of the helmet's shield and the wearer's face. A battery-powered fan provides a constant supply of air, and a system of prefilters and filters cleans the air before it is fed to the wearer. Dust helmets aren't airtight, so you don't have to worry about suffocating if the fan suddenly quits. The positive air pressure produced by the fan also means that if the visor and hood don't form a perfect seal around your face, dusty air is unlikely to leak in.

PAPR models such as the Racal Airstream AH5 (see the photo on p. 56) and 3M's Airhat (shown in the photo on the facing page) locate the fan and filter in the back of the helmet itself, with battery power supplied from a separate belt pack. (Some light-duty units, such as Racal's "Airlite," house the battery pack in the helmet itself.) Other models, including the Racal Air-Mate 3, shown in the photo at left, house the fan, filter and battery in a separate belt-worn pack that connects to the helmet via a flexible hose. Regardless of the model you choose, the battery pack contains rechargeable ni-cads (nickel-cadmium batteries). Depending on the model, these batteries typically last from 4 to 12 hours between recharges. Like the batteries for most cordless power tools, ni-cad battery packs for PAPRs have a "memory," which means you should exhaust the battery completely before recharging, so that it won't lose a percentage of its ability to take a full charge (the new "smart chargers" now available are reputed to be able to keep a charging battery fresh for up to 30 days without diminishing its capacity).

One style of dust helmet (the Racal Air-Mate 3) locates the fan, filters and battery in a belt-worn pack connected to the helmet via a flexible hose. The helmet's flip-up shield makes it easier to answer the phone or have a conversation.

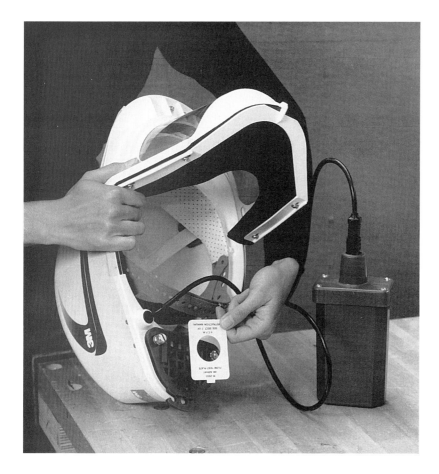

A PAPR filter check is done by placing a flow-test plate (or similar device) over the air intake, here on a 3M Airhat. With the fan running, the helmet is inverted; if the plate falls off, the filters need replacing.

The amount of airflow produced by the fan in a dust helmet varies by model, but is typically either 6 cfm or 8 cfm. Airflow diminishes as the filters become clogged; a simple pass/fail flowmeter (supplied by the manufacturer with the PAPR) allows you to check when it's time to service the filters (as shown in the photo above). The prefilters on some models can be cleaned by vacuuming or blowing them out. But, as with filter elements for respirators, the main filters on these units must be replaced when they're used up.

Despite the apparent degree of protection they provide, not all powered air-purifying respirators have NIOSH TC-21C approval. The Racal AGH1 and Airlite are rated only for "nuisance levels" of dust (as with comfort masks, see p. 40). Some models can be fitted with organic-vapor cartridges, so your expensive PAPR can do double duty in the finishing booth. One important caveat: PAPRs only filter the air, *they do not supply fresh oxygen.* You cannot work safely with a PAPR in an oxygen-depleted environment, such as in a spray-mist-choked finishing booth or an enclosed garage with an unvented heater or running car engine.

A dust helmet, such as the Racal Airstream AH5 shown here, can offer comfortable, dependable protection against respirable dust, even for bearded or eyeglass-wearing woodworkers who typically have trouble using respirators.

Pros and cons of choosing a PAPR

So why choose a powered air-purifying respirator when, for all the added expense, PAPRs don't provide fine-dust-filtering performance that's any better than a well-fitted respirator? Many bearded wood-workers choose PAPRs because they can't get a good face-to-mask seal with regular dust masks or they can't comfortably wear prescription eyeglasses with a half-mask respirator. Most PAPRs have plenty of room under their face shields for wearing eyeglasses (see the photo on the facing page). Other woodworkers prefer using PAPRs because they combine eye and respiratory protection in one device; models that use a hard-hat include head protection as well (if you work in a cold shop, you can buy a helmet liner to help keep your head warm). Because PAPRs provide a constant flow of fresh air, the face shield doesn't tend to fog up, something that woodworkers who wear regular safety glasses or goggles often complain about. Still others say that the positive air pressure makes it much less fatiguing to wear a PAPR compared to a regular respirator. And woodworkers who work in hot conditions enjoy the comfort of a continuous flow of fresh air streaming over their faces.

On the downside, dust helmets can be cumbersome to wear, especially those models that have large belt packs with protruding filters, which tend to bump into machines and benches as you navigate around the shop. There's another small and insidious problem with the belt-filter-style PAPRs: If you love chili, you'll have to watch yourself carefully—the location of the air inlet on the belt pack ensures that any flatulence will not go unnoticed. Then there's the communication problem. Not all models feature a flip-up visor, requiring you to remove the helmet and hearing protectors before you can talk on the phone, or even have a reasonably clear conversation. And you're likely to be assailed with nicknames like "aquarium head" and "space woodchuck" by your shop mates or, worse, scare the hell out of the occasional unannounced shop visitor.

Some woodworkers complain that the noise from the constant whir of a PAPR's fan is really annoying, especially in models that have the motor/fan mounted inside the helmet (many say that the sound is similar to the drone of a jet engine that you hear on a plane in flight). Also, regular muff-style hearing protectors can't be worn with some helmets (at least one unit, the Racal Air-Mate 3, can be fitted with helmet-mounted earmuffs). An alternative is to wear special behind-the-ear muffs, as shown in the photo on the facing page, or earplugs inside the helmet.

CHAPTER 4

Shop Ventilation and Air Filtration

Because of the profusion of new abrasive tools and machines, such as random-orbit sanders and wide-belt sanders, the average woodworker today generates more fine dust than ever. And regardless of how big and powerful a dust collection system you may have in your shop, a certain amount of fine dust always escapes into the air. Once aloft, fine dust is easily respirable, and since dust can remain suspended for a long time, your exposure can continue for hours after you're done sanding. Dust particles that don't end up in your respiratory tract will end up all over your bench, tools and floor in a fine film that once again becomes an airborne hazard each time you walk across the shop and resume work.

The best way to keep your shop clean and stay healthy is to get the fine dust out of your shop's air. Two practical methods for abating airborne dust in most woodworking shops are ventilation and air filtration. Ventilation is simply the process of exhausting dust-laden shop air; air filtration uses fan-powered filter devices to remove the lion's share of fine dust from air circulating around the shop. Both are considered secondary air-cleaning methods; neither is a replacement for collecting as much dust as possible at the source by means of some sort of dust collection system. But either method can dramatically improve the quality of the air in your shop—and your enjoyment of woodworking along with it.

Shop ventilation

Probably the simplest way to reduce the amount of fine dust in your shop is to catch it while it's airborne and blow it outdoors. Shop ventilation works by dilution, replacing dusty air with clean air from outside. This method is very low-tech, requiring only a strong fan, an intake outlet and an exhaust outlet. The idea is that the fan carries off airborne dust as it wafts around the shop and removes much of it before it has a chance to settle. Fresh air enters the shop through an inlet (an open window or door is fine), preferably located on a wall opposite the outlet, to create flow-through air movement.

Generally, you'd use shop ventilation only in conjunction with primary collection at the source, using shop vacuums or a central dust collection system. But if your fine-dust generation is modest, you can use ventilation as a primary means of capturing and expelling fine dust, albeit with limited effectiveness. Shop ventilation can help reduce the overspill from dust-spewing power tools, but the tool should still be connected to a dust collector or shop vacuum. For best protection, you should also wear a respirator while operating the tool.

A household box fan with a furnace filter taped over its intake can provide an effective means of taking fine sanding dust out of the shop air. Dust-removal efficiency is aided by taping cardboard baffles around the fan and by moving air toward the box fan with a second, high-velocity circulation fan.

Fan capacity

The larger the air-moving capacity of the fan you use, the more dusty air that is exhausted. High-capacity fans (or blowers, as they're sometimes called) are rated for the volume of the air they remove, measured in cubic feet per minute (cfm). Santa Cruz woodworker Cliff Friedlander uses a large (2,500 cfm) squirrel-cage fan to exhaust fine dust from hardwood and MDF created during the process of building kitchen cabinets (see the photo at left). Squirrel-cage blowers can be purchased new (see Sources of Supply on pp. 194-195), or scavenged from old air-conditioning equipment. Choose a fan that has enough cfm capacity to perform six to eight air changes an hour, as described on p. 69. If you use a high-volume fan to ventilate a shop that has a stove, water heater or furnace, it's imperative to allow plenty of fresh air to replace the exhausted air so that you don't create a downdraft that will bring smoke or toxic fumes down a chimney or ventilation pipe.

While a powerful fan can move a great volume of air, it has little power for capturing dust at its source. Therefore, move your dust source as close as possible to the exhaust fan. For example, to abate fine dust created during hand sanding, set up a work station next to a window or doorway. Use a box fan to suck the dusty air away from you and to the outdoors (see the photo on p. 59). The closer the fan to the dust source, the better.

You can increase the efficiency of a box-fan ventilation setup in two ways. One way is to tape cardboard baffles around the fan; the baffles will help to contain and direct the flow of air traveling by the dust source, and help the fan capture and carry away more particles. The other way to increase efficiency is to place a second fan behind your work area; this fan will blow fresh air past you and aid the flow of dusty air toward the exhaust fan. Just about any fan will serve this function, but you'll get the best performance by using an air circulation fan, as shown in the photo on p. 59. These compact fans are designed to move a good volume of air at high velocity (they are also useful inside the home to help spread cool or hot air from room to room). Just make sure not to place the fan so close to the work area that its powerful blast picks up fine dust and blows it around the shop.

Cabinetmaker Cliff Friedlander uses a large squirrel-cage fan to exhaust fine sanding dust from his shop in temperate Santa Cruz, California. An open window across the shop allows fresh air to enter.

Filtering ventilated air

The relatively small amount of fine dust exhausted from your shop by the fan probably won't be a problem, as long as the dust is blown into a large open area where it will disperse and settle harmlessly. But if your shop is close to your home (or near a neighbor's house), you'll definitely want to do the environmentally friendly thing and filter most of the dust from the air leaving your shop. Fortunately, adding a filter isn't difficult or expensive. Simply mount a standard fiberglass-media furnace filter that's as big as the inlet on your blower (or the outer dimensions of your box fan) to the intake side of the fan (I used tape to mount a filter to the box fan shown in the photo on p. 59). For even better fine-particle filtration, buy a better-quality pleated filter, such as a 3M Filtrete filter. You can buy any of these filters from your local hardware store, building supply or a heating, ventilation and air conditioning (HVAC) supply. The filter will not only keep a good percentage of dust particles from blowing outdoors, but it will also help keep the fan blades and motor from getting coated with dust. Note, however, that adding a filter reduces the fan's air-moving capacity slightly (see p. 69).

To keep dust and airborne pollen from entering your shop, you'll also want to fit a filter over your shop's air inlet. You can build a frame to hold the filter in place over the window or vent used as an air inlet. You can extend the life of your ventilation filters slightly by vacuuming or blowing them clean once in a while. Wear a respirator when you do, and replace the filters when they've become thoroughly clogged with fine dust.

Although easy to implement, the biggest shortcoming of shop ventilation is its limited application. Unlike an air-filtration device (described in the next section) that circulates air inside a closed shop, simple ventilation must displace the air blown outside by introducing fresh air into the shop. Hence, you won't want to be blowing all your shop air outdoors if it has been heated or cooled and/or dehumidified. (Note that by introducing fresh air, shop ventilation can provide a modicum of cooling on a hot summer day, if you locate your air intake in a shady spot.) Generally, shop ventilation is a technique best suited to woodworking in a temperate climate, or during the most temperate seasons of the year.

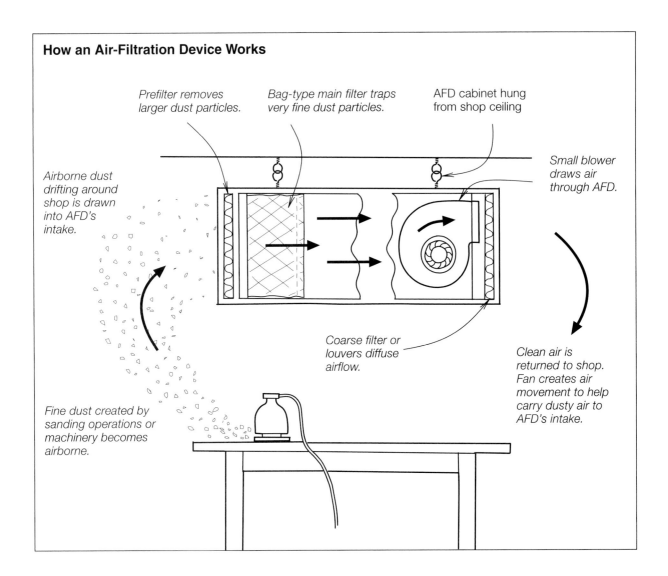

How an Air-Filtration Device Works

Prefilter removes larger dust particles.

Bag-type main filter traps very fine dust particles.

AFD cabinet hung from shop ceiling

Small blower draws air through AFD.

Airborne dust drifting around shop is drawn into AFD's intake.

Coarse filter or louvers diffuse airflow.

Clean air is returned to shop. Fan creates air movement to help carry dusty air to AFD's intake.

Fine dust created by sanding operations or machinery becomes airborne.

Air-filtration devices

Practically unheard of in small shops just a few years ago, air-filtration devices, also called air-cleaning devices or air cleaners, have long been used in industrial facilities for cleaning all manner of particles out of the air. Air-filtration devices (I'll call them AFDs, for short) are compact devices that are designed to be installed near the ceiling, where they don't take up much room in a crowded shop. They operate by drawing dusty air circulating around the shop through a series of filter media, and then returning clean air back into the shop, as illustrated in the drawing above. Because new air isn't introduced from outside, a heated shop stays warm and an air-conditioned shop stays cool. Ideally, an AFD exchanges all the air in the shop many times per hour, to keep free-floating dust in check.

As with shop-ventilation methods described in the previous section, air filtration should be used to augment dust control by a primary collection system, not replace it. Without any primary collection, you'll end up breathing unacceptably high levels of fine dust, even if you've installed an efficient AFD, since free-floating dust is likely to be inhaled on its way to being filtered out of the air. You're also likely to overwork the AFD by overloading its filters and diminishing its air-moving capacity. But by choosing the right air-filtration device and locating it properly in your shop (both discussed later in this chapter), you can effectively remove a great amount of the airborne dust that has eluded capture. If you run a commercial shop, air filtration is a great candidate for improving the quality of shop air to meet OSHA regulations for maximum levels of dust permitted in the workplace.

AFD anatomy

An air-filtration device is made up of three main components: a cabinet-style housing, a set of filters and a fan. Cabinets, typically made from thin sheet metal, are sturdy enough that units can be easily hung from the shop ceiling. To make the filters easier to remove and clean or change, many cabinets feature compartments at the front of the unit, as shown in the photo below. Air exhausted through the back of the

To make cleaning and replacement easier, most air-filtration devices house their prefilters in a slide-in compartment on the front of the unit. The JDS Air-tech 2000-350 shown here also has a side door that allows easy access to the unit's bag-type main filter.

cabinet passes through either a coarse diffusing filter, a fiberglass-media filter or a louvered outlet (see the photo on p. 74). The fans used in AFDs are the squirrel-cage blower type, powered by a small motor (typically between $\frac{1}{15}$ hp and $\frac{3}{4}$ hp). These motors are rated for continuous duty, so you can leave the unit running all day, if need be. The fan and motor are largely sheltered from dust because they are mounted downwind of the unit's filters. Some units, such as the Penn State Industries AC920, the Trend-lines AC1000 and the JDS Air-tech 2000-816 and 2000-1016, come with two-speed motors that allow you to set the performance of the unit to suit the amount of dust in the air. This feature might be useful if at times you do relatively little dust-raising work, yet at other times you run sanding machines all day and raise voluminous clouds of dust.

The motor and fans in most AFDs I've tried don't seem to generate much noise—typically about the same number of decibels created during a normal conversation between adults. You quickly became acclimated to the steady whir these units produce, so there's little need to turn them off during phone calls or conversations with shop visitors.

If you're a hobbyist who produces dust mostly by hand sanding or with small powered abrasive tools that are hard to collect from, such as a Dremel tool or die grinder, you might consider a benchtop AFD, such as Penn State's DC720, shown in the photo below. Such units don't take up space on a wall or ceiling, and store compactly when

Dust spewed from portable power tools that lack dust bags or hoses can be difficult to control. One solution for small tools, such as this Dremel tool, is to work close to a benchtop air-filtration device. Clear plastic baffles on the front of the unit direct the air through a pleated panel filter; clean air exits at the rear.

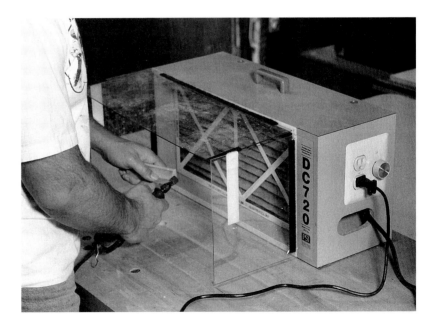

not in use. Benchtop AFDs are also handy if you occasionally like to do a little hand sanding at the kitchen table in the evening. The unit's built-in adjustable baffles help direct the airflow so that the device captures more fine dust and filters it out before it escapes and wafts around the room.

Two-stage filtration

AFDs capture dust particles in two stages: first with a prefilter and then with a main filter. (One unit, Hartville Tool's model 30916, has two pre-filters.) The prefilter is usually a spun-fiberglass, polyester-mesh or pleated-fiber filter, as commonly used for furnace filters. The prefilter takes the brunt of the dust load, trapping the larger dust particles ahead of the more expensive main filter. The main filter's task is to capture any fine dust left in the air; it is typically efficient at removing particles down to at least 3 microns. Main filters are usually the bag type (one is shown in the photo on p. 63). Some units use less expensive extended-surface, pleated-style main filters. A bag filter's multiple-compartment design (or a pleated filter's corrugations) gives it more surface area relative to its height and width, thus allowing it to trap more dust. The greater surface area also reduces a filter's airflow resistance, which allows the fan motor to work more easily. Lower air resistance also helps increase the volume of air moving though the AFD.

Filter efficiency How efficient is an AFD filter at trapping dust particles? All filters are rated for efficiency by detailed and complex testing procedures specified by the American Society of Heating, Refrigerating and Air-Conditioning Engineers (ASHRAE). Filter and AFD manufacturers employ independent testing laboratories to perform the ASHRAE tests to evaluate the efficiency of their different filters and AFD units. The test most commonly employed is the "dust spot efficiency test," which gives a good indication of the amount of particulate matter a filter is able to capture. The test results are interpolated into an overall efficiency rating for that filter. Filters commonly used for AFD main filters have efficiency ratings of 45%, 65%, 85% or 95%.

As with motor horsepower ratings, understanding how well any given filter performs is more complex than a single efficiency number can explain. Any filter's efficiency is different for different size particles. For example, even a relatively low-efficiency 45% filter is capable of removing 90% of the particles that are 5 microns and larger. By contrast, a 65% filter will remove 90% of the particles down to 1 micron, and a 95% filter will scrub out an impressive 99% of particles down to

1 micron from the air passing through it. Also remember that a filter's ability to trap small particles goes up as the filter becomes dirty, since the particles act as a sort of filter media themselves (see p. 43).

While even a 15% filter is 100% efficient at trapping particles the size of golf balls, it is a filter's ability to capture respirable dust (particles that are smaller than 10 microns) that you should be most concerned with. Manufacturers usually find it to their advantage to publish higher efficiency numbers when promoting their units, so be sure to check their claims carefully when evaluating an AFD's fine-dust-filtering abilities.

So how efficient does the filter in an air-filtration device need to be to clean the air in your shop? One air-filtration specialist I spoke with recommended that for stopping respirable dust, woodworkers should use an AFD with a filter efficiency of either 65% or 85%. If you are particularly sensitive to dust or prone to allergies, 95% filtration efficiency is recommended (some manufacturers offer a 95% main filter as an option). A 95% filter is efficient enough to cleanse the air of spores, mold and dust-borne bacteria as well.

It would seem logical to assume that the two filters in an AFD (the prefilter and the main filter) would create a sort of tandem effect resulting in better overall particle capture. However, the filtering efficiency of an AFD is primarily a function of the unit's main filter. The prefilter does affect (and can improve) the particulate-capturing potential of an AFD, but it is primarily used in AFDs for economy, since it is cheaper to replace this less efficient filter than it is to replace the more costly main filter.

Optional filters If your shop produces lots of very fine dust, say from running large stationary abrasive machines (such as stroke sanders, which can be difficult to collect from efficiently) or from power carving with abrasives, you might opt to fit your AFD with an electrostatic prefilter. Although they are much more expensive than regular furnace-type filters, electrostatic filters are washable and can be reused many times.

Fine dust floats in part because friction generated during sanding gives it a positive static electric charge; the particles repel each other. An electrostatic filter has a negative charge that neutralizes the charge on the dust, so it falls out of the airstream into the filters. This is the same principle employed by APSEE (Air Purification through Stimulated Emission of Electrons) machines, which are devices used in some factories to get dust to drop out of the air.

In spite of their name, electrostatic filters do not use electricity; rather, they are composed of electrostatically charged fibers contained in multiple layers. These layers have different ionic charges that attract dust particles in much the same way that balloons are attracted to a statically charged wool sweater. An electrostatic filter is also great for filtering out smoke, either from wood burned by cutting tools or from cigarette-toking woodworkers. The only important caveat for using these filters is that in shops where large amounts of solvent-based finishes are used it's possible for dust particles to bridge the filter layers and trigger a spark that could cause a fire.

Some manufacturers offer an optional charcoal filter for their AFDs. These filters are a blessing if you occasionally work with odiferous materials, such as pungent finishes and adhesives. These optional filters will reduce most odors, as well as abate fumes and smoke. As with organic-vapor cartridges (see p. 49), the activated charcoal in these filters doesn't filter fine dust very well. Therefore, you'll get the best performance by mounting a charcoal filter after the AFD's prefilter and main filter; install it in place of the diffusion filter found in most AFDs. Since the activated charcoal continues to work even when the filter is not being used (just like an organic-vapor cartridge for a respirator), keep the filter in a sealed plastic bag between uses. A warning: Don't ever try to use a charcoal-filter-fitted AFD to exhaust air from a spray-finishing booth, especially if you use solvent-based finishes; the motors in these units are not explosion-proof!

Filter cleaning and replacement Most prefilters and main filters can be vacuumed occasionally (on the side that faces away from the fan) to prolong their useful life. You can also clean a filter by blowing air through it from the exhaust side (the side of the filter that faces the fan), but you'll need to be careful because the jet of high-pressure air from a blowgun can easily rip holes through delicate filter media.

All filters need to be replaced once they're clogged to the point that the air flowing through them is restricted by about 50%. How can you tell when a filter is clogged to that degree? Expensive industrial AFDs incorporate an airflow gauge, known as a manometer, which reveals a reduction in air pressure inside the AFD caused by a dirty filter (see pp. 116-117). A less accurate but more practical, low-tech way of gauging airflow is with a few pieces of ribbon tied to the exhaust end of the air filtration unit. When a unit's filters are new, the ribbons fly straight out and flap vigorously in the rushing air (see the photo at right). Check the ribbons every once in a while, and replace the filters when the ribbons droop down or flap with about half of their original vigor. Another

Three short lengths of ribbon tied to the exhaust grill provide a simple way of gauging the airflow through an air-filtration device. When the ribbons sag and flutter less aggressively, it's a sign that airflow is restricted and that the unit's filters need cleaning or replacement.

way to do a quick filter check is to hold the filter a few feet from a 75-watt or 100-watt light bulb; a filter due for replacement will be hard to see light through (the embedded dust particles limit translucence).

Don't be surprised by the cost of replacement filters for your AFD (ideally, you should check the price before buying a new unit). Prices can vary from about $25 for a set of pre- and main filters for a small unit, to over $100 for some of the larger industrial-duty AFDs. One way to save money when buying replacements is to get them locally from an HVAC supply store. Chances are they'll be a lot cheaper than if you ordered stock replacement filters from the manufacturer. Just make sure that the filters you buy are exactly the same size (frame dimensions and thickness) and type as the originals. More important, make sure you buy filters that are at least as good (ASHRAE-rated for the same degree of efficiency) as the filters originally fitted to your AFD. If you substitute a cheaper filter, say a pleated furnace filter for a bag-type main filter, you'll degrade the AFD's dust-capturing efficiency. Conversely, you can improve the dust-grabbing performance of an AFD by replacing low-efficiency original filters with more expensive, higher-efficiency filters (often offered by the manufacturer of the AFD). But be aware that high-efficiency filters tend to be more restrictive, so you end up trading high efficiency for less airflow through the unit. When in doubt about filter substitutions, consult the manufacturer of your AFD for advice.

Sizing an AFD for your shop

Just as you must choose the right size central dust collector to suit the size and capacity of the ductwork that connects it to your machines, you must choose the right size air-filtration device to suit the size of your shop. Like central collectors, AFDs are sized by the amount of air that they move through them, measured in cubic feet per minute (cfm). The idea is to select an AFD large enough to make six to eight air changes per hour (the number of changes per hour recommended for typical woodshop conditions). This means moving the entire volume of air contained in the shop through the unit that many times per hour. Why so often? First, because new dust is being created all the time in a working shop. Second, because the filters in an AFD aren't perfect at removing all the particles in one pass, so the air must pass through the filters several times or more before most of the fine particles are captured.

To figure out how large an AFD you'll need for your shop, you'll need to start with a few calculations (summarized in the formula on the facing page). First, compute the total volume of your shop in cubic feet

FORMULA FOR SIZING AN AIR-FILTRATION DEVICE TO YOUR SHOP

$$\frac{\text{Cubic-foot volume of shop (length x width x height [in feet])} \quad \times \quad \text{Number of recommended air changes per hour (6 [hobby use] or 8 [full-time use])}}{60 \quad \text{(Division necessary to convert cubic feet per hour into cubic feet per minute [cfm])}} = \text{Cubic feet per minute (cfm) air-movement capacity of air-filtration device}$$

by multiplying its length, width and height. If the shop's ceiling is taller than 12 ft., use 12 as the height. If the layout of the shop is L-shaped or divided into sections, compute the overall volume by adding up the volume of the individual sections. Next, multiply the total shop cubic footage by the number of air changes per hour the unit is to accomplish. If you're a hobbyist or weekend woodworker, multiply by 6; if you run a full-time business or production shop, multiply by 8. The result reflects the total volume of air that the AFD needs to move an hour. But since AFDs are rated in cubic feet per minute, divide this number by 60 to get the correct cfm rating.

As an example, a shop that's 20 ft. long by 16 ft. wide with a 9-ft. ceiling has a volume of 2,880 cu. ft. Multiplying that figure by 8 air changes an hour yields 23,040, which divided by 60 shows that you'd need an AFD that's rated for *at least* 384 cfm.

I use the phrase "at least" in this example because the cfm ratings stated in an AFD manufacturer's literature typically indicate the amount of free air the unit is capable of conveying. In other words, the quantity of air moved through a unit sans filters. Because a working unit draws air through two or more filters that restrict airflow, filtered cfm averages between 63% and 91% of free-air cfm. Furthermore, a dirty filter is more restrictive than a clean one, so the cfm performance of a well-used AFD is likely to be even lower. Therefore, to be certain that the air-filtration unit that you select will fulfill your needs, select a model that offers 20% to 30% more free-air cfm than the actual airflow you need for your shop, as calculated above.

Two can be better than one If you have a large shop (say, over 7,500 cu. ft.), don't be surprised if your calculations reveal the need for a really big air-filtration device, one with a cfm of 1,000 or more. While there are quite a few AFDs on the market that can handle that airflow, you are likely to get better performance by using two units instead of one. Industry experts often recommend using two or more small AFDs in large shops because it's easier to locate them closer to different sources of airborne dust—say, one near the workbench where hand sanding is done and another near stationary sanding equipment. By mounting AFDs strategically, you can shorten the distance that dust-laden air must travel before it is inducted. Also, in multiple-employee shops, dusty air is less likely to pass through areas where people are working (and breathing) on its way to the AFD. Just as important, multiple AFDs can be used to work together to increase air movement: The exhaust from one unit can actually boost the intake of the other unit, thus improving air circulation and dust capture. Multiple units are also recommended for better airflow in irregularly shaped shops, where it can be difficult to keep air circulating (see p. 76).

Building your own device

The basic design for an air-filtration device—a fan and some filters in a box—is so simple that many small-woodshop owners opt to save a little money and build their own units. More power to them. But while you can get away with mounting a scavenged attic-exhaust fan and a cheap furnace filter in an old orange crate, you'll get much better performance if you choose components carefully and follow a few basic guidelines. The drawing on the facing page shows a simple AFD that's designed to handle light to moderate dust production in a small shop, say, up to the size of a two-car garage. If you're inventive and don't mind doing a little experimenting, you can modify these plans and build a larger unit to suit your needs.

The cabinet for the shopmade AFD is constructed from six pieces of ³⁄₄-in. plywood, cut to the dimensions shown and glued and screwed together. Three frames, made from ¹⁄₂-in. by ¹⁄₂-in. strips, create a pair of slots that contain the unit's filters. A small hinged door on the side of the unit provides access to the filters for cleaning and replacement. The fan is mounted to the inside back of the cabinet over the rectangular cutout for the exhaust. A louvered grill (available from a home supply store) fastened over the exhaust opening keeps debris and fingers out of the fan and allows you to direct the air exhaust to encourage air circulation (see p. 74). Eyebolts, fastened through the top of the cabinet, provide mounting anchors, if you plan to hang the unit from the ceiling (see p. 77).

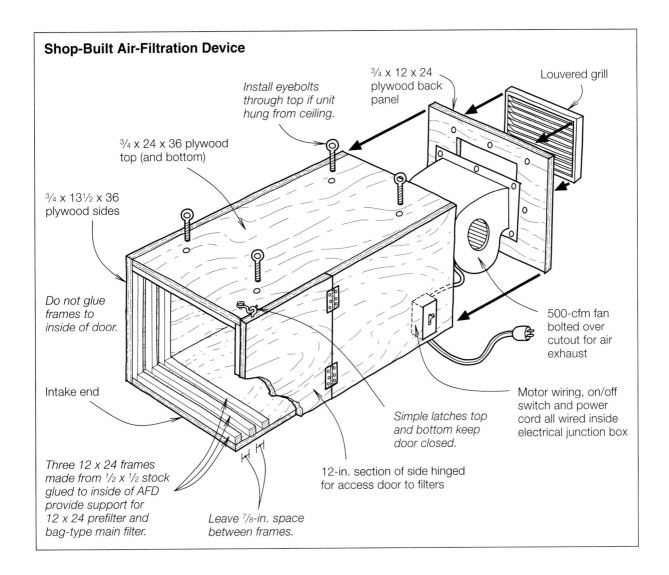

Shop-Built Air-Filtration Device

Install eyebolts through top if unit hung from ceiling.

³⁄₄ x 12 x 24 plywood back panel

Louvered grill

³⁄₄ x 24 x 36 plywood top (and bottom)

³⁄₄ x 13½ x 36 plywood sides

Do not glue frames to inside of door.

Intake end

500-cfm fan bolted over cutout for air exhaust

Motor wiring, on/off switch and power cord all wired inside electrical junction box

Simple latches top and bottom keep door closed.

12-in. section of side hinged for access door to filters

Three 12 x 24 frames made from ½ x ½ stock glued to inside of AFD provide support for 12 x 24 prefilter and bag-type main filter.

Leave ⅞-in. space between frames.

To afford reasonably good filtration, the shopmade AFD has two filters, each 12x24x1 in size. A simple fiberglass-media furnace filter is used for the prefilter. For best fine-dust-capturing ability, the unit uses a 90% to 95% efficiency bag-type filter as a main filter, which must be specially ordered (see Sources of Supply on pp. 194-195). At around $35, this bag filter is fairly pricey; you may wish to substitute a less expensive (but less efficient) pleated-media, extended-surface filter (such as the 3M Filtrete). Both kinds of main filters offer relatively low air resistance, so the fan can maintain a good rate of airflow even when the filter becomes dirty.

While just about any fan that's capable of moving 500 free-air cfm can be used as an air mover, a small squirrel-cage-type blower (W. W. Grainger order # 4C445) is a good choice; a blower with a mounting flange on the outlet makes it easier to mount the unit to the cabinet. It's easier to bolt the fan to the plywood rear panel before assembling the cabinet, using lockwashers to prevent fan vibration from loosening anything (see the photo below). If you decide to use another size or type of fan, make sure that the cfm capacity of the fan suits your air-filtering needs, as outlined in the previous section. Because of the added restriction that the filters will cause, you'll need a fan that has at least 20% to 30% higher free-air capacity than the filtered cfm you plan to get from your finished AFD. (Also, different filters present different degrees of resistance, which will affect the final performance of your shopmade AFD.)

You can wire the shopmade AFD with a non-metallic sheathed cable (such as Romex), as long as all connections are made inside an electrical junction box. If you opt to control your AFD from a timer switch (as described on p. 77), you can run a line for the fan directly to the

The heart of a shop-built air filtration device is a small squirrel-cage fan, which is easier to mount before assembling the cabinet. The device uses a furnace-type fiberglass prefilter and a bag-type main filter (shown on the bench to the right).

timer, in which case you won't need to install an on/off switch on the unit. If the unit is to be mounted within reach, you may wish to install an on/off switch in a junction box mounted on the side or bottom of the cabinet. The switch is a single-pole, single-throw switch that's rated to handle the amperage and voltage of the fan's motor.

Building an AFD from a kit   If you don't have the patience to build an AFD from scratch but don't have the money to buy a ready-made one, you can take the middle road and build an AFD from a kit. The Wood-smithShop catalog sells a kit for an AFD fitted with a 465-cfm fan (free-air cfm), which makes it large enough for working in a garage-sized shop. The kit includes everything you need to build the unit (including one set of filters) except hardwood for the filter frames and ¾-in. plywood for the cabinet that houses everything. The kit costs about half of what you'd pay for a similar-sized ready-made AFD.

Installing an AFD

To get the best performance from an air-filtration device, you have to mount it in the right location in your shop. The device stands the best chance of filtering the greatest percentage of dust from the air, if most of the air in your shop is circulating through it. Unfortunately, most shops are square or rectangular, with corners where air is apt to stagnate and allow the dust to settle out (only to become airborne again when disturbed). But there are several ways to encourage good air circulation to and from an AFD that will minimize air-stagnation problems.

Here are a couple of general rules about placement of an air-filtration device that apply to nearly all woodshops. First, try to locate the AFD between 8 ft. and 10 ft. from the floor (no lower than 6 ft.). If you have a shop with low ceilings (8 ft. or under), mount the unit to the ceiling or no lower than two-thirds the way up from the floor. If your shop has high ceilings, don't make the mistake of mounting the unit higher than 10 ft. or 12 ft. Fine dust created at ground level won't circulate much above 12 ft. to 14 ft. up, and higher mounting reduces an AFD's filtering performance significantly as well as making access to the unit for servicing more difficult and precarious.

For best performance in a rectangular shop, locate the AFD along one of the longer walls, orienting the unit so that the intake (the end that draws in air) is approximately one-third of the way from the end wall (see the drawing on p. 74). The suction produced by an AFD just isn't

Locating an Air-Filtration Device in a Rectangular Shop

Locate AFD on long wall, with intake one-third distance from short wall.

⅓   ⅔

Dusty air
drawn into
intake

Clean air
exhaust
encourages air
circulation
around shop.

⅔   ⅓

*If second AFD is used,
locate on opposite wall with
intake one-third distance
from short wall.*

A louvered grill on the exhaust end of an air filtration device, such as the Trend-lines AC1000 shown here, can be adjusted to improve the air circulation pattern around the shop.

strong enough by itself to pull dusty air from a great distance. This arrangement tends to enhance air movement toward the unit's intake by using the more powerful stream of air exhausted from the fan to create a circular airflow around the shop. Even if you can't position the unit ideally, locating it close to a wall will probably create better air circulation than placing it in the middle of the shop.

Some air cleaners have adjustable grill louvers on their exhaust end, such as the Trend-lines AC1000 shown in the photo at left. If your unit has louvers, set them to direct the air exhaust to encourage circulation around the room. If your shop has forced-air heating or air conditioning, make sure that the air exhaust from those units doesn't run counter to the flow of exhausted air from an AFD, or cause undo turbulence that could adversely affect good air circulation to the AFD.

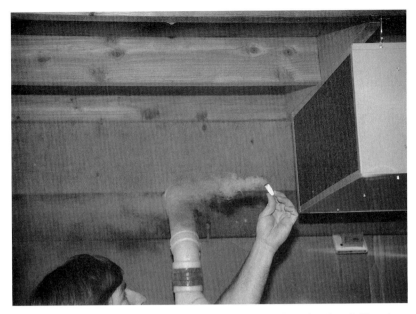

You can test to see how well air around your shop is circulating to and from an air-filtration device by lighting a smoke stick and observing the movement of smoke around the shop.

If you're not sure how well air is circulating to and from an AFD, you can check the airflow by observing how well smoke circulates around the shop. You can try using a lit cigarette or a few sticks of incense, but you'll get a better supply of smoke from a smoke stick (available from Lab Safety Supply, see Sources of Supply on pp. 194-195), as shown in the photo above. Turn on the AFD and hold the smoke source up to the exhaust end and observe the movement of the smoke. It should continue moving around the shop and eventually move toward the AFD's intake. Also try holding the smoke source at the end of the shop nearest the AFD's intake. Smoke should move toward the unit, albeit slowly. If stationary smoke haze reveals dead air zones, try relocating the AFD or using a circulation fan to bolster air movement, as described below.

If you're using only one AFD in your shop and are generating fine sanding dust in a location that's quite distant from the unit, you can enhance the dust-gathering performance of the AFD by using an air-circulation fan. Place the fan close to the dust source and point it in such a way as to blow the dusty air toward the AFD, as shown in the photo on p. 76. Try to set up your work station so that the fan is between you and the AFD. Avoid putting yourself between the fan and the AFD, because this encourages dusty air to be drawn toward you (where you're likely to breathe it) rather than away from you.

A compact, yet powerful, air-circulation fan can improve the performance of an air-filtration device (AFD). The fan blows dusty air from the bench area toward the AFD, increasing its capture efficiency.

AFDs in large and irregular shops In large rectangular shops, you can achieve the filtering capacity you need and further encourage circulation around the shop by placing two air cleaners on opposite long walls; each unit need produce only half the overall cfm you need (see p. 70). As with a single unit, locate the intake of each AFD one-third the distance to the short wall, as shown in the drawing on p. 74. Two or more AFDs are also likely to be needed if your shop is extra long and narrow (so-called "shotgun" shops), is irregularly shaped (with L-shaped or T-shaped layouts) or has partitions that divide different work areas. Air circulation is created in these situations by mounting AFDs in strategic locations, such as at corners where divided spaces meet, and using fans to encourage air movement through stagnant air zones.

Mounting an AFD Because the ideal location for an AFD in most shops is near a wall, the easiest way to mount a unit is to place it atop a shelf or on brackets fastened to the side wall. To deaden fan noise amplified by placement on a thin wood or metal shelf, set the AFD on rubber pads or furniture cups placed at the corners. Bolt or tie the unit down, so it won't vibrate or get knocked off accidentally.

If you wish to hang an AFD from the ceiling, most units have holes in their cabinets for eyebolts. For safe mounting, drive heavy-duty eye-screws into ceiling joists and hang the AFD's eyebolts from these with spring-loaded safety hooks (see the top photo at right). Unlike open hooks, safety hooks must be manually snapped open before the unit can be taken down. Make sure the unit isn't hanging low enough to smash into; the sharp-edged metal cabinets found on most units could render a nasty gash. Since most AFDs are fairly heavy (typically between 40 lb. and 85 lb.), place the unit on a stack of boxes during installation, rather than trying to heft it while connecting the safety hooks. Your vertebrae will thank you for it.

When to run an AFD

Because air-filtration devices can be so effective at collecting the fine dust that has escaped primary collection, you'll definitely notice a difference if you leave the AFD running during and after working; you won't see that fine coating of dust all over your machine tables and benchtops. And if your shop is in your garage or basement, your family won't be dusting the furniture nearly as often (it's amazing how readily extra-fine dust particles penetrate fine cracks and under doors and travel around a house).

You should run an AFD whenever you are operating machinery for more than a few minutes, and when you're using portable power tools, such as routers and sabersaws. All these bladed and bitted tools generate fine dust along with the larger chips they spew out. You especially need to run an AFD whenever you're doing any power sanding, which is the greatest source of fine dust in the shop. Even if your portable sander has built-in collection, most sanders spit out dust faster than most means of collection can capture it.

If you do your sanding (or heavy machine work) close to the end of the workday, you can abate floating dust by letting your AFD work overtime. Since it can take quite a bit of time for an air-filtration device to filter all the air in a shop thoroughly, it's not a bad idea to let the unit run for an hour or two after you've stopped working. To avoid the inconvenience of having to turn the unit off (or the cost of running it overnight), you can control it with a timer. You can buy a spring-wound timer with a capacity of up to 12 hours (available from W. W. Grainger) and a hold feature that allows you to turn the unit on manually for as long as you like (a timer is available as an option on Total Shop AFDs). Mount the timer in an electrical box, just like a regular light switch (see the bottom photo at right), with the power line from the AFD connected directly to the timer. Locating the timer near your shop's front door makes it easier to remember to set it for timed operation when you're ready to call it a day.

Spring-loaded safety hooks and eyebolts provide a secure means of attaching an air-filtration device to the ceiling, yet allow it to be taken down for more convenient cleaning or servicing.

An electric timer (conveniently mounted near the door) allows you to run an air-filtration device for a specified amount of time, so fine-dust capture can continue after you leave the shop.

CHAPTER 5

Portable Dust Collection Devices

Small, portable vacuums are the poor man's dust collectors. They are relatively inexpensive, versatile and don't take up much valuable real estate in shops that must share limited floor space with machinery and perhaps the family automobile. The smallest of the small portable hand-held units make quick work of dirty benchtops, and perform double duty cleaning up household spills or vacuuming sand from the trunk of your car. Canister-style shop vacuums are terrific for all kinds of shop pick-up chores, from collecting dust from portable and small stationary machines to sweeping floors (without raising a cloud of fine dust as a broom does!). And if you need more sawdust-sucking power, you can buy a larger portable collector that'll handle some full-sized jobs, like keeping a small table saw's sawdust output under control.

In spite of the straightforward nature of these simple suction devices, there are more than a few tricks for getting the most out of them, including a slew of devices and methods for making them quieter and easier to use, as well as for expanding their abilities and chip-holding capacity. Some of these devices are available commercially; others are things you can build yourself.

Shop vacuums

Shop vacuums are much like their household counterparts, but with a few important differences. A shop vacuum, often wrongly referred to as a "shop vac" (Shop-Vac is a trademarked brand name; it's the same as calling all facial tissues "Kleenex"), has a larger capacity and a more powerful motor than most canister-style household vacuum cleaners. More important for shop cleanup, all shop vacuums work just like two-stage central dust collectors. "Two stage" means that large chips and shavings are deposited in the canister before the air passes through the filter, as shown in the drawing below. No debris actually passes through the vacuum's fan, where a sucked-up chip or stray nail could wreak havoc (see the discussion of single-stage vs. two-stage systems on pp. 102-105). Many models feature a blower port—a hose connection where the air expelled by the vac is discharged. This low-pressure, high-velocity air can actually be used for a low-velocity air table, as described in *Woodshop Jigs & Fixtures* (The Taunton Press, 1994).

A shop vacuum's light weight and compact size make it portable enough to excel at shop clean-up time. Most units come with wheels built into the bottom of their canister, or they have a cart or wheeled assembly mounted to the bottom or side of the unit. Portability is a

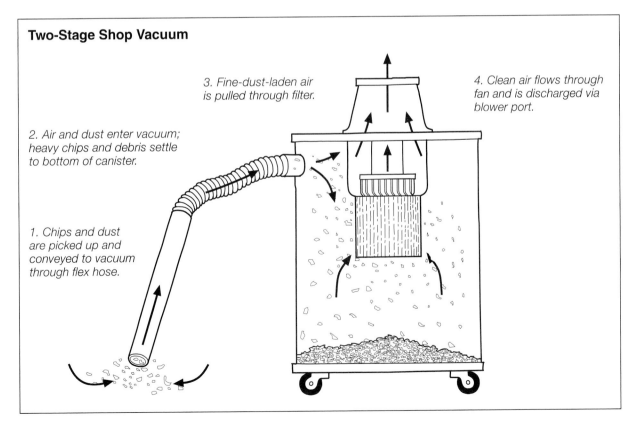

Two-Stage Shop Vacuum

3. Fine-dust-laden air is pulled through filter.

4. Clean air flows through fan and is discharged via blower port.

2. Air and dust enter vacuum; heavy chips and debris settle to bottom of canister.

1. Chips and dust are picked up and conveyed to vacuum through flex hose.

great part of a shop vacuum's usefulness, so if you plan to cart the unit around the shop a lot, check the size and quality of the wheels before you buy it. Cheap, hard plastic wheels on pressed-metal swivels can wear out quickly. And if your shop floor has an irregular surface, these small-diameter wheels can jam into crevices or hang up on bumps and upset the canister, making shop cleanup more frustrating. Some models, such as the Milwaukee 8911 and the Bosch 1702, have large rear wheels and a push-cart-like handle, making them very easy and stable to scoot around the shop.

Although they're extremely handy for shop cleanup and for collecting dust from portable power tools, shop vacuums can't take the place of portable or central collectors, which have more powerful induction motors and fans that produce the larger volume of air needed to collect chips and sawdust from shop machinery. While a shop vacuum produces an impressive amount of suction, thanks to a high-pressure airflow created by a high-rpm fan powered by a universal motor, the volume of air that's conveyed is low. (To understand better how air velocity and volume work together to carry dust and chips, see the sidebar on p. 100.) Low air volume, coupled with small-diameter hoses, means that shop vacuums are usually not up to handling the large quantities of chips and shavings produced by most full-sized woodworking machines. Also, the motors used in shop vacuums typically create a tremendous amount of noise (which can, however, be abated by methods discussed later in this chapter).

If your expectations are modest, you can often get away with using a shop vacuum to collect from a single small machine, such as a table saw, radial-arm saw or router table. But a thickness planer is usually a different story. The heavy shavings take more suction to remove than most shop vacuums can generate. And even if the vacuum works reasonably well, the small canister on most units will fill up from the waste of planing just a few boards. If your budget dictates that a shop vacuum is the only collector available, build a good dust hood (see pp. 169-173), keep the hose short and take small cuts on the machine to generate a lower volume of chips.

Power and capacity

We've all read the hyped-up figures in advertisements for shop vacuums—clearly another example of the kind of hype we've had to endure for years concerning the horsepower of portable power tools like routers. The confusion often stems from the power rating scale the manufacturer chooses to use. "Peak horsepower" seems to be the most popular choice, since that represents absolutely the most power output you're ever going to realize from any motor (albeit, in some cases, for a few seconds before the motor burns up).

The number of amps the vacuum's motor is rated gives you a slightly better gauge to compare different models: A shop vacuum with an 11-amp motor is undoubtedly stronger than one with a 6.5-amp motor. But for comparisons between units that have very similar-sized motors, amp ratings don't tell you how efficient the unit is at translating motor power into suction performance. Fan and air-system design, housing configuration, bearing quality, hose size and filter type all conspire to make some vacuums better performers than others. These factors also affect qualities that are subjectively important to the user, such as the vacuum's noise output and service life.

Probably the single best indicator of vacuuming performance is the static pressure the unit is capable of generating. Static pressure is typically stated in "static inches of water lift," which is a measure of how high the vacuum can draw water into a vertical tube against the force of gravity. Generally, the more inches of water a vacuum can draw, the better the sawdust-sucking performance it will deliver (this is only a test—not all vacs are designed to suck up water!). A top-performing shop vacuum (such as the Bosch 1702) may be capable of drawing more than 70 in. of water—at least half as much again as competing models with similar-sized motors. While few manufacturers rate their units this way, you can compare test results for static pressure for more than a dozen popular shop vacuums in a product-test article in the April 1995 issue of *Wood* magazine.

Hose size Besides power rating, another important factor that determines how well a shop vacuum actually picks up wood debris is hose diameter. The larger the diameter of the hose, the greater the physical capacity the vacuum will have for picking up larger chips, shavings and even small cutoffs. If you plan to use your vacuum for general shop cleanup or to collect chips from a jointer or table saw, you'll want to use a vacuum with a 2½-in. diameter hose. The 2½-in. hoses, which come standard on only about half of the models currently on the market, are fairly crush-resistant, but they aren't very durable since they're typically made of thin, easy-to-puncture vinyl wrapped around a spiral wire. If you need better durability, you can fit your vacuum with industrial flexible hose (made of PVC or polyester neoprene), as described on pp. 152-154.

One downside of a 2½-in. hose is that its maw is big enough to suck things off benchtops and machine tables that you don't want to dispose of, such as small parts, tools and small pets. The large opening does, however, make them good for collecting cutoffs or small parts,

Collecting small parts

Lest you think your shop vacuum is only good for collecting sawdust, it can also provide a simple and foolproof solution to a common woodworking problem: cutting off small parts on a table saw or radial-arm saw. For example, when cutting small blocks (like ABC blocks for a child), the "good" part is a small cutoff from a longer piece of stock. The problem is that these small parts are easily grabbed by the sawblade and chewed up or thrown violently across the shop. To remedy the problem, set up the shop vacuum to capture these small parts, and suck them out of harm's way.

Start by cleaning out your shop vacuum (so you won't have to pick the good parts out of a canister full of dust and debris). Remove the disposable bag, if need be. Then, temporarily clamp the 2½-in. dia. vacuum hose so that the open end is positioned near the point on the saw where each part will be cut off (see the photo at right). Now turn the vacuum on and take a trial cut. If parts aren't pulled away fast enough before the sawblade grabs them, try repositioning the hose closer to the blade, or fitting it with a smaller-diameter nozzle (which will increase the velocity of the airflow).

Not only does this technique make it safer to cut small parts, like wooden plugs, short dowels and loose tenons, but it also virtually guarantees that you'll have fewer rejected parts (due to the sawblade's nipping). And all the small parts end up in the vacuum's tub, where they won't get lost and are easy to gather. Just don't try this trick with a single-stage dust collector (where all the air and debris pass through the blower before depositing in the filter bag); if you do, you'll hear some horrible noise as the parts are shredded as they hit the fan (bigger parts are likely to destroy the fan!).

You can use a shop vacuum to suck up small workpieces, such as the minute wood cubes shown here, before they are snagged by the blade and chewed up or thrown. The hose is taped temporarily to a miter gauge and positioned near the point where the cut is completed.

as described in the sidebar on the facing page. One trick I use to suppress my vacuum's hunger is to stretch a small piece of ¼-in. wire mesh called "hardware cloth" (available at a good hardware supply store) over the end of the hose (see the photo at right). A rubber band holds the wire mesh in place. You can use even finer mesh as needed, say to prevent the accidental pickup of small screws or other hardware. It really beats scrounging through a dusty canister searching for missing tools—or Fluffy, your pet hamster!

The smaller-diameter hoses—1 in., 1¼ in. and 1½ in.—that come standard on many shop vacuums (including the Porter-Cable 7810, the Wap SQ14 and the Bosch 1702) generally create very high air velocities, which make these units good for capturing small chips and fine sawdust. These smaller hoses are also more flexible and less cumbersome than 2½-in. hoses, which make them great for collecting dust from portable power tools (see pp. 84-86). Just don't try to use these thin hoses for collecting large debris, because you'll clog the hose. With some models, you can buy a larger-diameter hose as an optional accessory (practically any shop vacuum can be jury-rigged with a 2½-in. hose, even if the maker doesn't offer one).

One of the unpleasant side effects of having a plastic hose with dust moving through it at a high velocity is that it tends to create static electricity in a dry environment, which can result in some nasty shocks to the user. If your vacuum's hose has a wire helix that is exposed inside the hose, try running a ground wire from the hose's spiral wire to the motor housing or frame of the vacuum. (This remedy probably won't work if the wire helix is sandwiched between layers of hose material.) If the vacuum's motor isn't grounded (it has a two-prong electrical plug), you'll need to fit a new electrical cord with a ground wire running from the motor frame to a three-prong plug.

Canister capacity As with horsepower ratings, manufacturers are apt to fudge a bit when it comes to the capacity of the canisters on their shop vacuums. Canister capacity is typically stated as "gross capacity" measured in gallons. Actual capacity is usually less. For example, my aging Sears shop vacuum, rated to hold 16 gal., actually holds more like 14½ gal. once the pleated-paper filter element is in place.

The capacity of the shop vacuum you buy should depend on what you want to use it for. Small-canister vacuums, in the 6-gal. to 10-gal. range, have adequate capacity for shop cleanup or for collecting small chips and fine dust from portable power tools (and they are small enough to fit under a workbench and compact enough to transport around a really small shop). If you wish to collect chips and shavings from small stationary machines, I'd recommend a canister that holds at least 12 gal., and preferably 16 gal. If you prefer a really big shop vacuum to

Stretching a piece of wire mesh over the end of a vacuum hose prevents it from accidentally sucking up small tools and hardware.

a portable collector (see pp. 94-97), the Delta 49-255 and the Ryobi IDV28 (shown in the photo on p. 90) feature 28-gal. canisters—large enough to contain the prodigious output of a small planer paring down a pile of rough boards. If you already own a powerful, but small-capacity shop vacuum, you might be able to expand its capacity by using a preseparator canister, as described on pp. 110-111.

Collecting from portable power tools

A significant use for shop vacuums is in collecting small chips and fine dust from portable power tools, such as routers, saber saws, belt sanders and random-orbit sanders. Most modern versions of these tools come with built-in dust collection ports. On power sanders, this port is often the mount for the tool's small dust collection bag. You can usually remove the bag and plug a hose into the port. Some tools require an adapter to make this connection (if the hose doesn't attach snugly, you can usually hold it in place with a small flexible-hose clamp, as shown in the photo below). Other portable power tools, such as routers and saber saws, require special adapters to provide them with dust collection (Makita even makes a dust-extraction attachment for rotary drills, used for dusty masonry-drilling operations). You can also build custom hoods for portable tools and add dust collection directly to shop-built jigs and fixtures, as described on pp. 188-190.

To reduce the bother of having to drag the hose around while using the tool, its preferable to use a small-diameter flexible hose, somewhere between 1 in. and $1\frac{1}{2}$ in. in diameter. Many models offered these days come standard with hoses of this size. If your unit has a

You can enhance the dust collection from a portable power tool with a built-in dust bag by connecting the tool's dust port to a shop vacuum. A small hose clamp holds the flexible hose in place.

2½-in. hose, you can purchase a smaller-diameter hose and fit it to your vacuum; if it isn't a standard accessory, a few wraps of duct tape or cobbling up a connection fitting from some PVC pipe should do the trick. When I connected a Makita 1-in. dia. hose to my 2½-in.-ported Sears shop vacuum and switched it on, the motor whined and strained considerably. If this happens with your setup, I'd suggest adding extra ports to let air bleed into the hose—I simply drilled a few extra holes into my PVC connector fitting, adding new ones until the straining motor quieted down to its normal dull scream.

At first, dragging around the hose makes the power tool feel terribly unwieldy. To ease the bulkiness of the hose, try suspending it with a bungee cord attached to the ceiling above your bench or work area, as shown in the top photo at right. Just make sure to attach the bungee cord securely, so it won't spring back suddenly and cause injury, and leave lots of slack in the hose, so you won't suddenly reach the end of your tether as you come up to the end of a long board you're cutting, shaping or sanding. If you can dedicate a hose to a single power tool, attach the tool's electrical cord to the hose with duct tape or wire or plastic ties. Attaching the two together makes it less likely for either to snag or hang up as you work.

Automatic vacuum control switches Another way to streamline the process of collecting dust from a portable power tool is to control the shop vacuum with an automatic switch. This special electronic switch detects the current of the power tool as it is turned on and off, and switches the vacuum on at the same time. Even slicker, most electronic switches feature a built-in delay when cutting off power to the vacuum, thereby allowing the suction to clean out any dust or chips left in the hose (some switch models even allow you to adjust the delay period).

You can buy an automatic switch as a plug-in accessory. The Automater line of switches come as small boxes that plug directly into 110-volt power (see the bottom photo at right). The box has two receptacles: one for the shop vacuum and one for the portable power tool. You can also buy units that will control a 220-volt induction motor, such as found on many portable and central dust collection systems. Several shop vacuums currently on the market come with similar automatic switches built directly into them, including the Fein 42989, the Makita 420 and the Porter-Cable 7810, shown in the photo

Suspending the vacuum hose and electrical cord of a portable power tool with a bungee cord (hooked on a rafter or ceiling joist above the bench) will keep them from fouling the tool.

The Automater electronic switch turns a shop vacuum on and off along with the power tool that's plugged into it. Plugging a powerstrip into the auto switch allows several tools to remain connected at once, so you don't have to replug a tool each time it is used.

Some shop vacuums, such as the Porter-Cable 7810 shown here, feature a built-in automatic switch. The portable power tool is plugged into a receptacle on the vacuum, and the switch turns the vacuum on and off in concert with the tool.

Fitting a Y-connector (made from plastic pipe fittings) to the intake on a shop vacuum allows the connection of two hoses, so that both tools served remain ready to run with dust collection.

above. Regardless of the brand or model, any automatic switch has a maximum number of amps it will handle (both for the power tool and the vacuum). If you plan to run a power tool that's particularly power-hungry, make sure to check the capacity of the switch before you buy it.

If you often switch between several tools when working at your bench, you can plug them into an electrical powerstrip (see the bottom photo on p. 85). Plug the powerstrip's cord into the tool receptacle on the automatic switch (if you plan to run multiple tools at the same time, just make sure their combined amperage doesn't exceed the limit of the auto switch). To circumvent the hassle of having to switch vacuum hoses when working with multiple tools, you can make a Y-connector that will allow two or more hoses to be connected to your vacuum at one time. I fashioned a very serviceable Y-connector (see the photo at left) from several plastic pipe fittings. A sanitary Y creates the secondary connection; a slip-fit basin connector is just right for mounting a 1¼-in. hose on the Y. In my experience, you don't lose enough suction by connecting two or three hoses to require plugging hoses that are not currently in use (in fact, when using small-diameter hoses with a vacuum that has a 2¼-in. port, connecting multiple free-flowing hoses seems to help; using only one small hose constricts the airflow too much).

Vacuum filters

Portable shop vacuums employ an extensive array of filter materials, including pleated paper cartridges, foam or paper sleeves, cloth filters and tank liners and disposable paper bags. Each individual type of filter has particular advantages and disadvantages, as outlined in the chart below. To improve performance, many shop vacuums have two-stage filtration, using a prefilter, such as a cloth liner or a disposable bag, to screen out debris ahead of the main filter (foam sleeve, pleated paper, etc.). This prefilter makes the main filter less susceptible to clogging, so it needs cleaning less often. Employing a two-stage filter also extends the life of the more expensive main filter. Several different vacuum models, including the Fein 42989 and the Wap SQ14,

SHOP-VACUUM FILTER MATERIALS		
Filter Media	Advantages	Disadvantages
Pleated paper cartridge filter (often used alone; sometimes with a prefilter)	Large surface area, for better flow-through; can be blown or washed out and reused. Excellent filtration when pleated filter combined with disposable bag.	Relatively expensive to replace; paper folds can be damaged by sharp-edged debris sucked into vacuum.
Foam sleeves (always used with a paper or cloth prefilter)	Inexpensive; easy to clean and replace; good for wet pickup.	Need to be used with a paper sleeve or tank liner as prefilter.
Paper sleeves (often used as prefilters for foam sleeves)	Inexpensive; simple.	Paper can tear easily; installation can be tricky.
Cloth filters (usually used as prefilters)	Inexpensive; easy to install. Good filtration when combined with foam sleeve.	Only fair filtering performance, even when used with foam or paper sleeve filter.
Cloth tank liners (used as prefilters)	Easy to install and clean; large filtering area less subject to clogging. Good filtration when combined with foam or pleated filter.	Expensive to replace if badly torn.
Disposable filter bags (used in conjunction with another filter element)	Effective prefilter that extends life of main filter; convenient means of emptying debris from vacuum (especially good for disposal of fine dust).	Bags tend to be pricey (between $3 and $7 each); sharp-edged scraps can tear the bag. Difficult to retrieve items accidentally sucked into vacuum.

feature two-stage filters that are capable of filtering out fine dust particles down to 1 micron in size. Hence, these vacuums are a great choice for capturing fine dust from power sanders. Models that use a disposable bag also make emptying out a canister's worth of sanding dust a much tidier task.

Unfortunately, the single filters found in most shop vacuums do a less-than-perfect job of removing all the respirable dust from the air passing through them. In fact, they can even perform a disservice by stirring up fine dust and forcefully blowing it around the shop. Therefore, you'll probably need to wear a dust mask, ventilate the shop or use an air cleaner to protect your lungs from fine dust, especially during sanding operations. Alternatively, you can relocate your shop vacuum outside or move it to a room or closet adjacent to your shop (just make sure the room is ventilated; an airtight enclosure will prevent exhaust from the vacuum from exiting). You can run flexible hose (or 2½-in. PVC pipe) into the shop, to connect to machines or portable power tools; keep the runs relatively short—under 15 ft. for average-size vacuums. The relatively small volume of air that a shop vacuum is capable of removing from your shop won't increase your heating or cooling bills significantly, so you don't have to worry about returning the air from the unit to the shop (see pp. 127-128). A bonus of removing the vacuum from the shop is the reduced noise. You can operate the unit remotely by running an extension cord and plugging it into a switched outlet in the main shop, by switching it on and off automatically (see pp. 85-86) or by using an electronic remote control (see pp. 165-166).

Keeping it clean Just as it becomes harder to breathe through a respirator when the filters are clogged, the suction performance of any shop vacuum diminishes as its filter(s) become more and more choked by dust and debris. Some vacuums, such as the Makita 420S and the Porter-Cable 7810, have built-in filter-shaking mechanisms to dislodge particles from their pleated filters to reduce clogging between major cleanings (see the drawing on the facing page). You can make any vacuum's main filter element easier to clean—as well as protect it from damage—by pulling an old nylon stocking or a leg cut from a nylon pantyhose over it (see the photo at left). Queen-size pantyhose is fine for smaller-diameter (4-in. to 7-in. dia.) filters; for larger-diameter (7-in. to 9-in. dia.) filters, you'll need to buy extra-large (or size XX-Large) pantyhose (if the fit is loose, use a big rubber band to hold the pantyhose in place). The fine nylon mesh of the pantyhose keeps chips from damaging or getting stuck in pleated-paper filters, which can be quite difficult and time-consuming to clean out. Just pull the stocking off before cleaning the filter. Replace the stocking when it gets too many runs in it.

Pulling a nylon stocking over a pleated-paper filter prevents coarse chips and shavings from clogging the filter and makes it easier to clean.

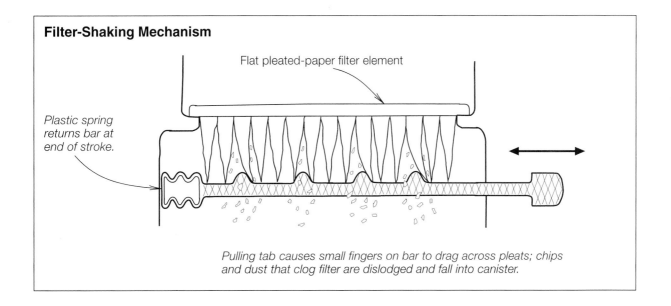

Filter-Shaking Mechanism

Flat pleated-paper filter element

Plastic spring returns bar at end of stroke.

Pulling tab causes small fingers on bar to drag across pleats; chips and dust that clog filter are dislodged and fall into canister.

Once a filter has become clogged by fine dust, the simple way to restore its performance is to remove the filter element and shake, blow or vacuum off the dust (known as "dust cake") that's built up on it. Thin paper-sleeve prefilters can be gently shaken clean, but they should be changed once they get torn or really dirty. To avoid raising a ton of fine dust inside the shop, take your shop vacuum outside before emptying its canister, and be sure to wear a respirator. Remove most of the sawdust buildup dry, using a brush to clean between the corrugations on a pleated-paper filter (work carefully and use a brush with bristles that aren't too stiff, as the paper is fairly easy to tear). To clean out the really fine dust that embeds itself in the filter fibers, foam and most paper filters can be flushed out with water. Don't apply too much force, say from a high-pressure garden hose, lest you tear the element. If you do get a small hole or tear in a paper or foam filter, wait for it to dry and then tape the hole with duct tape or glue on a small patch (use yellow glue for paper; silicone sealant for foam). Replace the filter if it's been damaged extensively or after a long period of heavy use. If you can't find a replacement for a cylindrical or flat pleated-paper element, check the stock at a local auto-supply store; you can often come up with a perfectly suitable substitute for the official replacement.

Some vacuums use disposable bags that make it very easy to empty the canister. However, these disposables can be very expensive to replace, costing up to $7 each for some models. Since the bag doesn't really have to match the size and shape of the canister precisely, you can save money in some cases by substituting a cheaper disposable bag from a different make and model of vacuum (use duct tape to adapt the fit of the bag's intake hole to suit the vacuum). Since most vacuums use the bag as a prefilter, carefully shake or blow the bag clean, and patch any small holes or tears with tape or glue before replacing it. If you're using the vacuum to pick up only larger shavings and debris, leave the disposable bag out entirely (to reduce the risk of the bag being torn) and let the vacuum's main filter do all the work.

Accessories

Most shop vacuums come with a whole gang of accessories, many of which are similar to the extras that come with standard household vacuums. These usually include dust brushes, crevice tools, floor nozzles and extension wands, all of which make the average clean-up chore easier. For example, extension wands make floor cleanup a less backbreaking chore, and can keep you off that rickety ladder when sucking up cobwebs and dusting on top of hanging fluorescent fixtures (where fine dust can be a real fire hazard). And the crevice tool is a blessing for cleaning out small dust-packed spaces between the bench and wall, or for retrieving a small tool or fastener that's rolled behind a cabinet. If your shop vacuum didn't come with all the accessories you need, you can probably buy them as optional items from the same company that made the vacuum. You can also often use accessories from other manufacturers; just make sure they're made to fit the same size and style hose. Another alternative is to make your own accessories from inexpensive PVC pipe and fittings, such as the floor sweeper shown on pp. 32-33.

Cutting down on shop-vacuum noise

Because most shop vacuums are powered by universal motors that operate at high speeds (typically upward of 10,000 rpm), they emit a surprisingly piercing, nerve-grating whine. Add to this the already bothersome roar of a portable power tool, and the noise level quickly approaches the cacophony of a heavy-metal rock concert. This high noise level makes it nearly impossible to hear a ringing door buzzer or telephone.

Just as you can quiet down a noisy jalopy with a new muffler, you can quiet down your noisy shop vacuum the same way. Ryobi offers a muffler device as an accessory for their shop vacuum. To retrofit other vacuums, Beam Industries makes a special device called the "Sound Off" muffler (see Sources of Supply on pp. 194-195) that connects to a vacuum's exhaust port (sometimes labeled "blower"). An optional fitting adapts the unit for 2¼-in. ports, but a few winds of duct tape around the fittings supplied or a plastic pipe coupling will adapt the Beam to fit practically any shop vacuum. A bracket and hose clamp are included with the muffler to allow mounting to the vacuum's canister.

Quieting the nerve-grating racket produced by some canister-style shop vacuums can be done by adding a muffler. Here, Beam's Sound Off muffler is mounted to a Ryobi shop vacuum.

The Sound Off muffler works very well on vacuums that have their motors mounted inside the canister, with the exhaust port atop the unit (such as the Delta 49-225 or Ryobi IDV28 shown in the photo). In my non-scientific trials (using an inexpensive noise-level meter purchased from Radio Shack), I found that the Beam muffler reduced the sound-output level of the Ryobi by more than 10 dB—a significant improvement. Vacuums with top-mounted motors (such as most Sears models; see the photo on p. 28) benefit less from the Beam muffler; much of their noise emanates directly from the exposed motor housing. Also, you can't fit the Beam muffler on vacuums that don't have a regular exhaust port.

Another way to reduce a shop vacuum's noise (as well as any fine dust that gets by its filter) is to relocate the vacuum to a closet or different room, as described on p. 88. If you usually keep your shop vacuum under your bench, you can reduce its mighty roar to a whisper by covering it with a sound-deadening enclosure, such as the one shown in the drawing below. An enclosure should completely cover the vacuum

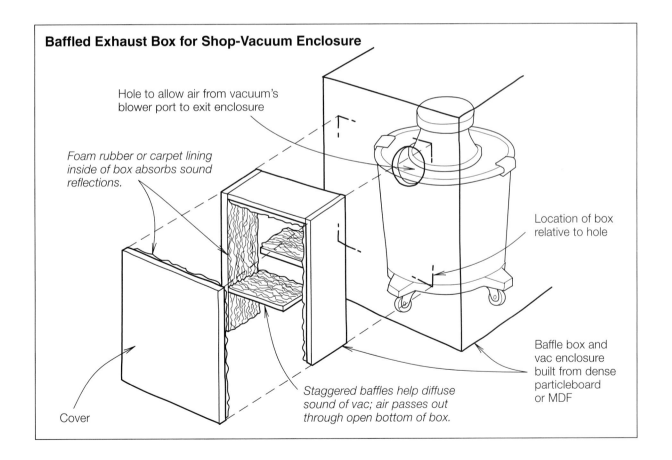

Baffled Exhaust Box for Shop-Vacuum Enclosure

Hole to allow air from vacuum's blower port to exit enclosure

Foam rubber or carpet lining inside of box absorbs sound reflections.

Location of box relative to hole

Cover

Staggered baffles help diffuse sound of vac; air passes out through open bottom of box.

Baffle box and vac enclosure built from dense particleboard or MDF down to a solid floor (if the vacuum must rest on a wood floor or shelf, put a couple of pieces of thick carpeting under the unit to keep motor noise from being conducted and amplified by the vibrating wood). The enclosure should be well sealed at the bottom, and it should provide a sound-reducing baffled air-exhaust cover (as shown in the drawing on p. 91) and a tight-fitting port for the vacuum hose. To contain a small unit, build a simple cover that fits over the unit like the domed lid on a fancy serving dish. To keep larger wheeled vacuums portable, build a door into one end of the enclosure, sealed when closed with weatherstripping (sort of a "vacuum garage"). To be most effective, any enclosure should be built from a dense material, such as particleboard or MDF. Line the inside with thin foam rubber, carpet or soundboard (sometimes called beaverboard; available at building-supply stores) to deaden the sound reflections inside.

Hand-held portables

Small hand-held portable vacuums are the equivalent of handguns in the woodworker's clean-up arsenal. Although they don't have much in the way of sawdust capacity, hand-held units, such as Black & Decker's "Dustbuster" models, are useful tools to complement a regular shop vacuum at clean-up time. Cordless portables are particularly handy. Not having a hose and electrical cord to contend with makes these units terrific for quick benchtop cleanups—for example, for sucking up small piles of carving shavings, or for removing waste from mortises you're chopping by hand (see the photo at left). Even though the suction power of some cordless models I've tried leaves much to be desired, I've been favorably impressed with the power and capacity of B&D's "Classic Plus" Dustbuster, which operates on 4.5 volts (most other models run on 3 volts). Keeping the handheld in its recharging station (located near the workbench, if possible) will keep it ever ready for use. Like most other cordless tools, you should occasionally allow the battery to drain entirely, to overcome the effects of ni-cad battery memory (where constantly "topping off" the battery reduces its capacity to take a full charge).

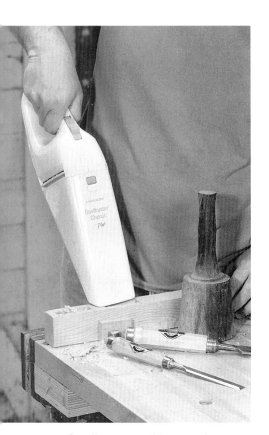

Cordless portables, such as this Dustbuster Classic Plus, are great for benchtop clean-up chores or for removing waste from joints cut by hand, such as these mortises.

One caveat when buying a hand-held portable for the woodshop is to avoid the small bagged models, such as Royal's Dirt Devil. While these portables are great for household vacuuming chores, the big problem for shop use is that all debris must pass through the unit's small fan before it's blown into the collection bag (like a single-stage collector; see p. 102). If you suck up chips larger than lentils, they won't pass through the fan and they'll bang around inside the unit until it's switched off, when they'll fall out onto the floor. By contrast, most

Using portable power tools at the job site is a much cleaner proposition if you connect the tool to a portable vacuum. The Makita 420S has straps that allow it to be worn like a backpack, and has an automatic switch built in.

Dustbuster-style handhelds have a chamber and filter ahead of the fan, so as long as the debris fits through the unit's intake opening, it'll be collected without a hitch.

A relatively new addition to the woodworker's clean-up arsenal is the Makita model 420S. This portable vacuum is small enough to be carried with one hand or worn as a backpack, allowing you to haul it around the shop or the job site with ease during cleanup (see the photo above). The unit includes a receptacle for plugging in a power tool and a built-in electronic switch that turns the vacuum on and off with the tool. By connecting a portable power tool's dust port to the vacuum's small-diameter flexible hose, you can do all kinds of trimming and finish work inside your home (or in a client's home) without making piles of sawdust.

Portable dust collectors

The next step up from a shop vacuum is the portable dust collector. These popular units are larger than a standard vacuum, both in terms of chip-holding capacity and motor size and fan strength. Models like the Shopsmith DC 3300 (see the photo on p. 29) or the barrel-top Delta 50-179 (shown in the photo at left below) sport durable ½-hp or ¾-hp induction motors, as compared to the compact universal motors used in most shop vacuums. This power, coupled to a larger, stronger fan wheel (rather than the small plastic fans used in most shop vacuums), allows portable collectors to suck up a much larger volume of air and chips.

Many portable collectors are two-stage units: Chips flow into the collection drum or bag first, where large chips settle before fine dust is trapped by the filter bag (see the discussion of single- and dual-stage

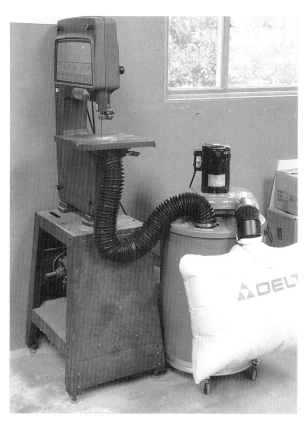

Popular for their compact size and good collection strength, canister-style portable collectors, like the Delta 50-179 shown here, allow efficient chip collection from most machines without the cost of installing a central system.

Compact portable collectors, such as the Penn State DC3 shown here, are easy to wheel around the shop and hook up to small machines like this horizontal belt sander.

collectors on pp. 102-105). But there are also single-stage portable collectors, such as the Makita 410 and Asian-built units like the Grizzly G1163 or the Penn State DC3, shown in the photo at right on the facing page. These portables work in the same way as do many larger-size central dust collectors: They suck chips and sawdust directly through the fan and into a filter/collection bag(s). Single-stage portables are usually very compact, but they lack the power and air-moving capacity of full-size central dust collector units, which are necessary for conveying dust from a ductwork system (see Chapter 6).

There are at least two good reasons you may wish to buy a portable dust collector. First, portable collectors are less expensive than central units, both in terms of purchase price and installation. A single-stage portable with a 1-hp motor costs less than a good cordless drill, and you need only buy a length or two of flexible hose to hook it up—there's no expensive ductwork to install. Second, their compact size and mobility make them nearly as portable as shop vacuums, but they're better able to handle the large volume needed to collect chips from full-sized woodworking machines. Their small size also makes portable units very flexible, because they can be readily wheeled around the shop and hooked up only when and where they are needed. This feature is especially good for weekend warriors who must work in a garage or a space that's used only part of the time for woodworking. Many portable collectors are small enough to fit under a workbench, or in a closet when not in use.

On the downside, the chip-holding capacity of portables with small canisters leaves much to be desired. Also, some compact units, such as the Penn State DC3 (see the photo at right on the facing page), can be difficult to empty, since they have no canister and chips and dust must be emptied directly from the filter bag. One way to increase chip-holding capacity and make sawdust easier to empty from such units is to add a dust preseparator canister ahead of the collector, as described on pp. 110-111.

Another problem is that running a noisy portable collector in close proximity to a noisy machine can generate enough decibels to make the user feel sonically abused, even with earmuffs on! A couple of possible solutions are to build a removable sound-deadening enclosure for a portable collector similar to the one described for a shop vacuum (see pp. 91-92), or to relocate the collector to a closet (see p. 88).

Hooking up a portable collector

How you hook up a portable dust collector depends, as always, on how you work and which machines you wish to collect dust from. Most woodworkers I've visited keep a short length of 4-in. flexible hose attached to the intake on the collector, which they interchange

A portable collector is much handier to hook up when you add quick-disconnect fittings to the hose ends. The fittings allow you to switch the collector between machines with just a twist of the wrist.

between the dust ports on the machines. Adapters can be used to allow a 4-in. hose to fit onto a machine with a 2½-in. dia. port (often found on smaller tools designed for home-shop use). If you have several machines you wish to serve, you can make hose reconnection faster and easier by installing quick-disconnect fittings, such as the ones shown in the photo at left. These devices (available from Air Handling Systems; see Sources of Supply on pp. 194-195) install on the ends of a flexible hose with a hose clamp—just a twist attaches or detaches the hose coming from the portable unit to a short hose coming from the machine or other dust source.

Because of its limited power and capacity (compared to larger central collectors), most woodworkers probably won't want to use a portable collector with more than one machine at a time. The exception would be hobbyists working with small machines and tools that don't produce much dust, such as scrollsaws or portable power tools; in that case, you can split collection using one or more Y-fittings on your hoses. In any case, try to keep your hose runs short. The longer the hose, the more the friction that's generated, which diminishes vacuum strength (see the discussion of static-pressure loss in the sidebar on p. 100). Also, using small-diameter hose or tubing can zap the dust-capture strength of most portable collectors. In my first attempt at installing a collector in my shop, I connected a ½-hp portable to a 12-in. planer via 3-in. PVC plastic drain pipe that was 15 ft. long; the only way the collector could keep up with chip production was if I set the planer to take a *very* light cut.

Controlling connections with a switchable manifold

If you find yourself working between several full-sized shop machines, say when ripping and dressing lumber using a table saw, jointer and small planer, you might want to install a small system of ducts and blast gates, as discussed in Chapter 8. But a less complex way to control collection to several machines is with a manifold, a device that directs the airflow from the portable collector to only one machine at a time, saving you the trouble of installing blast gates or having to switch hose connections each time.

A manifold consists of a box that provides connection for hoses coming from the collector and the machines, and a gate that directs suction to only the chosen machine. A simple manifold that can serve three machines is shown in the drawing below. The box is built from ¾-in. shop-grade birch plywood and accepts hoses from three machines (it could probably be adapted to work with four or five machines). A sliding gate made of ¼-in. plywood controls the airflow, and a dowel locks the gate into position. Plastic pipe connectors glued and screwed into holes in the box provide mounts for flexible hoses connected to machines and the collector. Adjustable hose clamps attach the hoses and allow their removal (to clean residual dust out of the manifold). A similar manifold (designed to suit your application) could also be used with a small central dust collection system.

Three-Outlet Dust Collection Manifold

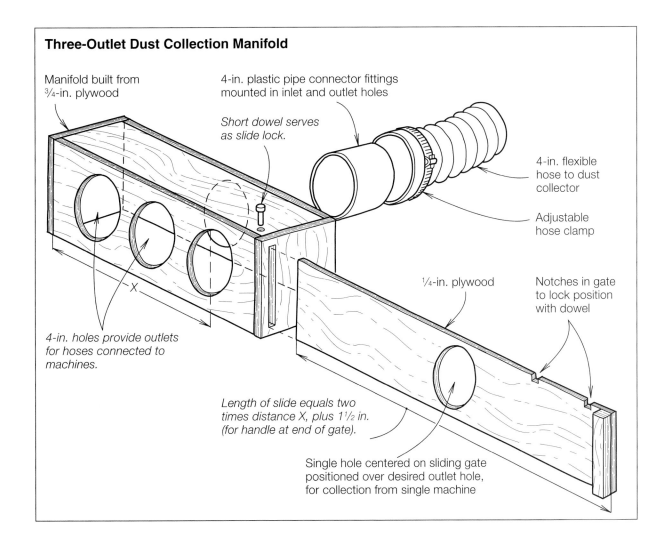

Manifold built from ¾-in. plywood

4-in. plastic pipe connector fittings mounted in inlet and outlet holes

Short dowel serves as slide lock.

4-in. flexible hose to dust collector

Adjustable hose clamp

X

¼-in. plywood

Notches in gate to lock position with dowel

4-in. holes provide outlets for hoses connected to machines.

Length of slide equals two times distance X, plus 1½ in. (for handle at end of gate).

Single hole centered on sliding gate positioned over desired outlet hole, for collection from single machine

CHAPTER 6

Central Dust Collectors

The best way to achieve the goal of a clean, dust-free working environment is to capture the dust as it's created, before it can escape and end up all over your shop. You can use a portable collector to capture sawdust at one or two machines or employ a shop vacuum to gather dust from portable power tools, but the best permanent solution for handling all the dust-producing machines in your shop is to install a central dust collection system. Having all your machines connected to a central collection system is almost as good as having a cleaning service on hand to tidy your shop: Every time you run a machine, the collector whisks chips and dust away, depositing them in a barrel, bin or bag, for neat and convenient disposal.

As shown in the drawing on the facing page, a central collection system consists of a network of ducts that connect to all machines and dust sources in the shop. The ductwork conveys dust and debris captured at the source back to the central collector. Collection begins at each machine with a hood or pickup that helps contain and capture chips and dust. A flexible hose connects the machine to a blast gate, which opens or closes airflow to that machine. Air and dust then flow through rigid ductwork, consisting of branch ducts that feed from different locations in the shop into a main duct that goes directly to the central collector.

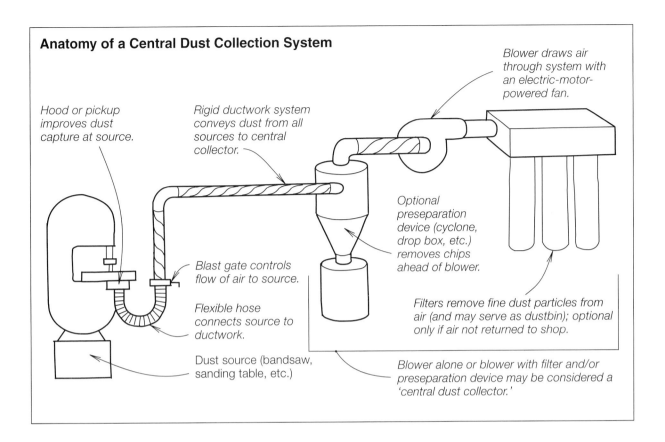

Anatomy of a Central Dust Collection System

Hood or pickup improves dust capture at source.

Rigid ductwork system conveys dust from all sources to central collector.

Blower draws air through system with an electric-motor-powered fan.

Blast gate controls flow of air to source.

Flexible hose connects source to ductwork.

Optional preseparation device (cyclone, drop box, etc.) removes chips ahead of blower.

Dust source (bandsaw, sanding table, etc.)

Filters remove fine dust particles from air (and may serve as dustbin); optional only if air not returned to shop.

Blower alone or blower with filter and/or preseparation device may be considered a 'central dust collector.'

The anatomy of a central collection system may seem simple, but there's more to installing a complete system than just running duct-work made from any old pipe you happen to have around the shop (like that surplus muffler pipe you have in the attic) and hooking it up to a collector that you bought simply because it was the one that was on sale at your local tool store. Air—the medium by which chips and dust are collected—has very specific characteristics that must be un-derstood and harnessed correctly to achieve efficient collection (see the sidebar on p. 100). And the central collector you choose to run your system must suit the size and capacity of the ductwork (see pp. 105-107). You also have many choices to make about the configu-ration and features of your central collector. The type of collector you buy (or assemble from separate components) affects not only the per-formance of the system but the ease and safety of using it as well. Ideally, all these decisions should be made carefully before buying and installing the ductwork and components for a complete central col-lection system. In this chapter we'll focus on the dust collector itself; in chapters 7, 8 and 9 we'll consider the design and installation of the entire system.

Air is the medium that makes all dust collection possible. The amount of air that flows through a system, how fast it flows and how much friction it encounters in its journey are all factors that are crucial to understanding how an efficient dust collection system works. These factors enter into play when sizing and laying out ductwork (as discussed in Chapter 7), as well as when choosing the right collector to suit the system (see p. 105).

Here are some principles of moving air that are important to understand when designing a central dust collection system:

1. Moving air has volume, measured in cubic feet per minute (cfm). Generally, the larger the volume of air traveling through a pipe, the more dust and chips it can carry. Therefore, machines that produce a greater volume of chips (such as planers and shapers) require more air volume (500 to 1200 cfm or more) to capture and convey them to the collector. Dust collectors with bigger motors and fans generally can move a larger volume of air. And the larger the diameter of a duct, the larger the volume of air and chips it can carry.

2. Moving air has speed or velocity, measured in feet per minute (fpm). The faster that air moves through ductwork, the better that larger shavings and chips will remain entrained in the airstream. Too slow an air speed and chips settle out and accumulate, eventually clogging the pipe. But too fast an air speed generates more friction than necessary. The air velocity recommended for small-shop dust collection systems is 3,500 fpm for the main duct and 4,000 fpm for branch ducts.

3. Moving air is subject to friction, measured as inches of static pressure (SP). Static-pressure loss is the energy lost to friction as air and chips travel through a duct, around corners and through transitions (such as where branches merge with the main duct). The power of a central collector is also rated in terms of the inches of static pressure that it can overcome.

Central dust collector basics

A central dust collector is like a big shop vacuum, but with some important differences. A shop vacuum doesn't have the chip-holding capacity or power of a central collector. It uses a small, high-rpm universal motor (the same kind used in most portable power tools) and fan to draw sawdust through a small-diameter (1-in. to 2½-in. I.D.) flexible hose that can easily clog with large shavings. In contrast, a central dust collector employs a powerful induction motor (as used in most stationary machines) and a special large-volume fan, called a blower, to convey chips and sawdust through larger-diameter (3-in. to 6-in. or more) ductwork.

A shop vacuum moves a small volume of relatively high pressure air (between 45 in. and 80 in. of static pressure) through its small-diameter hose, whereas a central collector moves a high volume of low pressure air (around 5 in. to 10 in. of static pressure in a typical small system), which is adequate for moving chips through larger-diameter hoses and ductwork (see the sidebar above). While a shop vacuum is certainly adequate for clean-up chores or collection from small tools, it just doesn't move the volume of air necessary to collect and convey the huge quantity of chips generated by full-size stationary machines.

Central dust collector anatomy

Most central dust collectors are made up of only a few basic components, as shown in the drawing on p. 99. At the heart of the system is the blower—the fan that creates the vacuum to entrain dust and chips in air and convey them through the system. Blowers designed for dust collection have paddle-wheel-style fan wheels (also called impellers), which revolve inside a metal housing with an inlet and an exhaust port. In all but industrial-type blowers, the fan wheel is driven directly by a powerful induction motor (better-quality collectors use TEFC— totally enclosed, fan cooled—motors, which are sealed against dust for longer service life). Some portable collectors (see Chapter 5) also use this kind of blower and induction motor, but most of these don't possess enough power or air-moving capacity to function as effective central collectors.

The blower's inlet may be connected directly to the ductwork that conveys sawdust from the machines, or to a preseparation device, such as a cyclone, drop box or canister, that removes debris and chips ahead of the blower for safety and better performance (see pp. 106-112). The blower's exhaust is usually connected to one or more filter bags or an assembly called a filter bag house to remove fine dust from the air before it passes through the filter media and back into the shop or the atmosphere (see pp. 113-119).

You can purchase a central dust collector as a complete, ready-to-use unit, with all components hooked together and attached to a base, or you can assemble your own collector from separate components. One advantage of building your own collector is that you can mount components separately, to fit into narrow, odd-sized or cramped spaces. The most basic collector you can build consists of a blower alone connected directly to shop ductwork. The cost of simplicity is that this system must exhaust air outdoors, so that you don't pump your shop full of sawdust. For a return-air system (see pp. 127-128), you must add some form of filtration. And for even better system performance and longer filter life, it's desirable to add a preseparation device ahead of the blower.

Ready-to-run central units are available in dozens of different models from home centers, woodworking mail-order catalogs, industrial dust collection suppliers (see Sources of Supply on pp. 194-195) or your local hardware and tool store. Central collectors come in different sizes and capacities (see the sidebar on p. 106), and with different features.

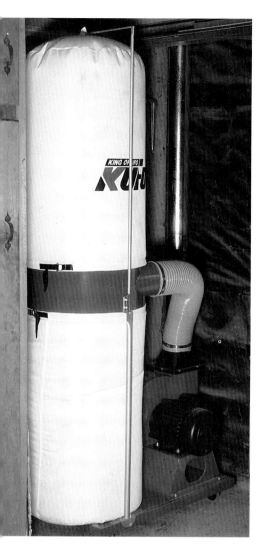

Single-stage dust collectors offer affordable collection in a ready-to-use package. A two-bag KUFO 2-hp collector is shown here.

But the most important difference between models is whether or not they incorporate preseparation, which determines if the unit is a single-stage or a two-stage collector.

Single-stage collectors

As shown in the drawing on the facing page, single-stage collectors draw air and sawdust directly through the blower, then expel them into a collection bag or canister and filters. In contrast, a two-stage system incorporates a preseparator, which removes chips and debris so that only finer dust and air pass through the blower and on to the filters.

The primary advantage of single-stage dust collectors, such as the one shown in the photo at left, is that they are relatively simple and inexpensive to buy (they are the ubiquitous Asian-made collectors you see in most woodworking supply catalogs). On smaller collectors (1 hp to 2 hp), a pair of bags provide a collection bag and the filter medium. Larger collectors ($2\frac{1}{2}$ hp to 3 hp) use multiple pairs of bags to provide more chip-holding capacity and greater filtration area.

The single-stage design has several disadvantages, however. First, abrasive particles (collected along with fine dust during sanding operations), small wood cutoffs and stray bits of "tramp" metal (small screws, nails, brads, etc.) come in direct contact with the fan as they are sucked through. This barrage of particles not only causes an alarming amount of noise, but it can also damage the blower impeller and housing, or at the very least accelerate wear on these components, especially if the unit has a plastic fan wheel. A more serious problem is that bits of metal accidentally passing through the fan can create a spark that can trigger a powerful explosion and fire (see p. 20). To reduce the risk of explosion, most two-stage units use a non-sparking cast-aluminum fan wheel; many single-stage units have plastic fan wheels. Unfortunately, sparks can still occur if metal particles bounce off the inside of a sheet-metal blower housing. Fortunately, you can convert any single-stage collector into a two-stage unit by adding a cyclone or other form of preseparation, as described on pp. 106-112.

Because they are built for the home-shop market, most single-stage units lack the fine-filtering ability of industrially rated dust collectors (technically, they are "chip collectors"). Single-stage collectors typically have filter bags made from materials not engineered for fine-particle filtration and use them as collection bins as well. As these bags fill up, collection performance suffers, since there is less surface area for air to pass through. Worse, increased pressure inside the bag can force fine dust particles to be blown through the filter media into the air (see p. 115).

Single-Stage vs. Two-Stage Dust Collectors

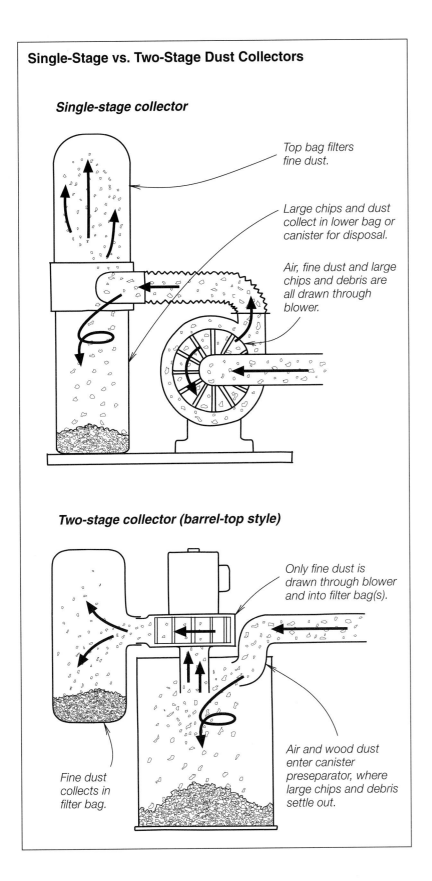

Single-stage collector

Top bag filters fine dust.

Large chips and dust collect in lower bag or canister for disposal.

Air, fine dust and large chips and debris are all drawn through blower.

Two-stage collector (barrel-top style)

Only fine dust is drawn through blower and into filter bag(s).

Fine dust collects in filter bag.

Air and wood dust enter canister preseparator, where large chips and debris settle out.

Barrel-top collectors, such as this Dust Boy model 1004 2-hp unit, provide the safety and performance of two-stage collectors in a compact unit.

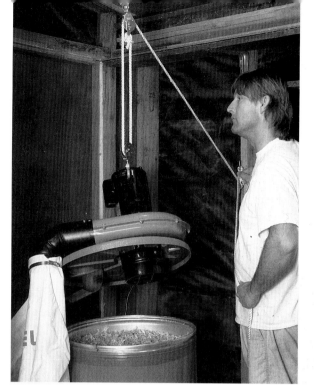

To ease the task of lifting the heavy lid of a canister-style collector (with blower and motor attached) use a small block and tackle. To keep the lid suspended while chips are dumped, tie the rope off to a cleat screwed to the wall.

Two-stage collectors

A two-stage system is designed to eliminate the problem of impeller damage and sparking by drawing only fine dust particles through the blower. Larger chips and stray debris are taken out and deposited in a canister before they can reach the blower. The preseparation of chips and sawdust from the airstream is usually accomplished by a cyclone or separation canister (see pp. 106-111). In addition to making life easier for the blower (and less dangerous for the woodworker), a two-stage collector also sends far less sawdust to the filters, so they clog less readily and need cleaning (or, for filter bags, emptying) less often. On the downside, two-stage collectors are generally more expensive than single-stage models. Also, units that incorporate large cyclones, such as the Delta 50-901 (see the bottom photo on p. 109) or systems assembled from separate components tend to take up more valuable shop real estate than compact single-stage systems.

Barrel-top collectors A two-stage unit that's very popular in small shops because of its compact design is the barrel-top collector, such as the Delta 50-180, 50-181 and 50-182 models and the Dust Boy (shown in the photo at left above). These collectors preseparate chips into a barrel or drum before sending air and finer dust on to the blower and filter. A flexible hose connects the unit to the shop's ductwork. Barrel-top units are compact because the blower and filter bag are mounted in a single unit. If the chip-holding capacity of the canister is too small for your needs, you can easily increase it by substituting a larger barrel or fiber drum. You can also make a large-capacity bin by building a plywood box with a round cutout on top. Make sure to use thick weatherstripping around the cutout, so that the collector lid forms a tight seal with the bin.

One disadvantage of barrel collectors is that you have to lift off the heavy blower each time you need to empty the canister. You can get around this problem by lifting and suspending the top with a rope and a block and tackle (anchored to the ceiling above the collector), as shown in the photo at right on the facing page. A metal cleat screwed to the wall near the collector provides a place to secure the rope to hold the top up while you dump out the barrel.

Choosing a collector

Once you've decided on the style and type of collector system you want to install, you still have to pick a model that's powerful enough to work efficiently with your ductwork. How powerful a collector you need depends primarily on three factors:

1. How much sawdust your shop produces. The more (and larger) chips and dust a woodworking machine produces, the greater the volume of collection air needed to capture and convey them.

2. How far the ductwork must convey sawdust from the source (a machine, floor sweep, sanding table, etc.) to the central collector. The farther (or more circuitous) that distance, the stronger the collector's blower must be to overcome the friction generated by the air passing through the ductwork.

3. The number of machines that the collection system must handle simultaneously. Running several machines at once requires more air volume—and collector power—than running a single machine.

All these factors are determined by the design of your entire central system, which means you can't pick the right collector for your system until you've designed the system and planned out the ductwork (as described in Chapter 7). This information allows you to choose a central collector powerful enough to run your system efficiently (see the sidebar on pp. 106-107).

Collector power and performance

Because all central dust collectors have blowers powered by electric motors, the obvious way to distinguish the size of various collectors is by the size of their motors—1 hp, 3 hp, and so on. But there are two figures that provide a far more important measure of a collector's capacity and strength than horsepower: the volume of air that a collector moves (in cfm), and the number of inches of static pressure (SP) that the collector is rated. A collector with a higher cfm rating will handle more dust output, or collect from more machines simultaneously than one with a lower cfm rating. A collector with a higher SP rating will handle a larger, more convoluted (or inefficiently designed) system of ductwork than one with a lower rating.

Here's where it gets tricky: A collector's air-moving capacity (cfm) *changes* depending upon the amount of air friction (SP loss) that the blower must overcome from the ductwork. (Imagine how much harder it is to take a tiny sip of soda through a 3-ft.-long straw than it is to take a big gulp through a regular 8-in.-long soda straw.) When a collector is working harder, it moves less air volume. This variable air-moving capacity makes it impossible to choose the right-sized collector for your system based on cfm and SP ratings alone. Worse, manufacturers usually print cfm ratings for their collectors that reflect the amount of air the collector moves *when it's not connected to ductwork* (operating at zero SP loss). This is known as "free-air cfm." Static-pressure ratings can be similarly misleading because they often represent the maximum power the collector is capable of generating when

moving no air at all (at zero cfm). This is like the suction power you feel when you put your hand over the end of a running vacuum cleaner's hose.

Fan performance curves

The best way to make sure that a blower or dust collector you're interested in buying will be powerful enough for your system is to ask the manufacturer or dealer for a fan performance curve, such as the one shown in the graph on the facing page. A test of actual collector performance, this graph plots the amount of air a collector's blower will convey under different work loads. A fan performance curve may reveal that a blower capable of moving 1,100 cfm at low SP loss (say 2 in.) may deliver only 500 cfm when running a system with twice as much SP loss.

Once you know what your system's cfm requirements and SP losses are (as calculated on pp. 136-143), it's a simple

Preseparation of sawdust

Most wood debris that's drawn into a central collection system contains elements that range in size from gum-wrapper-sized shavings to microscopic dust. A preseparation device removes all large shavings and chips, as well as the majority of coarse sawdust, from the dust source before the air passes through the blower and into the filters. While commercially made two-stage collectors, by definition, incorporate some sort of preseparation, you can also add a preseparation device to a single-stage collector, or to a central collection system assembled from separate components.

There are two practical methods for preseparation of wood chips. The simplest way is to use a drop box or a dust preseparator canister, which creates a reduction in air velocity that causes heavier particles matter to choose a collector by comparing these numbers to a collector's fan performance curve. For example, if the largest dust producer in your shop is an 18-in. thickness planer (which requires about 750 cfm), the collector whose fan curve is shown in the graph would be powerful enough to handle that machine, as long as the ductwork to that machine had 5 in. or less of SP loss.

Unfortunately, not all manufacturers or dealers can readily supply you with a performance curve for their dust collector models (and there's no easy way to predict actual performance by extrapolating from the unit's free-air cfm rating). If you're willing to take the risk, you can simply buy a collector that you think will get the job done and see if it performs adequately when connected to your ductwork. In this case, it's prudent to select a unit that's at least 50% more powerful than you think you will

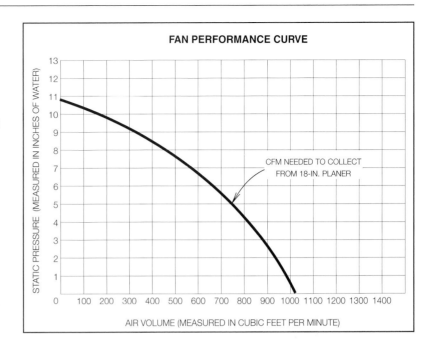

FAN PERFORMANCE CURVE

CFM NEEDED TO COLLECT FROM 18-IN. PLANER

STATIC PRESSURE (MEASURED IN INCHES OF WATER)

AIR VOLUME (MEASURED IN CUBIC FEET PER MINUTE)

need—just make sure ahead of purchase that the dealer will exchange the collector if it isn't right for you. If you already own an undersized collector, you might be able to coax better performance out of it, as discussed on pp. 158-159.

If you'd rather play it safe, don't buy a dust collector from a dealer or manufacturer who can't supply a performance curve graph for the unit. You might spend more time shopping, but you're much more likely to end up with a collector that will run your dust collection system effectively.

to fall out of the airstream. A more efficient method is to use cyclonic preseparation, which works by swirling air and dust around so that chips and particles slow down (due to friction) and drop out. Only the lightest fine wood dust particles (which don't have much inertia) remain entrained in the stream of air. (Imagine a pea and a cannon ball at the center of a spinning merry-go-round; the heavier cannon ball will fly off the merry-go-round with far more force than the lighter pea.)

Many dust collectors incorporate some sort of cyclonic preseparation in their design. Barrel-top portable and central collectors employ a deflector just inside the intake that causes air to swirl and dust to settle (it's the first stage of their two-stage collection). Even some single-stage units have a spiral dust deflector inside the shroud that supports

The spiral dust deflector inside the bag holder found on many single-stage collectors encourages large debris and coarse dust to swirl and settle to the bottom of the lower bag.

the collection bags (see the photo at left). This deflector encourages larger chips to swirl and settle in the lower bag. But neither of these devices is as effective as a true cyclone.

Cyclones

A separate component that can be added to any collection system, a cyclone is a sheet-metal cylindrical canister with a funnel-like bottom that looks like it should be part of an Ozark mountain whiskey still (see the drawing below). Air and debris coming from the shop's duct-work enter the upper part of the cyclone tangentially, which creates a vortex. As the high-velocity airstream bounces off the wall of the cyclone, the air compresses, and heavier wood debris and coarse dust settle out and drop through an opening at the bottom of the cyclone's funnel, into a barrel or drum for easy disposal. Only air and very fine dust (typically 15 microns and smaller) still entrained in the airstream exit the cyclone, passing up through a pipe that runs partway down the center. A duct then carries the mostly clean air on to the blower. Cyclones are so efficient, removing up to 99% of the dust sent through them, that their exhaust can sometimes be discharged directly into

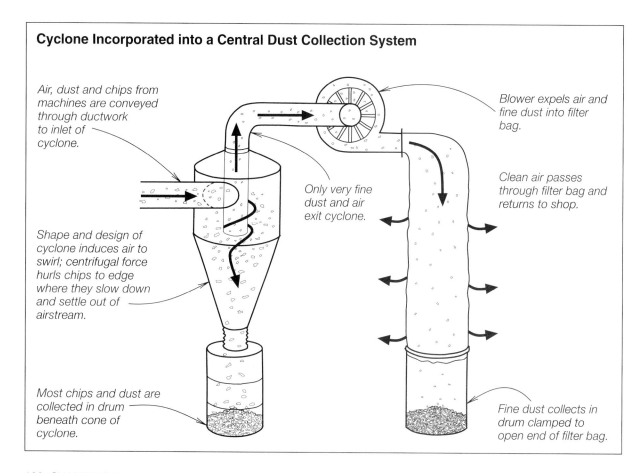

Cyclone Incorporated into a Central Dust Collection System

Air, dust and chips from machines are conveyed through ductwork to inlet of cyclone.

Blower expels air and fine dust into filter bag.

Only very fine dust and air exit cyclone.

Clean air passes through filter bag and returns to shop.

Shape and design of cyclone induces air to swirl; centrifugal force hurls chips to edge where they slow down and settle out of airstream.

Most chips and dust are collected in drum beneath cone of cyclone.

Fine dust collects in drum clamped to open end of filter bag.

the outside air. More often, the blower sends air on to the filters, for final removal of very fine, health-threatening particles before returning the clean air to the shop.

If you want to assemble your own collection system from scratch, you can buy a cyclone as a stand-alone unit, and connect it to an existing blower and filter assembly (see the photo on p. 126). You can also add a cyclone to a single-stage collector by connecting it between your shop's ductwork and the blower intake, as shown in the top photo at right. Cyclones come in different sizes, each designed to handle a specific amount of airflow; you must buy the right size cyclone to suit the capacity of your blower (see the sidebar on pp. 106-107). Also, when designing your central collection system, you must remember to add an extra one or two inches of static-pressure loss—the price that cyclones extract for their preseparation services.

To save you the trouble of sizing and mounting a cyclone and blower as separate components, some manufacturers offer dust collectors with integrated cyclones paired with blowers, such as the Torit model 13, the Murphy-Rodgers MRC-7B3 and Delta's 50-900 series of collectors (the 3-hp 50-901 is shown in the bottom photo at right). These collectors are designed for medium and large shops and look like the big cyclones you see on large cabinet factories or big institutional woodshops. Because the blower and cyclone are carefully tailored to each other, it's the surest way to get predictable performance in a cyclonic separation system. Most units have a top-mounted fan mated to a compact, but efficient cyclone. A hose from the bottom of the cyclone drops chips and debris into a drum, while the air from the blower is sent to a large filter bag fitted over a second drum, for ease of emptying the finer dust.

If you have a small shop with light to modest dust collection needs and you're up to the adventure of building your own cyclone, Woodsmith-Shop offers a kit for building a small cyclone suitable for a 500-cfm system. You'll have to supply your own 1-hp blower (available from numerous sources; see the Sources of Supply on pp. 194-195), but the kit does include plans for a cabinet for the cyclone and top-mounted blower, as well as plans and filter fabric for a simple filter box. I've read magazine articles on building cyclones from scratch, but I don't recommend you undertake this; building and connecting the complex sheet-metal parts is a very tricky project best left to an experienced sheet-metal worker.

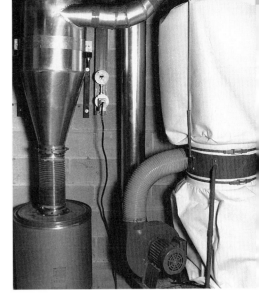

A preseparation device, such as a cyclone, can be added to an existing single-stage system. The Oneida cyclone shown here is connected to a 2-hp Asian-made collector fitted with oversized filter bags.

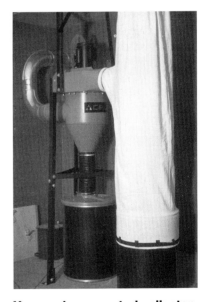

You can buy a central collector with a built-in cyclone, such as the Delta 50-901 shown here. The cyclone is extremely efficient at preseparating chips and coarse dust, sending only fine dust through the blower and to the filters.

Dust preseparator canisters

If you don't want to buy a regular cyclone, you can still add the advantages of preseparation to your small central collector (or portable dust collector) by fitting a dust preseparator canister (the "poor man's" cyclone). This device is compact, inexpensive and easy to hook up to your present collector. It consists of a canister with a tight-fitting lid and inlet and outlet pipes and fittings. A flexible hose from the ductwork brings incoming air and debris through an intake on the lid. The big stuff swirls around inside the can and drops out. Cleaner air exits into a flexible hose (fitted to an outlet on the lid) that connects to the blower and filters. The lid comes off easily for emptying the can. Disposal is even neater if you line the can with a disposable plastic garbage bag.

Adding a dust preseparator canister not only transforms a one-stage collector into a two-stage system, but also adds chip-holding capacity that many smaller central collectors and portables lack. The trade-off is that there is some loss of collection power due to the added energy it takes for air to travel through the canister. Also, a portable collector loses its portability when tethered to a preseparator can. One solution is to connect the preseparator can permanently to the biggest chip-producing machine in your shop (probably the thickness planer or table saw). You can connect your portable collector to these machines via the preseparator can's exhaust hose when needed; the rest of the time, the unit remains portable, so you can wheel it around to wherever it's needed. It is possible to get modest performance with a preseparator can hooked up to a shop vacuum, but you'll need a powerful unit (with a motor rated at no less than 10 amps). I've used preseparator cans with standard 2½-in. dia. shop-vacuum hose (smaller hoses won't work) with modest results when connected to a router table or 8-in. table saw; don't expect thorough collection of chips from a planer or shaper.

Build one or buy one   You can build your own preseparator canister using a 34-gal. fiber drum or a 55-gal. steel drum with a tight-fitting, yet removable lid. A pair of 4-in. dia. ABS or PVC fittings are installed into the lid of the canister, as shown in the drawing on the facing page. A PVC elbow installed in the top of the can provides an intake; turning the elbow as shown creates a rudimentary cyclonic action. A 4-in. connector fitting mounted into the top of the can provides an exhaust for the hose that connects to the blower.

If you don't care to build your own setup, you can buy a commercially made preseparator lid (see Sources of Supply on pp. 194-195), as shown in the photo on the facing page. This cast-ABS-plastic device fits atop a regular 30-gal. steel trash can. It comes with ports sized to accept 4-in. hoses, but you can use special reducer fittings (designed

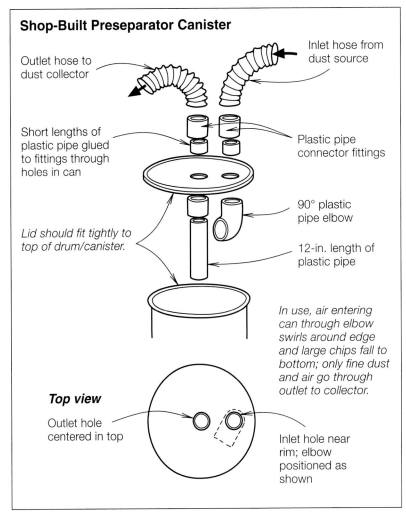

Shop-Built Preseparator Canister

Outlet hose to dust collector

Inlet hose from dust source

Short lengths of plastic pipe glued to fittings through holes in can

Plastic pipe connector fittings

Lid should fit tightly to top of drum/canister.

90° plastic pipe elbow

12-in. length of plastic pipe

In use, air entering can through elbow swirls around edge and large chips fall to bottom; only fine dust and air go through outlet to collector.

Top view

Outlet hole centered in top

Inlet hole near rim; elbow positioned as shown

A dust preseparator canister lid fits atop a 30-gal. trash can and adds capacity to a small collection system as well as preseparation ahead of the blower.

for inexpensive flexible hose) or cobble up connectors using regular PVC or ABS plumbing fittings to adapt the ports to accept other diameter hoses. You'll get slightly better performance if you run some wide, thin weatherstripping around the inside rim of the lid, so that it seals better to the top of the can.

Drop boxes

In lieu of a cyclone or preseparator canister, you can build a simple drop-box preseparator. This kind of device, shown in the drawing on p. 112, is essentially just a box with an intake, an exhaust and an internal baffle. For best performance, the size of the box and proportions of the box's width to baffle length should be calculated using the formula shown. While relatively crude and easy to construct, an airtight drop box is capable of removing up to 60% of wood particles from the air ahead of the system's blower and filters.

A drop box provides a simple, shop-built preseparation stage for removing chips and debris ahead of the blower. This unit mounts the box directly on top of two drums, which provide ample chip-holding capacity.

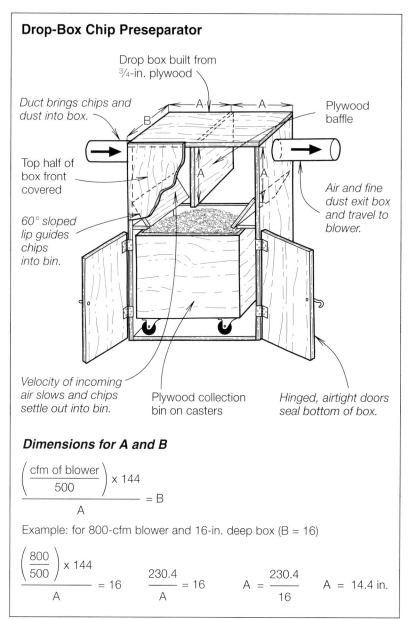

Drop-Box Chip Preseparator

Drop box built from ¾-in. plywood

Duct brings chips and dust into box.

Plywood baffle

Top half of box front covered

Air and fine dust exit box and travel to blower.

60° sloped lip guides chips into bin.

Velocity of incoming air slows and chips settle out into bin.

Plywood collection bin on casters

Hinged, airtight doors seal bottom of box.

Dimensions for A and B

$$\frac{\left(\dfrac{\text{cfm of blower}}{500}\right) \times 144}{A} = B$$

Example: for 800-cfm blower and 16-in. deep box (B = 16)

$$\frac{\left(\dfrac{800}{500}\right) \times 144}{A} = 16 \qquad \frac{230.4}{A} = 16 \qquad A = \frac{230.4}{16} \qquad A = 14.4 \text{ in.}$$

As in a regular cyclone, coarse dust and shavings drop out and fall to the bottom of the box. To make disposal neater and more convenient, build a chute into the drop box so that debris is deposited directly into a bin. Alternatively, you can build the box to fit above one or more trash drums, as shown in the photo at left. One drop-box design I've seen installed in a second-story shop has a chute built under the drop box where chips collect; the chute opens below to allow chips to be deposited directly into a cart or the back of a pickup truck for easy disposal.

Collector filtration

Unless you live in a temperate climate where you can simply run the exhaust from your central collector directly outdoors, adding a filter is the last step in creating a closed air loop between the dusty air collected at your machines and the clean air that's returned to your shop. A good filter removes the very fine respirable dust from the airstream (preferably after most chips and dust have been removed by preseparation), transforming it into clean air that's perfectly healthy to breathe. To ensure good fine-dust filtration and optimum system performance, you must choose your filter system carefully, as well as match the amount of filtration to the size of your system.

There are lots of different filter media to choose from, either for replacement filter bags for an off-the-shelf system or for a custom filter assembly you build yourself. Also, there are several ways that you can increase the filter area and improve the performance of your system without taking up too much valuable shop space.

Fabric filters

The most common way to filter dusty air is to pass it through fabric filter material. The fabric can be sewn into a bag, as is standard on most small-shop collectors; on single-stage units, the bag serves as a collection bin as well as a filter. Alternatively, filter material can be sewn into tubes that attach to a box (also called a plenum) that distributes air to multiple filters, an arrangement commonly called a filter bag house.

Among the dozens of fabrics available for industrial dust and fume filtration, four are commonly used for woodshop filter bags and tubes: cotton sateen, woven polyester, knitted polyester and felted polyester (see the photo below). Cotton sateen fabric, or cotton duck, is a canvas-like material that was often used in years past for filter bags on some of

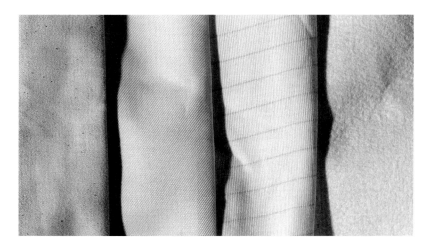

Not all filter fabrics are equally effective at straining respirable dust from the air. Here are four popular fabrics for dust filtration, arranged from worst to best filtration (from left to right): cotton sateen, woven polyester, knitted polyester and felted polyester.

the less expensive collectors. Cotton bags are inexpensive and work fine for collecting chips and sawdust, but they do a poor job of filtering fine dust. Particles smaller than 30 microns are typically blown right through the weave (remember, particles smaller than 10 microns tend to do the worst respiratory damage). Fortunately, many manufacturers and tool dealers offer better-filtering polyester fabric bags as optional replacements for cotton bags.

Since the price of cotton has gone up in recent years, even the least expensive single-stage collectors come with woven polyester bags these days. Woven polyesters are slightly better at handling fine dust than cotton fabrics, but neither fabric is manufactured to industrial specifications for filtering wood dust. Woven polys are durable, a plus on two- or four-bag single-stage collectors, where the lower bags serve as dustbins as well as filters.

Knitted polyester fabrics are durable and very good at filtering out respirable dust particles. Knitted filter bags are thick-woven and look something like giant tube socks. Sometimes, carbon fibers are incorporated in the weave to help dissipate static electric charges (see the dark lines on the fabric sample in the photo on p. 113). While good for handling a moderate volume of fine dust, knitted polys are not widely used for woodworking filter systems.

Felted filter fabric is matted together from countless fine polyester fibers pressed into a thick material. While more expensive than knitted polys, felted polyester fabrics really shine when it comes to fine particle filtration. Felted filter fabrics are available in a wide range of weights and types that are designed and manufactured specifically to meet the filtration needs of the woodworking industry. They are used almost exclusively in large industrial systems, and are readily available for smaller systems as well (they are optional on many new units). Filter bags or tubes sewn from a 12-oz. or 16-oz. felted fabric are a terrific choice whether you're buying filters for a new central collector, upgrading an existing system or building a bag house for a new system. Felted filter fabrics that are singed or glazed slightly on the inside surface (by briefly exposing the fabric to a flame) release dust cake readily, making them a good choice for systems that must handle lots of fine sanding dust.

If you wish to retrofit the bags that came with your collector (or fit bags or tubes for a new system), your best bet is to buy them from one of the many companies that sew filter bags for industry (see Sources of Supply on pp. 194-195). These companies generally stock different fabric materials in many styles and sizes of bags or tubes. Smaller, local filter companies can usually make bags or supply yardage to suit custom applications.

Cartridge filtration

An entirely different approach to filtering dust from collection air is to use replaceable cartridge elements. Cartridge filtration has been used in industrial applications for many years, and just recently one company (Oneida) has started to offer a cartridge-filtered collector designed for smaller woodworking shops. A typical cartridge (shown in the photo at right) is much like a pleated filter used in a shop vacuum. The primary advantage of cartridges is that they squeeze a lot of square feet of filter area into a small physical package, which makes them a good choice if the space you have available for a central collector is extremely limited. The primary disadvantage is that cartridge filters are more time-consuming to clean than fabric media. Further, the pleats can be difficult to clean thoroughly, giving them a greater tendency to clog. They are also more expensive to replace than most other fabric filter media.

Dust cake and filter cleaning

In a properly engineered dust collection system, small-particle filtration can actually improve as the filters get dirtier. This is true because the film of dust, or dust cake, that forms on the inside of a filter bag begins to act as a sort of filter itself: The particles that accumulate block the passage of progressively finer and finer particles (see the drawing on p. 43). Unfortunately, in small collectors with a less-than-optimum amount of filter surface area (see the sidebar on p. 116), the chips and dust cake that accumulate inside the bags just make it more difficult for clean air to exit through the filter media. This restriction in airflow, known as "filter blinding," creates more pressure inside the bag, which the blower must work harder to overcome. The end result is higher static-pressure losses and a drop in the overall performance of the dust collection system. An unfortunate health consequence of higher bag pressure is that it tends to push fine dust particles right through the filter media.

There are two ways to minimize system pressure losses and particle infiltration: One is to make sure you have enough filter area to handle the volume of air passing through the filters. The more surface area a filter has, the more minute passages it has for air to flow through it (see the sidebar on p. 116). The other way to minimize pressure losses and particle infiltration is to clean the filters regularly. In industrial dust collection systems, filter bags or tubes are cleaned by means of special devices, such as shakers, pulse jets and reverse air systems. In a small shop, the standard cleaning method is to grab a filter bag or tube and shake it gently. The secret is to clean the bag thoroughly, yet leave a fine layer of the dust cake intact, so that the bag's extra-fine-particle-filtering ability continues to work.

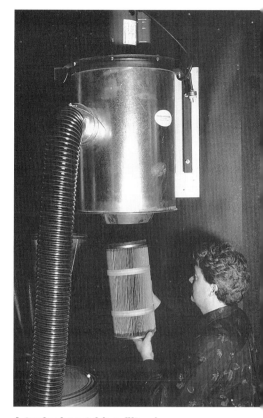

A typical cartridge filter is much like a pleated filter used in a shop vacuum. Here, a cartridge filter is mounted inside a small cyclone/blower made by Oneida Air Systems designed to operate with the cartridge in lieu of other filtration.

When do filters need cleaning? Generally, the more sanding you do and the more fine dust is collected, the more often the filters in any collection system need attention. Because they blind more quickly, you should empty the lower bags on single-stage systems when they're only one-third full, and shake both upper and lower bags clean. After a certain amount of time, most filter materials clog to the point that they need replacement. When replacing pull-on bags, make sure the straps are tight: A loose strap may allow a bag to blow off, which will send a horrific cloud of dust all over the shop.

If your filter assembly is a large bag house, a more reliable way to tell when your filters need attention is to use a static-pressure gauge, such as a Magnehelic (see Sources of Supply on pp. 194-195). A small-diameter flexible hose connects the gauge to the bag house, allowing the Magnehelic to measure the amount of pressure inside (see the

---

How much filter area does your system need?

It's important for any dust collection system to have an adequate amount of filter surface area to reduce air pressure caused by the natural buildup of dust cake as the filters get dirty. The amount of filter area, measured in square feet of fabric (cartridge filters are rated by their equivalent square-foot area), is always considered in respect to the system's air-handling capacity (in cfm) and stated as a ratio of "air to cloth." To calculate the air-to-cloth ratio, divide the cfm of the collection system by the number of square feet of filter area. For example, an 800-cfm system with 100 sq. ft. of filter has an 8:1 air-to-cloth ratio, or 8 cfm for every 1 sq. ft. of filter.

Note that the ratio changes depending on how much air is actually moving through the system. Your collection system may have a high air-handling capacity (say, 1,200 cfm), but if you use only one machine at a time, your air-to-cloth ratio should be based on the volume of air used by your largest dust source (say, a planer that uses 500 cfm).

What's the best air-to-cloth ratio for your system? A ratio of 10:1 is a good choice for an average system, and it's easy to calculate: Just take the system's cfm and discard the last digit. However, employing this ratio requires that two conditions be met. First, your filter bags should be sewn from a 12-oz. or 16-oz. felted filter fabric or other industry-rated medium (see p. 114). Second, you are filtering dust and chips created by general woodworking operations (with a mixture of particle sizes, from

big chips to fine dust). Further, large shavings and coarse sawdust must be removed ahead of the filters by pre-separation (via a cyclone, drop box, etc.). Systems that must handle great amounts of very fine sawdust or sanding dust, such as from working MDF or solid-surface materials (e.g. Corian), will do better to use a lower air-to-cloth ratio (more filter to cfm), such as 7:1, to provide more surface area to handle the greater volume of fine particles.

A coating of fine dust on benchtops after the collector has been running awhile or a puff of dust rising from a filter bag as the collector is turned on is a good indication that your current filter arrangement is undersized. When in doubt, add more filters; they can only improve your system's performance and efficiency.

A Magnehelic gauge is a good way to monitor pressure inside a filter bag house, and can tell you when it's time to clean or replace filters.

photo above). As the filters get blinded, the pressure goes up. By marking the needle's position on the gauge dial when the filters are new, you'll know when it's time to clean the filters—when the gauge shows a 75% to 100% pressure increase. If pressure doesn't decrease significantly after filter cleaning, it's time to replace the filters.

Filter bag houses

Once you have calculated how much filter area your system needs (see the sidebar on the facing page), it's likely you'll want to increase the filter area. An easy way of nearly doubling the amount of filtration in a single-stage collector is to remove its standard bags and fit oversized replacement bags (see the top photo on p. 109). Oneida Air Systems sells replacements that fit most Asian single-stage collectors (see Sources of Supply on pp. 194-195). The downside of adding larger filter bags is that they take up a lot more shop space than stock bags. Cartridge filtration is one method that can provide lots of filter area in a small package, but it's difficult to retrofit to an existing collection system.

A better way to add more filtration in a compact space is to replace a one- or two-bag filter with a bag house fitted with many small-diameter filter tubes or bags that pack more surface area into a small physical space. The smaller bags or tubes are fitted to an airtight box called a plenum, which receives air from the blower via a rigid or flexible duct. A plenum box reduces the velocity of the dusty air entering it, eliminating particle infiltration due to high-speed air blowing directly against the inside of the bags. Also, a plenum box evenly distributes the air to multiple filter bags, spreading dust cake more evenly and reducing filter blinding. The only shortcomings are that multiple individual filters can be time-consuming to clean and costly to replace.

A plenum box provides mounting and air distribution for a series of tube filters. Made from plywood or purchased as a sheet-metal box (as shown here), a plenum can be hung from wall or ceiling.

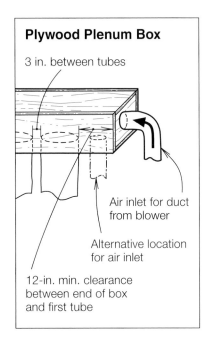

Plywood Plenum Box

3 in. between tubes

Air inlet for duct from blower

Alternative location for air inlet

12-in. min. clearance between end of box and first tube

Plenums and shaker boxes There are two popular plenum designs for bag houses that use filter tubes or bags. A plenum box, such as the one shown in the photo above, mounts to a ceiling or wall in the shop and uses filter tubes that mount below it. You can buy a sheet-metal box (see Sources of Supply on pp. 194-195) or build a plywood plenum box yourself (see the drawing above). The filter tubes attach to metal flanges called thimble rings. The open bottom ends of the tubes are fitted over 5-gal. plastic pails, which collect very fine dust. Adjustable hose clamps secure the tubes to both the thimble rings and the pails. Unless massive amounts of sanding dust are being collected, the pails need to be emptied only once in a great while.

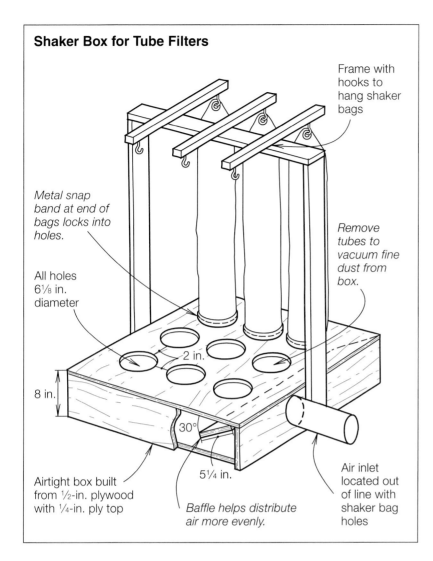

Shaker Box for Tube Filters

Frame with hooks to hang shaker bags

Metal snap band at end of bags locks into holes.

All holes 6⅛ in. diameter

Remove tubes to vacuum fine dust from box.

2 in.

8 in.

30°

Airtight box built from ½-in. plywood with ¼-in. ply top

5¼ in.

Baffle helps distribute air more evenly.

Air inlet located out of line with shaker bag holes

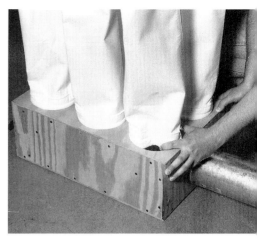

Many small-diameter filter tubes fitting into a shaker box provide lots of surface area in a small package. The open end of each tube has a springy metal band inside that locks into a hole to seal the bag to the shaker box.

Another style of plenum commonly used for bag houses is the shaker box, such as the one shown in the drawing above. This device consists of a plywood box with two posts that rise up to support cross-members from which tube filters are suspended by hooks through grommeted holes. You can also buy ready-made sheet-metal shaker boxes (as shown in the photo on p. 126). Each small-diameter tube filter has one end sewn shut and a grommet for the hook from which it hangs. The open end of each tube has a springy metal band inside that snaps into a hole in the shaker box (see the photo at right) for a dust-tight fit. The shaker box gets its name because dust shaken out of the tubes during periodic cleanings falls into the bottom of the box. You can clean the box by occasionally snapping out a few of the tubes and vacuuming them clean, or you can build a tight-fitting dust door or drawer into one end to allow easy disposal.

CHAPTER 7

Designing a Central Collection System

A central collection system is a lot like the human circulatory system: A collector works like a heart to pump dust and chips through a series of ducts that branch out around the shop like veins and arteries. Smaller branch ducts from each machine (or group of machines) connect to a larger main duct that conveys all debris back to the collector. The sawdust is then filtered from the clean air, which is usually pumped back into the shop. But like a cardiac patient with arterial constriction, a poorly designed ductwork system won't convey dust effectively and it can clog up entirely (in both the analogy and the example, this could result in a heart attack!).

This chapter will take you through all the steps required to design a central dust collection system for a small- or medium-size shop, from laying out the ductwork to determining the right size collector to run it. It doesn't cover dust collection systems for large commercial shops, which have more complicated needs. If you don't want to get in over your head (or if you need help), talk to an air-handling expert at a company that sells dust collection components (check the Sources of Supply on pp. 194-195 or look under "Dust and Fume Collection" in a metropolitan Yellow Pages). Air-handling specialists have years of experience in designing collection systems (which are required in all kinds of shops and factories, not just woodshops). Many of the companies that sell ductwork and accessories will also design shop systems for a small charge.

The design process

In order to operate at peak efficiency—and make best use of the power of a central collector—the network of ducts and hoses that connects all shop machines and work stations must be properly designed. Proper design means that the sizes, lengths, twists and turns of both the branch ducts and the main duct should be calculated and specified according to the established rules and formulas of air-handling systems.

However, anyone who has casually flipped through the pages of *Industrial Ventilation, A Manual of Recommended Practice* (the textbook assembled by the American Conference of Governmental Industrial Hygienists that is considered the technical "bible" on air-handling systems) might hazard a guess that brain surgery would be less complicated than designing a central collection system. Indeed, perform-

Sizing pipe and specifying fittings are the first steps toward assembling an efficient central ductwork system. Shown here are the various-diameter spiral pipes, welded fittings, flexible hoses, blast gates and hardware needed for one small-shop system.

ing all the calculations necessary for a complex system can get far more involved than most pamphlets or magazine articles on dust collection would have you believe.

Fortunately, designing a simple small-shop dust collection system doesn't have to be difficult, and can be accomplished with a minimal amount of mathematical calculation. By simple, I mean a collection system where only one machine is used at a time, or where only the machines on one branch of the system are used at a time. Larger, industrial systems are usually designed for running all or most machines at once, and must be designed for balanced airflows and specially stepped main lines—usually a very complicated task well beyond the scope of this book.

To make the process of designing a small-shop collection system easier, I've broken it down into six steps:

1. Drawing a layout of your shop, with the location of all the machines that will be hooked to the system (see pp. 123-125).

2. Deciding where the central collector will be located (pp. 125-128).

3. Planning the layout of the ductwork (pp. 128-134).

4. Sizing branch ducts (pp. 135-138).

5. Sizing the main duct (pp. 138-139).

6. Calculating the static-pressure losses in the system and choosing a central collector that suits the size and capacity of the system (pp. 140-143).

Once you've completed these design steps, you'll be ready to install and test your system, as described in Chapter 8. Information on building hoods and dust pickups for connecting your ductwork to your machines is given in Chapter 9.

I know there are droves of woodworkers out there who simply loathe the mere thought of using formulas or doing math of any sort. For these "calculation underachievers," I've included an easy out: a simple set of guidelines for setting up a modest but effective small-shop system (see the sidebar on the facing page). Whether you follow this streamlined approach or adhere to the traditional calculation method, you'll still need to begin the design process by making a shop-layout drawing, as described in the next section.

If the thought of having to perform complicated mathematical equations to design a dust collection system makes you feel queasy, here are some guidelines for designing a simple, but effective collection system. This system will work in most small woodshops that are about the size of a two-car garage (or smaller) and have one person working on only one machine at a time.

1. Choose a 1½-hp to 3-hp collector that delivers at least 600 to 800 actual cfm at around 5 in. or 6 in. of static pressure (see pp. 106-107). This should be enough air to handle collecting chips from a single machine at a time, with the largest air requirement being from a thickness planer or shaper.

2. Make sure that the air-to-cloth ratio of the collector's filters (made from 12-oz. or 16-oz. felted-polyester filter fabric) is around 10 to 1: 10 cfm for every 1 sq. ft. of filter area (see the sidebar on p. 114). If you're going to use a single-stage collector, you'll almost certainly need to add oversized felted filter bags or a separate filter bag house (see pp. 117-119).

3. Mount the collector in a safe location that's reasonably close to the machines it will serve (see pp. 125-128).

4. Run a 5-in. or 6-in. main duct from your collector and use the table on pp. 136-137 to size each branch duct. Use rigid ductwork (preferably not plastic) for all main and branch ducts. Use short lengths (2½ ft. or less) of flexible hose only when connecting the machines to their branches. Use large-radius elbows and 45° lateral tees on all ducts (see pp. 133-134). Fit a blast gate for each machine, and use efficient hoods and pickups on the machines that aid chip capture but don't starve the system of air (see Chapter 9).

5. Follow good practices for installing and sealing the system, as described in Chapter 8.

6. If some machines don't collect as well as others, read the section on tweaking the system, as well as the discussion of what to do if your collector is underpowered (pp. 156-159).

Even if you decide to follow these abbreviated guidelines, it still pays to read through the sections on system design (branch- and main-duct sizing and pressure loss, pp. 135-143), because you'll glean many good suggestions for improving system performance and ease of use.

Making shop-layout drawings

Just as you would draw up plans before building a cabinet or a piece of furniture, so should you make a drawing of the layout of your shop as the first step in designing your central collection system. This drawing should include:

• A plan view (from overhead) and an elevation view (from the side) of your shop (see the drawing on p. 124). You may need to draw two or three elevations (north wall, west wall, etc.) for a less-cluttered view. Include any sheds or adjacent structures that will house ductwork or your collector. Make sure to include the location of all doors and windows, as well as permanent light fixtures.

Shop-Layout Drawings

Plan view

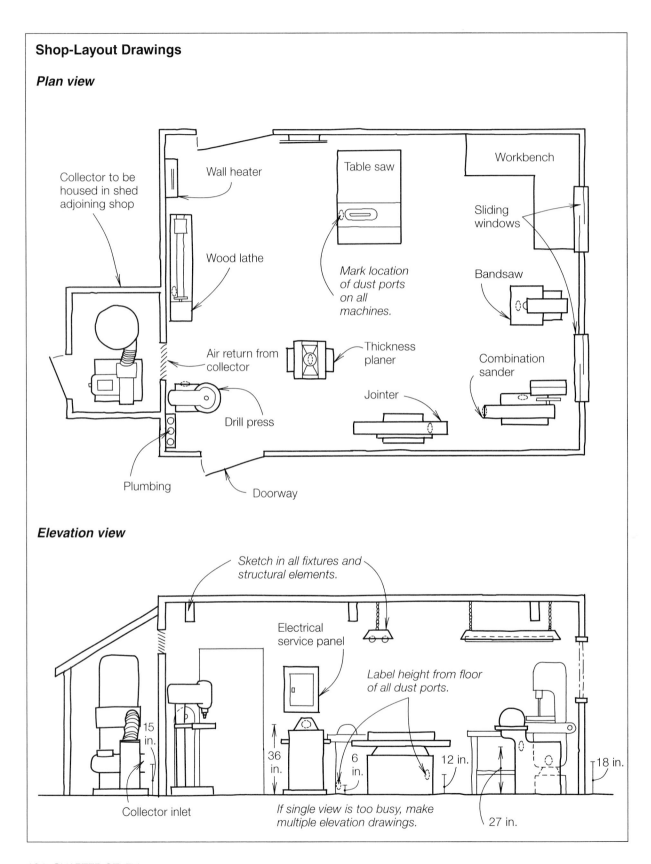

Collector to be housed in shed adjoining shop

Wall heater

Wood lathe

Table saw

Workbench

Sliding windows

Bandsaw

Mark location of dust ports on all machines.

Combination sander

Air return from collector

Thickness planer

Jointer

Drill press

Plumbing

Doorway

Elevation view

Sketch in all fixtures and structural elements.

Electrical service panel

Label height from floor of all dust ports.

15 in.

36 in.

6 in.

12 in.

18 in.

27 in.

Collector inlet

If single view is too busy, make multiple elevation drawings.

- A sketch of all machines in your shop that will have ductwork running to them (as well as any machines that might interfere with duct runs). Include the position of the machine's dust port (or proposed hood location). Also note any locations where ductwork would interfere with the operation of machines—such as an area around a sliding table on a table saw that must remain unobstructed.

- Include the position and dimensions of any structural elements, such as beams, rafters, joists, posts or soffits, as well as existing plumbing or electrical lines that might interfere with duct runs. If ductwork will be installed beneath the floor, include floor joists, ledgers and pipes and heating ducts on your drawing, as relevant.

You can make your sketch or drawing on any kind of paper, or do the sketch on a computer using drawing or CAD (computer-aided design) software. I like to sketch on graph paper with a main grid of $1/2$-in. squares and $1/8$-in. subdivisions (commonly used for architectural drawings). Using a scale of $1/2$ in. = 1 ft., you can usually draw an entire small shop on a single 11-in. by 14-in. sheet, yet still sketch in all the relevant details without the need for a magnifying glass.

Producing an accurately rendered shop-layout drawing is the groundwork for developing a detailed plan for the location of your collector and the layout of the ductwork around the shop, as outlined in the next two sections. To avoid a lot of erasing during the design phase, I suggest you sketch your collector/ductwork ideas on sheets of inexpensive translucent tracing paper taped over your shop layout. That way, if an idea doesn't pan out, you can simply remove and discard it. Also, you can easily compare and contrast the relative merits of two different designs by alternately overlaying them (most CAD programs allow overlays as well). The tracing-paper method also makes it easier to revise the shop-layout drawing, should you decide to move machines around to suit the proposed collection system better.

Locating the central collector

Before you lay out your collection system's ductwork, it pays to consider carefully the location of the central collector. Your decision will likely affect both the performance of the system and the convenience of operating it. Choosing a spot that best accommodates your collector physically is no good if it requires a complicated layout and makes for poor collection from some or all of your machines. And locating a collector centrally (for optimal duct runs and best performance) is no advantage if its noise level keeps you from switching it on, or if the collector is an obstruction that interferes with work. There are several factors to consider before deciding on a final location for the collector, including available space, proximity to machines, noise level and the need to return clean air to the shop.

Available space

In most small shops it's hard to find room for a collector. Of course, space is a bigger issue if you're going to try to shoehorn a 3-hp single-stage collector (with its four large filter bags) into a one-and-a-half-car garage shop than if you're considering buying a compact barrel-top collector. Assembling a collector from separate components—blower, cyclone and filter bags or bag house—lends a lot of flexibility because the various components can be located wherever they best fit the space available: under benchtops, in corners or hung from the ceiling. (If you do take this route, components should be mounted reasonably close to one another to keep static-pressure losses low; see pp. 140-143.)

Another way to conserve valuable shop real estate is to locate your collector in a space adjacent to your shop: a closet, a shed or, if you live in a warm, dry climate, even the great outdoors. Another possibility is to use a portable central collector that's wheeled outside when you work inside the shop. Just make sure to consider noise and air-return issues, as discussed in the following sections.

Separate components, here an Oneida shaker box for a tube-filter bag house (left), blower (center) and cyclone (right), can make it convenient to put a central collector into a crowded shop.

Proximity to machines

The farther a dust collector has to convey dust and chips through ductwork, the more power it requires. Therefore, for greatest system efficiency, it's best to keep duct runs as short as possible. This calls for some compromises when the ideal location for the collector doesn't coincide with the ideal location for the ductwork's main line. The issue will be more acute if you work in a really big shop (where the central collector may end up 65 ft. from the nearest machine it's going to serve), or if you're trying to squeeze the best possible performance out of a small collector.

Noise level

When you add up the whoosh of moving air and motor and fan whine, central collectors can get pretty noisy. Noise can be a problem whether you locate the collector inside the shop (and must suffer with the accumulated din of machines and the collector) or outside (and have to deal with neighbors' complaints). You can quiet either an in-shop or outdoor unit by building an enclosure around it (see the photo at right). The enclosure will better attenuate noise if lined with soundboard or acoustical foam (see the vacuum enclosure on p. 91). If the enclosure is sealed, you must provide a way for air to return into the shop or escape outdoors. A louvered vent, such as used to ventilate a laundry room, can be installed over an opening for exhaust air. Ideally, the vent should be about 10 times as large as the cross-sectional area of the collector's intake duct.

It's also possible to reduce collector noise with a duct silencer, a kind of muffler that is installed on the air-discharge side of the blower. Although similar in working principle to the shop-vacuum muffler (see pp. 90-91), duct silencers are very expensive—typically more than $400—and well beyond the budget of most small shops.

Returning clean air to the shop

If you locate your collector outside the shop and you live in an area with cold winters and/or hot summers, you'll want to return the clean air exhausted by the collector's filters back inside the shop. Otherwise, you'll need to heat (or cool and possibly dehumidify) the fresh air drawn in to replace the air that the collector has sucked out of your shop.

If you've chosen to save space by using separate collector components and locating the blower and/or cyclone in a separate outbuilding or outside, you can simply run a duct back into the shop and mount the filter bag house inside (as shown in the drawing on p. 131). If you live in a cold or hot climate, you'll want to insulate any exposed ductwork and components (such as the cyclone), so that the air passing through them isn't cooled or heated excessively before it returns to the shop.

Building a movable enclosure can cut down on the noise created by a dust collector located inside the shop. The plywood box shown here has notches cut in the sides, to allow it to fit tightly against the wall over ductwork, and is fitted with wheels, for quick access to the collector.

If you live in a temperate climate (as I do here in Santa Cruz) and have decided against an air-return system, it is imperative that you provide replacement air for the air removed from the shop by your collector. The replacement air can be supplied through a filtered vent, or an open window. Air replacement is crucial if your shop has ventilation pipes for water heaters, furnaces or stoves. A forced downdraft caused by inadequate air replacement could bring smoke and/or toxic fumes into the shop when the dust collection system is running!

Fire hazards

Because of the fire and explosion hazards associated with fine dust, never locate a collector near a source of sparks, such as a welding bench or grinding wheel, or near an open flame, such as from a water heater, stove or furnace. Also, never store combustibles such as rags and finishing materials in the same area as the collector.

Laying out the ductwork

Once you've got a pretty good idea of where you're going to put your collector, you're ready to lay out the ductwork to the machines. By now, you've probably decided on the height at which your ductwork will run; most woodworkers install their systems either above their machines, hanging ductwork from rafters or ceiling joists, or under the floor, suspending ductwork from floor joists. Hanging ductwork above machines is easy and convenient (you can even run ducts through attic spaces in shops with low ceilings), but branches that drop down to machines that are in the center floor area may get in the way. Under-floor installations solve this problem but are more time-consuming to install, unless you have a basement beneath the shop. It is also possible to install ductwork in a new cement slab floor (consult your air-handling specialist for details).

Whether the collection system is in a small shop or a large factory, it is designed with two kinds of ducts: the main duct, a single large pipe that runs from the collector through the length of the shop, and the branch ducts, multiple smaller pipes that connect each machine to the main duct. The ductwork system resembles the branches of a tree, with branch pipes running diagonally or perpendicularly from the main line to the area of the machine. A vertical pipe then drops down (or comes up through the floor) to a convenient height for fitting a blast gate and a short (1½ ft. to 2½ ft.) length of flexible hose to connect the machine to the branch (see pp. 150-154).

For now, you'll just be sketching in the proposed location of main and branch ducts as simple lines on both the plan and elevation drawings. To make things simpler when selecting fittings later, you'll want lines that represent a duct turning a corner to bend only at either 45° or 90° and lines depicting merging ducts to meet at 45° (90° only when absolutely necessary), with the angle pointing "downstream" (toward the collector; see the drawing below). Try to make all your duct runs as short as possible: The longer the duct, the more energy it will take the collector to convey dust and chips from the machine. Also, try to make all your duct runs as straight as possible: Every single twist and turn that the ductwork takes will require more collector energy.

The following scenarios are illustrated to give you some idea of different ductwork-layout strategies. Each has advantages that make it more suitable in some shop situations than in others.

Central main duct The drawing below shows one possible layout with the main line running directly across the center of the shop. This layout works best if most machines are grouped somewhere near the center of the shop (especially if they are in line), away from the walls, and there's room for a collector along the short wall or in an adjacent outbuilding. It provides for the shortest possible main line, with

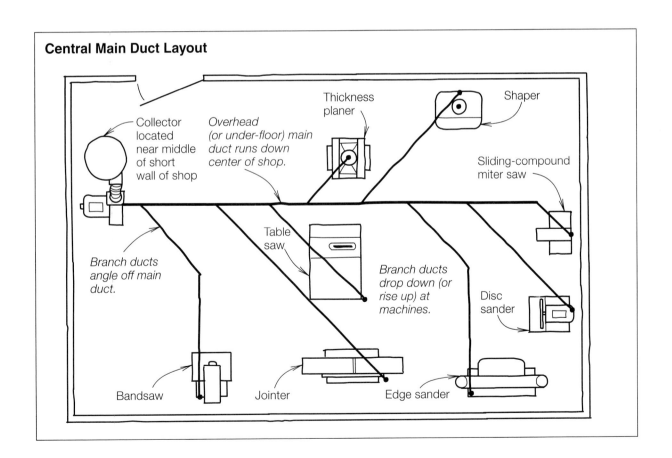

Central Main Duct Layout

Collector located near middle of short wall of shop

Overhead (or under-floor) main duct runs down center of shop.

Thickness planer

Shaper

Sliding-compound miter saw

Branch ducts angle off main duct.

Table saw

Branch ducts drop down (or rise up) at machines.

Disc sander

Bandsaw

Jointer

Edge sander

Diagonal Main Duct Layout

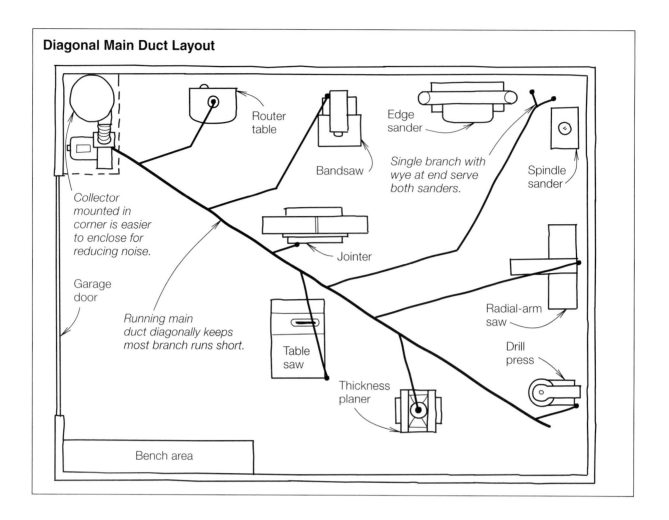

Collector mounted in corner is easier to enclose for reducing noise.

Garage door

Running main duct diagonally keeps most branch runs short.

Router table

Bandsaw

Single branch with wye at end serve both sanders.

Edge sander

Spindle sander

Jointer

Table saw

Thickness planer

Radial-arm saw

Drill press

Bench area

branch lines that drop (or rise) in the center of the shop or along walls as needed. But if your shop is wide and the machines are far apart, some of the branch lines in this scheme may end up being quite long. Depending on overhead (or under-floor) obstructions, you can run long branch lines diagonally (as for the branch to the jointer) or, by adding another 45° bend, run the branch perpendicular to the main (as for the bandsaw and edge sander).

Diagonal main duct The second layout, shown in the drawing above, has the main line running diagonally across the shop from corner to corner, with branch lines running diagonally off it. This arrangement locates the collector in the corner of the shop, where it's more out of the way and easier to enclose for sound attenuation (see p. 127). The branches from this diagonally running main line will be relatively short if most machines are grouped in the center of the shop, or along two or three walls, as shown. In cases where two machines are grouped close together at some distance from the main duct (such as

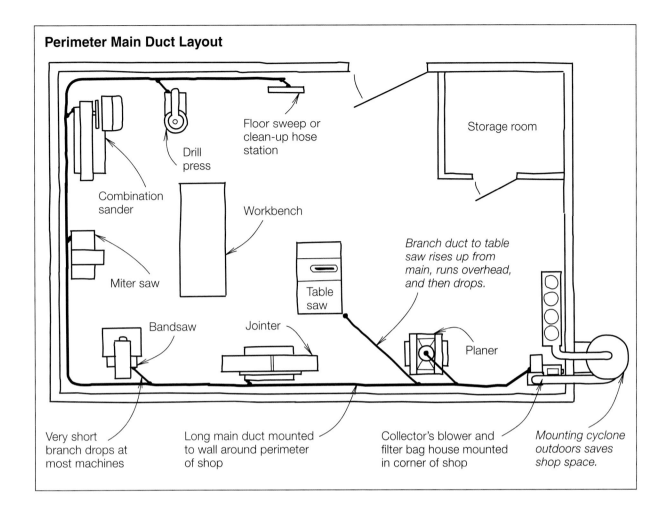

Perimeter Main Duct Layout

Floor sweep or clean-up hose station

Drill press

Storage room

Combination sander

Workbench

Miter saw

Branch duct to table saw rises up from main, runs overhead, and then drops.

Table saw

Bandsaw

Jointer

Planer

Very short branch drops at most machines

Long main duct mounted to wall around perimeter of shop

Collector's blower and filter bag house mounted in corner of shop

Mounting cyclone outdoors saves shop space.

the edge sander and spindle sander in the drawing on the facing page), it's possible to run a single branch duct to the tools, then split the branch duct to service both machines (see the discussion of wye branches on p. 133).

Perimeter main duct The main line in the drawing above runs around the perimeter of the shop. This arrangement is best if most of the machines are located along the walls. It also allows you to hang the ducting for the main line on the wall, rather than from the ceiling, which is preferable if your shop has no crawl space and low headroom. While the main line in this scenario is the longest of the three, it provides for the shortest branch lines to wall-hugging machines. On the downside, branches that serve center-floor machines (such as the table saw in the drawing) must reach up and overhead, and then down again—a long way to go with lots of efficiency-robbing twists and turns. An alternative is to move the machine closer to the wall and run the branch horizontally at main-line level (but you'll have to walk around it).

Woodworking machines aren't the only things you can connect to a central dust collection system. While planning the ductwork layout, you might also consider adding a floor sweep to the system (see the drawing on p. 131). A floor sweep is basically a large rectangular hood mounted at floor level with a flip-up door on the long side. Dust and small debris are swept up to the door, which is then opened to suck it away. Unless you buy a good-quality floor sweep ("good" meaning expensive) with a door that seals tightly, you should fit a blast gate to the branch to keep air losses down (see pp. 150-152).

If you'd rather avoid the clouds of fine dust that sweeping raises, you can add one or more clean-up stations to your shop in lieu of floor sweeps. Each station consists of a length of flexible hose (2½ in. to 4 in. in diameter) connected to a branch duct and controlled by its own blast gate (a wye branch or lateral tee allows the hose station to share a branch duct with a machine; see the photo below). Add a hook (or a tray or box) for hose storage to complete the station.

A large-diameter hose makes it easy to vacuum up dust and debris from benchtops or around machines. Just fit a piece of large-mesh nylon netting or steel-wire hardware cloth over the end of the hose to help you avoid accidentally sucking up small tools and parts. If you have lots of floor area to clean, you can construct a bigger version of the floor vacuuming pickup (see pp. 31-33) from 3-in. or 4-in. dia. plastic pipe.

You can also use the strong suction and high volume of air conveyed by a central collector to capture fine dust produced during sanding by hand or with portable power tools. Sanding tables and booths, portable dust hoods, as well as portable power tools themselves can be connected to a central system (see pp. 188-193). You might want to include one or two extra stations (each with its own blast gate and flex hose) near workbenches for connecting such devices.

Adding a vacuum hose to your collection system makes shop cleanup quick and easy. The 2½-in. flexible hose, controlled by its own blast gate, connects to ductwork via a lateral tee shared by a jointer.

Turning corners and connecting branches

Once you've finished the rough layout, it's time to add some detail to the simple duct-layout lines on your drawings by specifying many of the fittings that will be used to make bends and connect branches to the main line. Considering the size of the fittings you use is especially important if your duct must pass through cramped quarters (around a corner, under a beam) because many fittings are bulky and take up quite a bit of room. More important, the kind of fittings you choose has a major effect on how much friction air and dust passing through the system encounter (see pp. 140-143).

The general rule with turns and transitions in the ductwork is that the more gradual they are, the better. Changing directions suddenly takes more energy than changing directions gradually—think of how much more your car's tires squeal when you tear around a sharp curve than when you cruise around a gentle one at the same speed. When air and dust traveling through ductwork at high speed must round a sharp corner (or airstreams must merge at sharp angles), more friction is generated against the side of the pipe; hence a more powerful collector must be used to convey it.

Large-radius elbows To turn ductwork corners gradually, special large-radius elbows are used. These elbows have a much more gradual bend than standard HVAC pipe elbows, as shown in the photo at right. Large-radius 90° and 45° elbows for dust collection typically have a radius that is one-and-one-half times the pipe's diameter. For example, a large-radius 4-in. elbow has a 6-in. radius (as measured on the elbow's centerline). For even more gradual bends, some suppliers make elbows with a radius two times pipe diameter.

Special fittings To merge the airflow between connecting ducts, special air-handling fittings are used, including wye branches, lateral tees and tee-on-tapers (see the photo below). Wye branches are used simply to merge two ducts into one, say to connect a single branch duct to two machines. Lateral tees are used to merge dust sources on a branch or branch ducts with the main duct. They consist of a sleeve, with one or more connectors sticking out of the side for attaching the

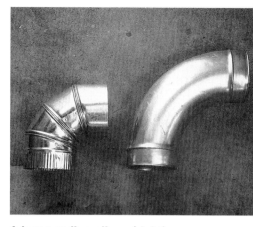

A large-radius elbow (right) allows air and dust to negotiate turns with less friction than a standard tight-radius HVAC pipe elbow (left), making for a more efficient collection system.

Choosing the correct fittings for merging ductwork is essential for efficient performance. Commonly used fittings include a wye branch (front center), a boot tee (left), a lateral tee (rear center) and a tee-on-taper (right).

branch duct(s). The most commonly used fitting is a 45° lateral tee, such as a "4 on 6" with a 4-in. branch and a 6-in. main duct; 90° tees (also called bullhead tees) are available, but they tend to create high friction losses in the system. Branch lines that must run at a 90° angle from the main line are best routed using a 45° lateral tee on the main duct and a 45° elbow on the branch. If you must run a perpendicular branch directly from the main duct, a special "boot tee" (see the bottom photo on p. 133) is a better choice. It has an angled gusset that eases the transition of air flowing from branch to main duct, creating less friction than with a 90° tee. Many other special fittings are available (or can be custom-welded) to suit all sorts of tricky installations.

In places where a branch duct joins a main branch that changes diameter, a tee-on-taper is called for. These fittings have one (or more) 45° connectors that join a tapered sleeve, such as a 6x5x4 with a main duct that reduces from 6 in. to 5 in. and a 4-in. branch. The larger end of the sleeve is oriented toward the collector. A tee-on-taper fitting is also useful for connecting machines with more than one pick-up hood to a branch duct (such as a radial-arm saw with a rear hood and blade-guard pickup; see pp. 178-179).

Whenever possible, the conventional way to orient a lateral tee or a tee-on-taper is to have the branch line split off horizontally from the main line (when viewed in elevation)—not directly downward. But on installations where the main line runs at the juncture of wall and ceiling, it's more practical to orient lateral tees so that branches angle downward, as shown in the photo on the facing page. The only shortcoming of this arrangement is that chips may settle into unused branches that are closer to the collector (any branches that accumulate dust are flushed out whenever they are brought into use).

The termination of the main line should connect to the last branch with a lateral tee. Installing an end cap on the straight portion of the fitting allows removal, in case you need to snake out a clogged main line. It's a good idea to terminate long branch lines this way, too. A lateral tee also allows the main line to be extended, should you add more machines in the future (see p. 159).

Mark out the location of the fittings on your drawing and figure approximate lengths for the straight pipe runs between fittings. Your next job is to figure out what diameter pipe and sizes of fittings to use. Pipe diameters also determine which type of tee (lateral or tee-on-taper) you'll need to use at each location where ducts merge.

When ductwork is run along a wall, branches can be dropped down vertically to machines below. This layout saves the room it takes to run branches horizontally and then drop them down to machines—the more conventional way of splitting off branch lines.

Determining correct duct diameters

Why be particular about the diameter of the pipes in your ductwork system? First, different machines produce different amounts of dust and chips: A thickness planer needs a greater volume of air to capture and transport its waste than a router table does. Second, air has to move at about the right speed through the pipe. If it moves too slowly, chips will settle out before they reach the collector; too fast, and the air creates more friction against the sides of the pipe than necessary, which reduces collection efficiency. The correct pipe diameter will carry the right volume of air to meet the chip output of the machine, and carry it at a speed just fast enough to keep dust and chips entrained (carried in the airstream without settling out). When determining the diameter of the pipes for your ductwork system, start with the branch lines.

Sizing the branch lines

In most small-shop systems, only one machine is used at a time, and hence only one branch duct will be drawing air at any time. The easiest approach to sizing branch ducts in such systems is to determine a pipe diameter that will meet the air-volume requirements of the machine (or machines) that the branch serves, and carry that air at a high enough velocity. Relying on the experience of dust collection experts, I've compiled the table on pp. 136-137, which lists the air-

CFM REQUIREMENTS AND RECOMMENDED DUCT DIAMETERS
FOR WOODSHOP MACHINES

Machine/dust source	Cfm requirements	Recommended duct size (for 4,000 fpm air velocity)
Table saw or panel saw		
up to 8-in. blade	350 cfm	3 in.
10-in. to 16-in. blade	350–500 cfm	4 in.–5 in.
Heavy-duty operation with dado	650 cfm	6 in.
or molding head		
Top pickup	100–200 cfm*	2 in.–3 in.
Radial-arm saw (rear hood and blade guard pickups)		
10-in. or smaller blade	350 cfm	4 in.
10-in. to 16-in. blade	550 cfm	5 in.
Thickness planer (single head)		
10 in. to 12 in.	500 cfm	5 in.
15 in. to 20 in.	600–800 cfm	5 in.–6 in.
20 in. to 24 in.	1,000 cfm	7 in.
Bandsaw (either single top hood or dual pickup)		
14-in. to 16-in. wheels	400 cfm	4 in.
18-in. to 24-in. wheels	550 cfm	5 in.
Band resaw; blade 2 in. to 3 in. wide	550–750 cfm	5 in.–6 in.
Jointer		
up to 8 in. wide	350–400 cfm	4 in.
8 in. to 12 in. wide	550 cfm	5 in.
Combination sander (6x48 belt, 9-in. disc)	600 cfm	5 in.
Disc sander (single or dual pickup)		
12 in.	350 cfm	4 in.
15 in. to 20 in.	550 cfm	5 in.
Horizontal belt edge sander (single or dual pickup)		
4 in. to 6 in. wide	550 cfm	5 in.
Vertical belt sander, up to 6 in. wide	400 cfm	4 in.–5 in.
Oscillating spindle sander,		
up to 50 sq. in. of abrasive	350 cfm	4 in.
Drum thicknessing sander (single drum)		
up to 12-in. drum, 200-sq.-in. area	400 cfm	4 in.
12-in. to 24-in. drum; 200- to 400-sq.-in. area	550 cfm	5 in.
24-in. or larger drum; 400- to 700-sq.-in. area	650 cfm	6 in.

CFM REQUIREMENTS AND RECOMMENDED DUCT DIAMETERS
FOR WOODSHOP MACHINES (continued)

Machine/dust source	Cfm requirements	Recommended duct size (for 4,000 fpm air velocity)
Drum thicknessing sander (dual drum)		
with single 5-in. or 6-in. dust port	800 cfm	6 in.
with dual 4-in. dust ports	700 cfm	6 in.
Wide belt sander		
12-in. to 15-in. wide belt	500–800 cfm	5 in.–6 in.
15-in. to 24-in. wide belt	800–1,200 cfm	6 in.–8 in.
Spindle shaper (single arbor)		
up to ¾-hp motor	400 cfm**	4 in.
1½-hp	550 cfm**	5 in.
3-hp	700 cfm**	6 in.
Router table or router-based joinery machine	200–350 cfm**	3 in.–4 in.
Drill press		
Small or large (also with mortising attachment)	350–400 cfm**	4 in.
Scrollsaw	200–350 cfm	3 in.–4 in.
Wood lathe		
Small	400 cfm***	4 in.
Medium	550 cfm***	5 in.
Large	650–750 cfm***	6 in.
Floor sweep	350–750 cfm	4 in.–6 in.
Clean-up hose		
2½-in. vacuum-type hose	125 cfm	3 in.
4-in. flexible hose	350 cfm	4 in.

   *   Add this cfm requirement to cfm needed for bottom hood pickup.
  **   Chip production varies greatly with type of cutter or bit used and rate of feed.
***   Varies with type of tool used and method with which cut is accomplished.

volume requirements in cubic feet per minute (cfm) for a wide assortment of woodworking machines. The chart also shows the correct branch-pipe diameter you should use to convey that air volume at approximately 4,000 feet per minute (fpm), which is the speed collection specialists recommend for air conveying dust and chips through branch-duct connections. (4,000 fpm is the optimum air speed; actual air velocity in the final system is likely to range between 3,500 and 4,500 fpm.) In cases where the machine might have more than one pick-up hood (for example, the horizontal belt edge sander), the table gives the correct branch-line size that will be split into two ducts, one to each hood. For branch ducts that will serve two machines with different cfm needs, pick the size needed to serve the machine with the highest cfm needs (in this case, the blast gates are used to control airflow to only one machine at a time). When in doubt about using, say, a 4-in. pipe or a 5-in. pipe for a branch, always choose the larger diameter. Write in all the required branch-line diameters on your sketch.

Sizing the main duct

With all the branch ducts sized, it's time to size the main duct that will connect them all to the collector. Starting with the section farthest from the collector, the main duct is sized to convey the amount of air required by the largest machine on the farthest-away branch, but at a slower velocity (3,500 fpm is recommended by experts as the optimum air velocity in the main duct). Because the air in the branch duct is traveling at 4,000 fpm, the size of the main duct is increased to convey it at a slower velocity. As shown in the drawing below, a 6-in. join-

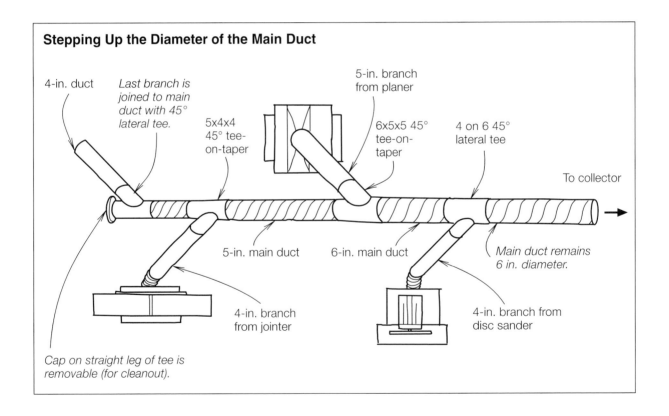

Stepping Up the Diameter of the Main Duct

4-in. duct

Last branch is joined to main duct with 45° lateral tee.

5x4x4 45° tee-on-taper

5-in. branch from planer

6x5x5 45° tee-on-taper

4 on 6 45° lateral tee

To collector

5-in. main duct

6-in. main duct

Main duct remains 6 in. diameter.

4-in. branch from jointer

4-in. branch from disc sander

Cap on straight leg of tee is removable (for cleanout).

MAIN-DUCT DIAMETER	
Largest cfm requirement	Main-duct diameter (for 3,500 fpm air velocity)
Up to 300 cfm	4 in.
Up to 475 cfm	5 in.
Up to 675 cfm	6 in.
Up to 925 cfm	7 in.
Up to 1,200 cfm	8 in.

ter that requires 350 cfm and has a 4-in. branch duct will call for a 5-in. main duct. The table above shows the correct main-duct diameters to handle different cfm requirements.

As you travel up the main duct to each branch, you increase the size of the main duct only if it must handle a higher volume of air from the branch. Referring to the example in the drawing on the facing page, the next branch duct serves a 500-cfm thickness planer, and therefore the main duct must jump up to a 6-in. dia. pipe. While you can use a simple reducer fitting to make the transition from 5 in. to 6 in., it's more efficient to use a 45° tee-on-taper (see the photo on p. 133). Note that even though the next branch in the example connects a smaller machine (a 350-cfm 12-in. disc sander) to the system, the diameter of the main duct does not decrease. It remains at the largest diameter necessary to serve the planer (the largest machine on the system) all the way until it reaches the central collector. On your shop-layout drawing, write in the diameter of the main duct along its entire length, noting the size of any reducers or 45° tee-on-taper fittings that you'll need along the way.

As you go through and size the main duct for your own system, it might be worthwhile to consider making a few changes in your shop layout. If your biggest machine, say a planer, were on the branch farthest from the collector, you would have to run your entire main duct in 6-in. pipe. However, if you move that machine to a closer branch, you could run smaller-diameter pipe for most of your main duct, only running the heavier and more expensive 6-in. pipe from the closest branch to the collector.

Calculating static-pressure losses

Once the ductwork is laid out and sized, the final step in designing your central dust collection system is to calculate the amount of resistance that air and dust traveling through the ductwork will encounter (measured as static-pressure loss; see the sidebar on p. 100). This information is then used to determine how powerful a collector you'll need to buy. If the collector isn't powerful enough to overcome the static-pressure (SP) losses inherent in the system, it won't perform up to expectations: The volume and velocity of the air moving through the ductwork will be inadequate, resulting in poor chip capture and chips settling inside ducts and possibly clogging them.

Calculating the SP loss in a small, one-machine-at-a-time system is based on developing a worst-case scenario: Under what circumstances will the collector have to work hardest? The answer is, when it is conveying dust and chips from the branch with the greatest resistance (with the highest SP loss), which is usually the longest, smallest-diameter branch with the most bends. Calculate the total amount of SP loss in the suspected worst branch by adding up the resistance in every single pipe, hose and fitting in that branch and the main duct between the machine and the collector (when in doubt about which is the worst branch, do the calculation for all suspected branches). Follow along with the example shown in the drawing on the facing page as we go through each step of the computation in the following paragraphs.

Static-pressure loss varies for air traveling through different diameters of pipe: the smaller the diameter, the higher the static pressure per foot of length. SP loss also varies for air traveling at different velocities: the higher the speed, the higher the loss. Therefore, we must add up SP losses for each diameter of branch duct and main duct separately. Starting with the branch duct, first add up all lengths of straight pipe. Multiply the total number of feet by the inches of SP loss per foot listed in the table on p. 142 for the corresponding branch-duct diameter. Next, figure the SP loss in the main duct by multiplying the number of feet for each diameter with its corresponding factor in the table. Using the same table, look up factors for different diameters of flexible hose used in the branch (to hook up the machine) and the main duct (if you're using flexible hose to connect the collector to the system), and add in these lengths.

Calculating Static-Pressure Loss

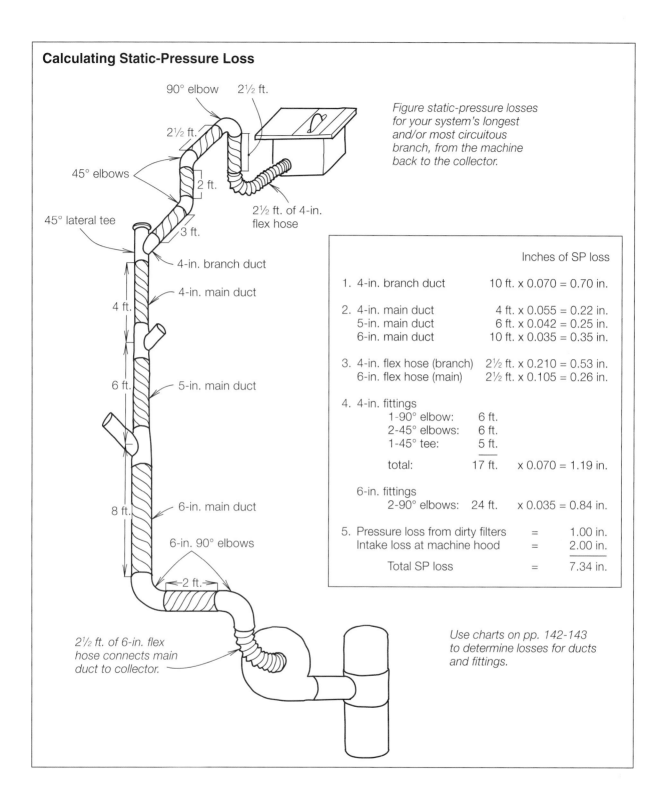

90° elbow   2½ ft.

2½ ft.

45° elbows

45° lateral tee

2 ft.

3 ft.

2½ ft. of 4-in. flex hose

4-in. branch duct

4-in. main duct

4 ft.

5-in. main duct

6 ft.

8 ft.

6-in. main duct

6-in. 90° elbows

2 ft.

2½ ft. of 6-in. flex hose connects main duct to collector.

Figure static-pressure losses for your system's longest and/or most circuitous branch, from the machine back to the collector.

Use charts on pp. 142-143 to determine losses for ducts and fittings.

Inches of SP loss

1. 4-in. branch duct   10 ft. x 0.070 = 0.70 in.

2. 4-in. main duct   4 ft. x 0.055 = 0.22 in.
   5-in. main duct   6 ft. x 0.042 = 0.25 in.
   6-in. main duct   10 ft. x 0.035 = 0.35 in.

3. 4-in. flex hose (branch)   2½ ft. x 0.210 = 0.53 in.
   6-in. flex hose (main)   2½ ft. x 0.105 = 0.26 in.

4. 4-in. fittings
       1-90° elbow: 6 ft.
       2-45° elbows: 6 ft.
       1-45° tee: 5 ft.

       total: 17 ft.   x 0.070 = 1.19 in.

   6-in. fittings
       2-90° elbows: 24 ft.   x 0.035 = 0.84 in.

5. Pressure loss from dirty filters   =   1.00 in.
   Intake loss at machine hood   =   2.00 in.

   Total SP loss   =   7.34 in.

STATIC-PRESSURE LOSS PER FOOT OF DUCT OR HOSE				
Diameter of duct	Inches of static-pressure loss per foot of rigid pipe		Inches of static-pressure loss per foot of flexible hose	
	For branch ducts (@ 4,000 fpm)	For main ducts (@ 3,500 fpm)	For branch ducts (@ 4,000 fpm)	For main ducts (@ 3,500 fpm)
3 in.	.100	.075	.300	.225
4 in.	.070	.055	.210	.165
5 in.	.055	.042	.165	.126
6 in.	.045	.035	.135	.105
7 in.	.038	.026	.114	.078
8 in.	.030	.022	.090	.066

Static-pressure loss is also different in the various types and diameters of fittings used in a ductwork system. The table on the facing page shows a number of common pipe fittings (in different diameters) and their SP losses, stated as an equivalent number of feet of straight pipe. Add up the equivalent number of feet for elbows and tees, separately for each diameter of main duct and branch duct. Then, add each diameter's equivalent number of feet together and multiply by the SP factor (from the table above).

Next, you need to factor in additional SP losses caused by dirty filters and energy lost as the air and chips enter the hood or pickup at the machine. There are ways to calculate these losses accurately, but for small-shop purposes, it's less complicated simply to assign average losses: 1 in. of SP for dirty filters and 2 in. of SP for entry losses. Don't add the SP loss for filters if the system doesn't have them and is exhausting directly outdoors. If your blower, cyclone and bag house are mounted in different locations (as shown in the drawing on p. 131), you must also calculate and add SP loss for every foot of pipe and fitting between these components. If your system uses a cyclone, drop-box or preseparator canister, add another 1 in. to 2 in. of SP loss as well.

EQUIVALENT LENGTH OF FITTINGS (FOR CALCULATING STATIC-PRESSURE LOSS)

Diameter of pipe fitting	90° 1.5 x radius elbow	90° 2 x radius elbow	45° 1.5 x radius elbow	30° lateral tee or wye branch*	45° lateral tee or wye branch*
	Equivalent number of feet of straight pipe				
3 in.	5 ft.	3 ft.	2.5 ft.	2 ft.	3 ft.
4 in.	6 ft.	4 ft.	3.0 ft.	3 ft.	5 ft.
5 in.	9 ft.	6 ft.	4.5 ft.	4 ft.	6 ft.
6 in.	12 ft.	7 ft.	6.0 ft.	5 ft.	7 ft.
7 in.	13 ft.	9 ft.	6.5 ft.	6 ft.	9 ft.
8 in.	15 ft.	10 ft.	7.5 ft.	7 ft.	11 ft.

* With lateral tees, use only for computing static-pressure loss of branch.

The final step is to add up all the SP losses for the system; in our example, they amount to about 7⅓ in. This is the amount of static pressure that our central collector must be capable of generating if it's going to collect dust efficiently from the worst branch. If it can do that, then it will surely handle collection from the shorter and/or straighter branches with ease.

Selecting the right collector for your system

Designing the ductwork for your system yields two figures that you'll need to choose the right-sized collector. The first figure is the volume of air (measured in cfm) that the collector must be capable of moving to convey sawdust from the most air-hungry machine on your system, as discussed on pp. 135-139. (If your system will collect from two or more machines at a time, this volume must equal the combined cfm of the machines.) The second figure is the number of inches of static-pressure loss in the system (as calculated in the section above) that the collector must be capable of overcoming to move the needed volume of air. Comparing these numbers to the performance curve of the collector you're considering purchasing will ensure that the unit will have adequate volume and power to run your system (see the sidebar on pp. 106-107).

CHAPTER 8

Installing a Central Collection System

Once you've designed the ductwork system and compiled a list of all the various pipes and fittings you'll need, it's time to put theory into practice and assemble and install the ductwork and hook it up to your central collector. Installing a system of ductwork is probably the cleanest kind of plumbing you'll ever do. But first, you have to decide what kind of ducting pipe to use, and then go about cutting, fitting and hanging it. After the blast gates and flexible hoses are chosen and connected, you'll be ready to test the system—and make changes if collection isn't up to snuff. As a final step, you can make your collection system easy to turn on and off by setting up a system of switches around the shop, or by installing a remote or automatic switching device.

Before you dive in, check with your local building department and fire marshall to see if you need a permit, and to make sure the system that you plan to install meets local building and fire codes. You'll also want to check with your insurance company to find out how system installation might affect your policy.

Ducting materials

There are only a few practical choices for ducting materials for woodshop dust collection systems: plastic pipe and spiral or snap-lock metal pipe. Choosing between them can be a very important decision, one that affects the ease of installation, the cost of the system and the safety of operating it.

Setting up the ductwork for a central collection system starts with the installation of the main duct. Save your back by raising the pre-assembled duct overhead by using a rope with a block and tackle set.

Plastic pipe

Probably the single biggest issue in small-shop dust collection is whether it's safe to use plastic pipe as ducting material. Drain and sewage pipe made from PVC or ABS plastic is inexpensive, readily available (though not in all fittings), easy to work with and easy to install; it's also already in use in innumerable small woodshops. In spite of its usefulness and ubiquitousness, plastic pipe can be a dangerous choice. Static electricity created by air and dust moving at high velocity through plastic duct can suddenly discharge and spark a fire or even a powerful explosion (see pp. 18-21). Chances for these disasters to occur are greater if the system is operating in a low-humidity climate or if a large volume of very fine sanding dust is being collected. Although shop fires are fairly uncommon, I've read enough accounts of small fires caused by plastic-pipe static combustion to make me very reluctant to condone the use of plastic ductwork, even for small collection systems. Losing a shop, your home—or your life—to a fire is just too high a price to pay for saving some time and money. If you already have plastic pipe ductwork in your shop and aren't willing to replace it with metal, the least you can do is to ground the pipe as thoroughly as possible, as described in the sidebar on p. 155.

Metal pipe

Static electricity does still occur in metal pipe (and explosions aren't impossible), but the difference is that grounded metal pipe dissipates the charge readily. This fact, coupled with the strength and simplicity of metal ductwork, makes it the best choice for dust collection duct-

Couplings offer a quick and easy way to connect lengths of spiral pipe. A male coupling is used, because straight pipe usually has female ends.

Much more affordable than heavier spiral metal duct, 24-ga. or 26-ga. HVAC pipe is readily available at hardware and home supply stores. The pipe is cut to length with tin snips before the center seam is snap-locked into place.

ing. Galvanized sheet-metal pipe is strong and light and not that difficult to install—if you're handy with a pair of tin snips or a hacksaw, a pop-riveter and a caulking gun.

Spiral pipe Among several types of metal pipe appropriate for collection system ductwork, heavy-duty spiral pipe, typically made from 22-ga. galvanized steel, is de rigueur for industrial systems and production shops. While it's very strong and durable, spiral pipe is also quite expensive, especially when you purchase heavy-duty welded fittings (usually made from 20-ga. steel). Industrial ductwork suppliers offer a tremendous range of fittings, including large-radius elbows, lateral tees and tee-on-tapers (see the photo on p. 133), so you can handle practically any situation. Couplings offer a quick and easy way of joining long lengths of spiral pipe, as shown in the photo above. Spiral pipe comes in many standard diameters from 3 in. to 16 in. (in 1-in. increments), which allow you to size your ductwork accurately, and in lengths up to 10 ft., which are good for long runs with less installation work.

Snap-lock HVAC pipe Although it's not as strong as spiral pipe, 24-ga. or 26-ga. snap-lock HVAC pipe (see the photo at left) is a good choice for most small-shop installations. It is significantly less expensive than spiral pipe, and its lighter weight makes it easier to hang on overhead installations. And lengths of pipe and fittings are joined by sliding together crimped ends, so you don't need to buy special couplings. On the downside, you can rarely find special fittings for HVAC pipe, such as large-radius elbows and 45° lateral tees (desirable for efficient airflow) at your local building supply store. Worse, many stores now carry lighter 30-ga. HVAC components, which are too thin for dust collection use and can actually suck flat, ruining your system. It's best to mail-order 24-ga. and 26-ga. pipe and special fittings from one of the mail-order sources listed in the Sources of Supply on pp. 194-195.

Cutting and installing pipe

Once you have all the pipes and fittings you need, you're ready to begin installing the system. It's usually best to install the dust collector first (bolting down components as necessary), then assemble and connect the main line, working out from the collector, and finally run the branch lines to the machines.

Start by assembling the main line on the ground or benchtop, mating straight pipe with fittings that will split off the branch lines. It's easier to lay out angled branch-line runs by setting the partially assembled ductwork atop an old piece of soundboard or cheap paneling and drawing in the spots where the branch lines will drop or rise vertically (see the photo below). You can then calculate the position of angled lateral tees or tee-on-tapers on the main line to produce correct branch-line placement. Cut any sections of pipe to length as needed, as described on pp. 149-150.

The main duct should be assembled on the ground and then lifted into place. Working on top of scrap paneling allows you to mark out the position of angled branches, making it easier to determine the length of pipes that join fittings.

Installations with ductwork that runs horizontally require pipe hangers to secure ducts in place. There are several different ways to hang ductwork, depending on your budget and the kind of walls you have in your shop.

If your shop has exposed stud walls and rafters or ceiling joists, it's easy to secure horizontal ducts using inexpensive plumber's pipe strap. Available at plumbing or hardware supply stores, pipe strap comes on a roll and looks like metal tape with holes in it. It's best to use screws with washers under the heads to hold the strapping to ceiling joists, stud walls and other members. Screws allow you to remove the straps when need be (don't use drywall screws, which are brittle and can snap unexpectedly).

To mount a section of pipe, run a U-shaped length of strap around a pipe to hold it flush against a member or surface. To hang a duct from rafters or farther down from the ceiling, wrap the strapping around it, crossing the straps as they're run up to the joist as shown in the top photo at right. Add several reinforcing straps on long runs of hanging pipe, to keep the pipe from swaying side to side (this is especially important if you live in earthquake country). For installation

of large main ducts, you might want to use heavy-duty hangers (which bolt together) and hanger straps (available from ductwork suppliers).

A good method for installing ductwork in shops with smooth (paneled or drywalled) surfaces is to attach thin wood strips to the walls or ceiling and secure the pipe to them. Strips of 1x2 are installed exactly where each duct will run, attached with nails or screws driven into studs or joists. The ducts are attached atop the strips using self-locking plastic tie straps (see the photo below). The ties are threaded through shallow cross-grain grooves cut into the inside of each strip before it is attached. Alternatively, you can shim the strips out from the wall a little, to allow the ties to be

put on wherever you wish. If you use this method to hang heavy, large-diameter metal pipe, you should substitute strong wire or adjustable hose clamps for the plastic ties.

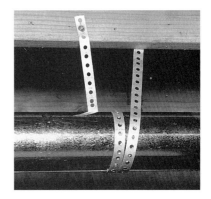

Plumber's pipe strap can be used to hold ductwork flush against a wall or ceiling, or to hang a duct down from the ceiling, as shown.

A convenient way to install ductwork atop a paneled or drywalled surface is to use 1x2 strips nailed or screwed along the path of the duct. The duct mounts atop the strips, which are grooved to allow fastening with self-locking plastic ties.

Once the main line is assembled, raise it into place with the aid of a friend or (for larger mains) a block and tackle, as shown in the photo on p. 145. If the main line is particularly long or takes a bend in the middle, it may be wiser to assemble and hang it in two steps. (If you're installing ductwork below a floor with a cramped crawl space, you may have to build it in place, piece by piece.) With the main line in place and level, fit pipe hangers, first at both ends, then every 10 ft. along the duct (as described in the sidebar on the facing page), to keep the ductwork from sagging. Now you can cut and fit each branch duct in a similar fashion, building it on the ground first, then hanging it in place. Secure the far end of each branch line with a hanger or strap.

Cutting pipe to length

Straight sections of HVAC pipe are easy to cut to length using a pair of tin snips (and wearing gloves): Simply mark and cut the uncrimped end as it lies flat, before the pipe is snapped together (see the bottom photo on p. 146). The crimped end slips into the uncrimped end of the previous pipe, with the crimps always pointing "downstream," back toward the collector. If the crimped end must be cut off (which is occasionally necessary to make connections), you can re-crimp the cut end with a special crimping tool, as shown in the photo below. This tool is available from stores that sell heating pipe and from Woodworker's Supply (see Sources of Supply on pp. 194-195). Before cutting the pipe, be sure to leave enough extra length for the new crimp.

Metal HVAC pipe that has been cut to length must have its 'male' end crimped before assembly. A special crimping tool is used, which is worked all the way around the pipe.

Assembling a Spiral-Pipe Joint

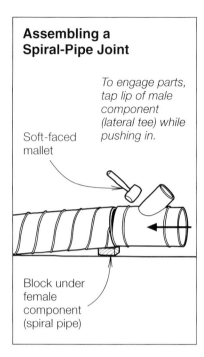

To engage parts, tap lip of male component (lateral tee) while pushing in.

Soft-faced mallet

Block under female component (spiral pipe)

Spiral pipe can be cut with a hacksaw, but it is quicker and neater to use a powered miter saw fitted with a special metal-cutting abrasive blade (available at hardware stores). After measuring and marking the pipe length, draw the line of cut around the pipe with a permanent marker pen, using a flexible magnetic strip as a ruler (the strip sticks to the pipe, which makes marking easier). To start a cut, lower the sawblade into the pipe, then rotate the pipe through the cut, following the marked line. Clean up the ends of each cut length by deburring the inside and outside edges with a half-round file, wearing gloves to protect your hands against sharp edges. Spiral-pipe parts are designed to fit together tightly, so it's often necessary to drive connections home. Working on the floor or on a benchtop, place a small wood block under the female component (usually the straight spiral pipe) and slip the end of the male component (usually a fitting) into it, as shown in the drawing at left. Tap the top part of the male end near its lip with a soft-faced mallet and push until the parts engage fully.

Fastening and sealing ductwork

On permanent installations, lengths of pipe and fittings should be fastened together with steel pop rivets (see the photo at left). Eighth-inch-diameter steel pop rivets are stronger than aluminum rivets, are quick and easy to install and leave only a small nub that doesn't protrude inside of the pipe as prominently as sheet-metal screws do. Pop rivets also drill out easily, if you change your mind or need to rearrange your ductwork later.

It's important to take the time to seal all pipe connections with a bead of silicone caulking (an unsealed system can loose 10% to 15% of its efficiency). Seal each branch down to the blast gate, and seal all seams on snap-lock HVAC pipes and adjustable elbows (if used). Make especially sure that pipe connections between the fan, cyclone and filter bag house are well sealed. It's easier to seal the main duct, as well as branch-duct subassemblies, on the ground before installation. Connections that are hard to reach can be sealed with duct tape. On underfloor systems, also run a heavy bead of caulk around the base of each duct where it comes through an exterior wall or up through the floor (to keep out drafts, moisture and bugs too!).

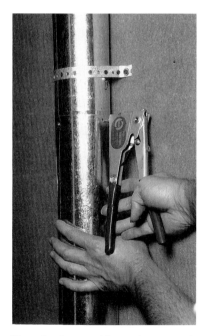

Pop rivets provide a strong and fast way to connect sections of ducting. Each rivet is inserted through a small hole drilled through the pipe and set into place using a special pop-riveting tool.

Blast gates

Once all the ductwork is in place, you need to cap the end of each branch duct with a blast gate, which will control the airflow to the machine on that branch. In small shops, fitting blast gates allows the collector to draw air from only one machine at a time. In large shops and industrial systems where many or all shop machines are run full time, blast gates are used to adjust the airflow at individual machines. Small shops may also use blast gates to balance the flow of air between two pickups on a single machine (see pp. 173-175).

Blast gates are simple valves with a sliding door that runs in a slot in the body of the gate. Sliding the door all the way in or out turns the collection vacuum off or on; sliding the door partway in or out allows partial vacuum, for airflow balancing. Commercially made blast gates come in plastic or metal; plastic gates are cheaper, but metal gates are more durable. Metal gates are available in three different styles, as shown in the photo below. The most common kind, the full gate, mounts between the ends of two pipes (or a pipe and a flex hose). A half-gate can be mounted in the middle of a rigid duct (by cutting a half-circle slot in the duct and pop-riveting the gate in place). Half-gates provide a convenient way to add gates to existing ductwork, though they don't seal as well as full gates. Yet another type, a self-cleaning gate, is a good choice for ducts that must convey fine dust from resinous or sappy woods such as pine. The fine, moist dust from these woods can stick into the slot on a normal blast gate and, over time, make it difficult to operate. The sliding blade on a self-cleaning gate is designed to be pushed all the way through the rear edge of the casting periodically to clean out debris that has accumulated in the slot.

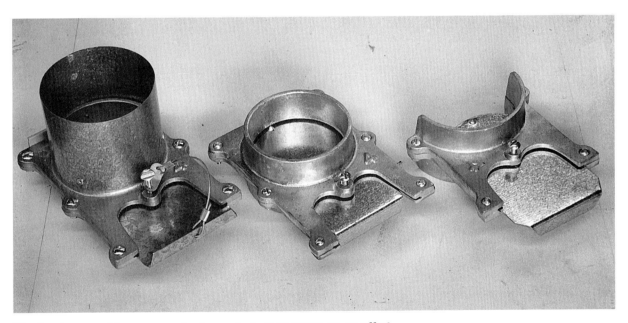

Blast gates provide a convenient way to turn vacuum on or off at each machine or dust source. Three styles commonly used are (left to right): a self-cleaning gate (shown with a collar for securing a flexible hose), a full gate and a half-gate.

In small systems where blast gates will be opened and closed often, it's best to locate them in an easy-to-reach spot near where you would stand to operate the machine (it's no fun to have to bend down to open a gate every time you want to run a tool). On machines that will be connected to their branch lines with flexible hose, the blast gate provides a natural transition: The duct is attached on one side, the hose on the other. Use pop rivets or sheet-metal screws to join a blast gate to rigid ductwork and adjustable hose clamps to attach flexible hose (pop-riveting a connector fitting or short length of pipe to the machine end of the blast gate makes for a more secure hose attachment). Ductwork near the blast gate should be anchored securely to the wall, machine base or other solid surface, so the gate can be operated without deflecting the duct.

Shop-built gates You can stretch a shoestring budget by building your own blast gates. The basic gate shown in the drawing on the facing page is built from plywood, Masonite and a scrap or two of hardwood. The holes bored or sawn through the plywood squares should be large enough to fit the end of the metal pipe (or the coupling used to attach flexible hose). Small tacks or escutcheon pins can be used to nail the inside end of the pipe to the plywood. A bead of silicone caulk around the outside of the pipe seals it to the gate. Screws through holes in the corners are used to assemble the gate with the Masonite slide in place (a small brad pin in the front edge keeps the slide from pulling all the way out). A grooved hardwood strip glued to the edge of the slide makes it easier to pull and push. To save the trouble of having to open gates and switch on the collector separately, you can install a switch directly on your shop-built blast gate connected to a low-voltage relay that turns on the collector (see pp. 164-165).

Flexible-hose connections

The final link between branch duct and machine is, in all but a few cases, a flexible hose connected between the blast gate and the dust port or hood on the machine. Although better-quality hoses aren't that flexible, they still allow the hose to twist and turn to make the connection—something that's often difficult to accomplish with rigid pipe fittings. Better yet, a flexible hose allows you to move the machine around a little, say to pull it away from the wall for adjustment, or to connect a hood that's mounted to an adjustable part of the machine, such as a hood attached to a table-saw cradle (see the photo on p. 176). And flexible hose is essential for connecting a collection system to a tool that moves, such as the head of a radial-arm saw. You can also use flexible hose to connect the main line to your central collector if it's in a location that would be difficult to connect using rigid duct and fittings.

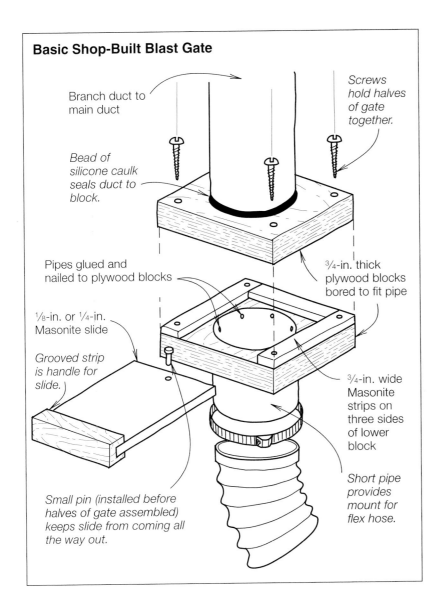

Basic Shop-Built Blast Gate

Branch duct to main duct

Screws hold halves of gate together.

Bead of silicone caulk seals duct to block.

Pipes glued and nailed to plywood blocks

¾-in. thick plywood blocks bored to fit pipe

⅛-in. or ¼-in. Masonite slide

Grooved strip is handle for slide.

¾-in. wide Masonite strips on three sides of lower block

Small pin (installed before halves of gate assembled) keeps slide from coming all the way out.

Short pipe provides mount for flex hose.

As with most things in life, with flexible hose you get what you pay for. The inexpensive flexible hose that's sold by many woodworking supply catalogs is very light duty, with thin plastic coverings that are easy to tear and don't hold up well to abrasion. Wood chips and abrasive particles shed during sanding operations create friction against the inside of the hose, and the debris can actually wear through a hose over time. The heavier-duty (and more expensive) types of flexible hose that are better for serious woodworking come with quite a number of different materials covering their steel-wire helix. Neoprene and thermoplastic rubber are both very durable and among the more popular flex-hose materials. For applications where the hose will be dragged back and forth or otherwise abused, you'll get better service life by buying rubber hose that has an external wearstrip (see the photo on p. 96). Polyethylene and PVC hoses, which come in clear material, are another affordable choice. Air Handling Systems offer a nice 2½-in. dia. PVC hose kit for a clean-up station (see the sidebar on p. 132). Although it's considerably more expensive (more than twice as much as rubber), elastomer-urethane hose has excellent abrasion resistance and is considerably lighter than rubber or neoprene hose. For hoses that require maximum flexibility (such as on panel saws and CNC routers), Hypalon hose is a good choice.

Most flexible hose can be cut to length easily using a razor knife to cut the material covering and a pair of diagonal cutters to slice through the wire helix. Once the wire is cut, carefully bend back about ¼ in. of the end to prevent a nasty puncture wound (I know from personal experience). The corrugated inside surface of twisting and turning flexible hose typically creates three times the friction of smooth-walled pipe, so keep flex-hose runs as short as possible (under 2½ ft.) to reduce static-pressure losses.

Grounding the ductwork

Proper grounding of the ductwork to stationary woodworking machines and to the central collector is necessary to discharge any static charge that may build up and cause fires or explosions. Just as important, metal pipe should be properly grounded to prevent serious shock from frayed or shorted electrical wiring.

One of the great advantages of installing sheet-metal ductwork is that it will conduct charges directly to the ground, as long as the machines and collector are grounded and there are no nonconductive components breaking continuity. Not all machines or collectors that have a ground lug on their electrical plug are properly grounded (electric ground at the motor may be insulated from the machine frame). Check ground by doing a continuity test using an electrical multimeter or continuity tester between the ground bar of your shop's breaker box (with the power switched off) and the frame of each machine, as well as the central collector. If the test doesn't show continuity, add a wire between the electrical ground wire and the machine's frame or sheet-metal housing. If there's still a problem, check the circuitry inside the breaker box to make sure all ground connections are in order (better yet, hire a licensed electrician to do it).

Nonconductive components, such as plastic or shop-built blast gates, flexible hose and plastic fittings in a machine's hood, can break continuity between ductwork and the ground. To restore the connection, run a short bridge wire between the machine (or collector) and the

Grounding a plastic-pipe system

If you have plastic-pipe dust collection ductwork in your shop, your best hedge against static-electricity problems is to ground the plastic pipe thoroughly. Grounding can be done by running a bare copper wire down the inside of each branch duct, as well as the main line, all the way back to the collector. Stranded wire has much better flexibility than solid wire; 14-ga. bare copper antenna wire (available at Radio Shack) is a good choice.

You can install ground wiring in a system where pipes can be disassembled by running wiring through each section of straight pipe separately. Thread the wire through small holes drilled near both ends of the pipe and stretch the wire tight. Leave the protruding wires long enough so that the ends can be twisted together and secured with insulated wire nuts after the pipe sections are joined or connected to fittings, as shown in the photo below.

In permanently installed plastic ductwork, you can run ground wire through the main duct by tying one end of the wire to a tennis ball and sucking it from the farthest branch back to the collector (with single-stage collectors, wrap some heavy mesh over the inlet to keep the ball from going into the fan).

To discharge static charges that may build up on the outside of the pipe (which attract dust to the surface of the plastic), wrap an additional wire tightly around the outside of each pipe as shown. Splice the ends to the inside wire at all fittings and to the ground at the machines and the collector. Seal all the holes drilled in the pipe with a dab of silicone caulk.

One final thing to consider: In larger systems or ones handling lots of abrasive particles, it's possible for the ground wire inside the pipe to be worn away, thus breaking contact with the ground. You may want to check your wiring for continuity every once in a while.

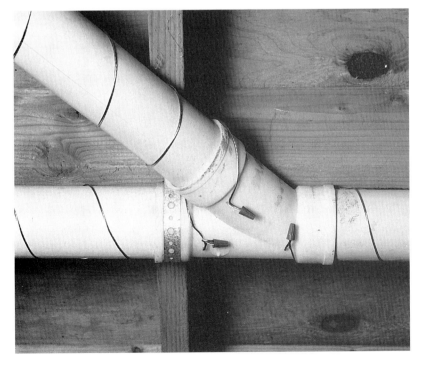

To prevent annoying and possibly dangerous static-electricity problems in plastic-pipe ductwork, run grounded bare copper wires through the inside of each pipe, wrapping the outside with bare wire as well. Use wire nuts to connect separate lengths.

metal branch duct (or the ground wire installed in plastic pipe). When using flex hose with a wire helix, scrape a little of the rubber or plastic covering off the inside to expose the wire so that it will make a ground connection when fastened to a metal blast gate and dust port or hood.

Testing and tuning the system

No matter how accurate your design calculations (see Chapter 7), the only way to evaluate a collection system is to fire it up and see how it performs. Just don't run your collector before your ductwork system is completely installed; running an unrestricted blower can quickly overwork the motor and even burn it out. For your first test, open up all blast gates, connect an ammeter (available from Radio Shack) to the power wires feeding the blower and flip the switch. The amperage read by the meter shouldn't exceed the motor's nameplate-rated amperage. If the amps drawn exceed the maximum, the motor could burn out if you happen to leave all or most of your blast gates open. To reduce the motor's workload (and amps drawn), decrease the airflow through the system by installing a reducer or partially closed blast gate at or near the blower inlet. Next, test each branch of the system by making a few test cuts at each machine. Watch for stray chips and plumes of dust thrown by the machine; these are signs that you may not have enough air moving through the branch serving the machine.

Calculating air velocity and volume

You can troubleshoot poor collection performance by measuring the air traveling through the duct with a manometer. As you'll recall, static pressure is measured in inches of water, and a basic manometer is nothing more than a U-shaped tube filled with water attached to an inch scale (see the photo at left). Air measurements are taken by connecting rubber hoses from the manometer to a device called a Pitot tube, which is inserted into an 1/8-in. hole drilled into the ductwork. Whenever possible, locate this hole at least 10 pipe diameters from the nearest transition (elbow, lateral tee, etc.). Insert the end of the Pitot tube into the hole far enough for the tip to be centered in the duct and pointing upwind (away from the collector). Take the measurement in a warm (70°F) shop; otherwise, use the conversion scale that comes with the Pitot tube (see Sources of Supply, pp. 194-195).

By connecting a single hose from the 90° leg of the Pitot tube to a single leg of the manometer, you can read static pressure directly; just add up the number of inches both above and below the zero mark on the scale. By connecting both tubes from the Pitot tube to both legs of the manometer, you can measure the velocity pressure inside the duct and use this measurement to determine air velocity (how fast the air is

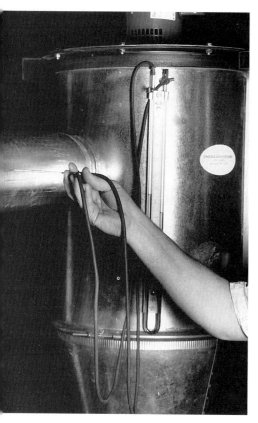

A tube-style manometer and Pitot tube can be used to check static pressure, air velocity and air volume moving through a duct. With the Pitot tube inserted into the duct through a small hole, fluid is displaced in the manometer tube, giving a reading on the scale.

traveling through the duct, in fpm) and air volume (how much air is flowing through the duct, in cfm). To determine air velocity, add together the number of inches above and below zero, then multiply the square root of this sum by 4005 (it's normal for the actual air velocity to range anywhere from 3,500 fpm to 4,500 fpm in branch ducts and 3,000 fpm to 4,000 fpm in a main duct). To get air volume, multiply air velocity by the square-foot area of the duct (sq.-ft. area = duct radius, in fraction of a foot, squared and multiplied by pi, 3.1416). For example, for a velocity-pressure reading of 0.9 in. in a 4-in. branch duct, you'd multiply the square root of 0.9 (which is 0.9486) by 4005, yielding an air velocity of 3799.14 fpm. For air volume, multiply 3799.14 by 0.087 (the sq.-ft. area of a 4-in. duct), to get 330.5 cfm.

Improving collection

If the air velocity and volume are fairly close to your design calculations yet chips still aren't collected efficiently, try redesigning the hood of the tool to contain and capture chips better (see Chapter 9). If air velocity and volume are lower than expected, first try disconnecting the hood from the branch to make sure that the hood itself isn't constricting the flow of air at the machine; redesign the hood as necessary. If collection remains poor even with a well-designed hood on the machine, you have several options for improving collection.

One option is to relocate the collector so that it's closer to the machines and dust sources. Alternatively, move the heaviest sawdust-producing machine (typically a planer, drum sander or large spindle shaper) to a branch that's closer to your central collector. Reducing the amount of ductwork between collector and machine reduces static-pressure losses—hence the better performance you'll get out of your collector. Performance will also improve if you make your duct runs straighter, since every twist and turn adds SP losses. A second option is to remove the machine with the poorest collection performance (probably the thickness planer) from the system and use a small dedicated collector to serve just that machine.

A third option is to increase the size of the central collector running the system (admittedly, not a welcome suggestion). Increasing collector size doesn't mean mounting a bigger motor on your existing blower housing. Since the motor turns at the same rate (probably 3,650 rpm), the fan will simply move the same amount of air as before and not improve things much. (On large belt-driven industrial systems blower output may be adjusted by changing fan speed with different-size pulleys. This adjustment isn't possible with a direct-drive blower, since most induction motors run at a fixed speed.)

You can, however, often squeeze higher performance out of your current collector. Here are two possibilities:

- You can improve the performance of most Asian-made single-stage collectors by retrofitting the blower's inlet plate and fan wheel, as shown in the photo below. A larger inlet plate allows the blower to

The performance of most single-stage collectors can be improved by retrofitting a few components. A new, dynamically balanced aluminum fan wheel, a larger-diameter inlet plate and oversized collection bags all work to allow the unit to move a larger volume of air with less resistance. (The old fan wheel and inlet plate are on the ground in front of the collector.)

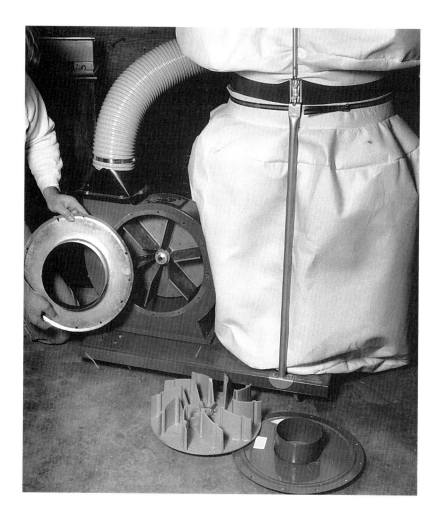

convey a larger volume of air, just like a bigger carburetor on an auto engine. And replacing a 10-in. fan wheel (found in some blowers) with a 12-in. aluminum wheel that has more paddle surface area also improves the air-moving capacity of the collector. (Inlet plates and fan wheels are available from Oneida; see Sources of Supply on pp. 194-195). One warning: Never run a retrofitted collector that's not connected to ductwork, since a totally unrestricted blower works harder and can burn out its motor (see p. 156).

- If your collector's filters are undersized (as filters in most single-stage collectors are), you can achieve modest gains by fitting larger dust bags, or adding a separate filter bag house (see pp. 117-119).

Future changes

You can always make future changes to a central collection system—it just takes more or less trouble, depending on the way you've laid out the ductwork. If you've planned ahead, your system will have the capacity for adding on extra branches to serve new machines. The easiest kind of change is adding on to the end of the main duct. If the last fitting on the main duct is a lateral tee or a tee-on-taper, simply remove the end cap and fit pipe to extend the main duct and add branches as needed. You can also add new branches without much fuss by using an ingenious add-on fitting called a 45° lateral saddle-tap tee (see Sources of Supply on pp. 194-195). The tee can be pop-riveted to the outside of an existing duct over a hole cut into the duct (see the photo below).

Adding new branches along the length of the main line is easily accomplished by cutting a hole into the main, and then pop-riveting a lateral saddle-tap tee fitting over the hole.

Switching a dust collector on and off

Once you have your system up and running, you can leave it on all the time, but you'll save lots of electricity by switching it off whenever it's not needed (and your shop will be quieter, too). The goal is to make the collector as easy as possible to switch on and off. Access is the key issue here, because you're less likely to use your collector if its switch is located across the shop from where you're working. There are at least half a dozen different switching methods that offer user convenience, including the simple mechanical pull cord and standard electrical switches as well as a bevy of remote-control and automatic electronic switching devices. The best method for you will depend on the size of your shop, the number of people that work in it and the size of your budget.

Pull-cord and paddle switch

One of the lowest-tech remote switches I've seen is based on the old-fashioned pull cords found in city buses and trolleys (where pulling a cord strung the length of the passenger compartment rang a bell or a buzzer to alert the driver that your stop was coming up). Employed in the shop, a pull cord can be used to activate a remote "paddle" switch (see the photo below) wired to the collector's motor, allowing you to turn it on or off from nearly anywhere in the shop.

A low-tech method for turning a collector on or off from anywhere in the shop is to build a paddle switch. Pulling on a cord routed around the shop presses the switch's hinged lever arm against an on/off switch, which is wired to control the collector.

Here's how the pull-cord system works: A cord is routed around the shop, threaded through a series of closed eyescrews driven into walls, ceilings and/or machine bases as necessary. Any strong cord will do (such as cotton or nylon mason's cord). Several cords can be connected to the cord that reaches the switch, so there's no limit to the number of machines the pull cord will control. The end of the cord farthest from the collector is anchored by a screw or tied to an eyescrew. The other end of the cord is attached to a plywood paddle (see the drawing below) hinged to one end of a metal electrical junction box (to give the pull action of the cord enough leverage to trigger the switch). The box houses a heavy-duty foot switch—the kind that pushes once for on, once for off. Pulling on the cord once turns the collector on; pulling again turns it off. If your collector has a 110-volt, 1-hp or 1½-hp motor, the switch can be wired to control the motor directly. For higher-horsepower and 220-volt motors, use the foot switch to control a relay (see pp. 163-164).

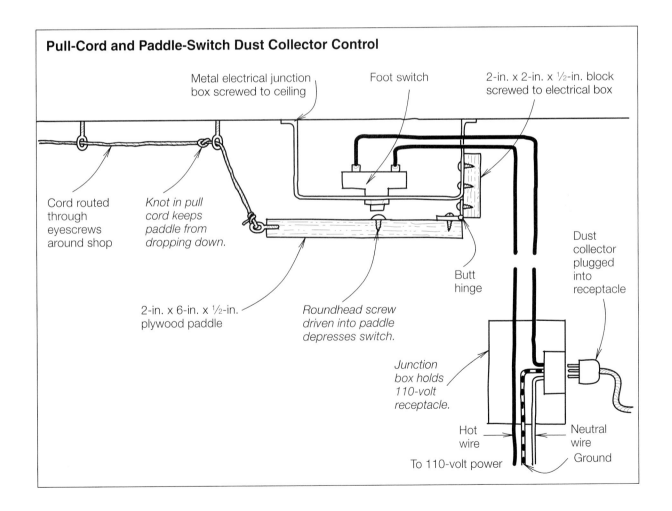

Pull-Cord and Paddle-Switch Dust Collector Control

Metal electrical junction box screwed to ceiling

Foot switch

2-in. x 2-in. x ½-in. block screwed to electrical box

Cord routed through eyescrews around shop

Knot in pull cord keeps paddle from dropping down.

2-in. x 6-in. x ½-in. plywood paddle

Roundhead screw driven into paddle depresses switch.

Butt hinge

Dust collector plugged into receptacle

Junction box holds 110-volt receptacle.

Hot wire

Neutral wire

Ground

To 110-volt power

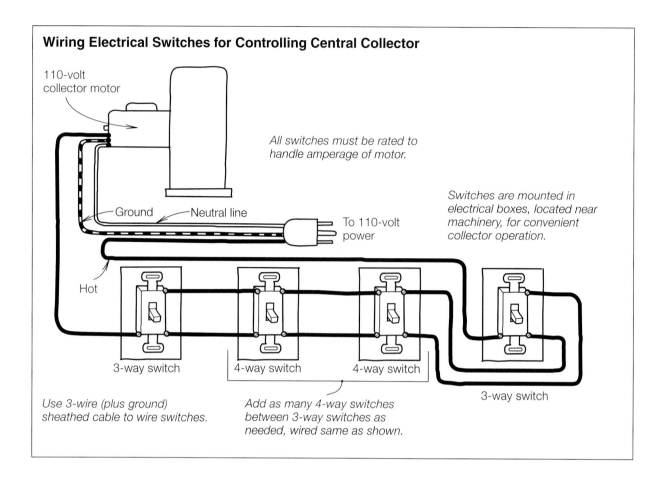

Wiring Electrical Switches for Controlling Central Collector

110-volt collector motor

All switches must be rated to handle amperage of motor.

Switches are mounted in electrical boxes, located near machinery, for convenient collector operation.

Ground — Neutral line

To 110-volt power

Hot

3-way switch

4-way switch

4-way switch

3-way switch

Use 3-wire (plus ground) sheathed cable to wire switches.

Add as many 4-way switches between 3-way switches as needed, wired same as shown.

Wiring multiple electrical switches

Another way to control your central collector from several different locations in the shop is to wire a series of three-way and four-way 110-volt electrical switches, as shown in the drawing above. For a 110-volt collector, the circuit is wired to control the current directly to the motor. For a 220-volt collector, the circuit can be wired to a relay that connects or disconnects power to the motor. The circuit is wired just as it would be to control a light, say in a stairwell in your home, from several locations. Any switch can be used to turn the collector on or off. So, for example, you can activate the collector from a switch near the table saw, then turn it off from a switch near the planer. You can wire practically any number of four-way switches in between the three-way switches at either end, as shown in the drawing.

While basic switch control of the collector is simple and thoroughly dependable, running sheathed cable is time-consuming and system components are expensive: A single four-way switch can cost $7 or more, and most switches are rated to handle only a 1-hp motor.

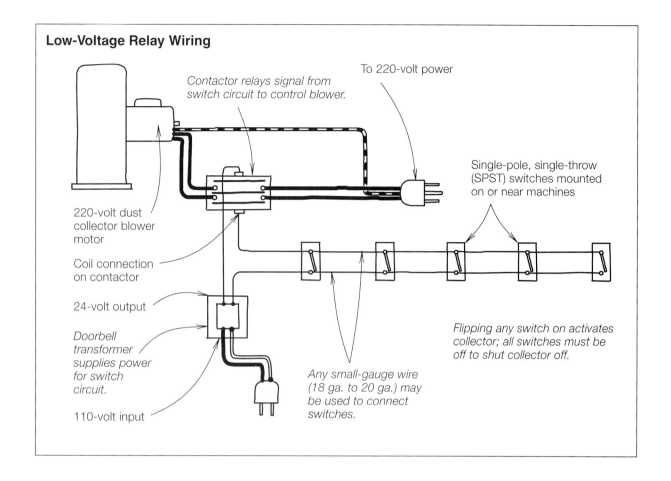

Low-Voltage Relay Wiring

Contactor relays signal from switch circuit to control blower.

To 220-volt power

Single-pole, single-throw (SPST) switches mounted on or near machines

220-volt dust collector blower motor

Coil connection on contactor

24-volt output

Doorbell transformer supplies power for switch circuit.

110-volt input

Flipping any switch on activates collector; all switches must be off to shut collector off.

Any small-gauge wire (18 ga. to 20 ga.) may be used to connect switches.

Low-voltage relay circuit

A popular—as well as cheaper and safer—version of the multiple-switch circuitry discussed on the facing page is to use a low-voltage transformer and wiring to relay the on or off signal to the collector's blower. In this system, a heavy-duty relay, called a contactor, is controlled by a series of switches mounted around the shop, as shown in the drawing above. Turning any switch on or off completes or interrupts the circuit to an electromagnet in the contactor, engaging or retracting one or two contact points that switch the blower motor on or off. A single-contact contactor is used to control a 110-volt motor; a two-contact unit (shown) is required for a 220-volt motor.

Choose a contactor with a 24-volt AC coil and use a 24-volt household doorbell transformer to power it (available at most hardware stores or from Grainger; #3A356). Because there's virtually no electrical-shock or fire hazard from low-voltage AC electricity, relay-switch wiring can be done with inexpensive 18-ga. lamp cord (or even 20-ga. speaker wire). The wire is run around the shop and held in place with staples.

For switches, you can use any basic single-pole, single-throw (SPST) switches you choose: regular household light switches, or SPST toggle switches (such as Radio Shack #275-602). You can mount switches in surface-mounted electrical boxes or plastic electronic project boxes (available from Radio Shack). For greatest convenience, locate the switches close to each machine's starter switch.

The downside of a relay system is that while any switch will turn the system on, you must use the same switch to turn the collector off again. This might get confusing if you're going between two or three machines at a time. To reduce confusion—and make switching on the collector easier—many woodworkers choose to incorporate low-voltage switches directly into the blast gates.

Switches built-into blast gates

As long as you have to open and close blast gates when you turn on machines anyway, the gates might as well do double duty. Relay-controlling switches can be built into commercial or custom blast gates, as shown in the photo below. Furniture maker Roger Heitzman

A low-voltage relay system is easier to use if you build switches directly into blast gates. The handle of the sliding gate presses against a microswitch screwed to the gate's frame, turning the collector on or off whenever the gate is opened or closed.

screwed a low-voltage microswitch (available from Radio Shack; part #275-017) to the frame of each of his custom-made blast gates. The handle of the gate bears against the head of the switch: Push the gate all the way closed, and the switch is off; pull the gate open, and the switch turns the collector on. The switches are wired just as they are shown in the relay-circuit drawing on p. 163. Wires can be run right along the ductwork and held in place with self-locking plastic ties.

As with a regular low-voltage relay system, you must turn the collector off by closing the same blast gate you opened in the first place. You can open other gates, and use other machines in the process, but you'll still have to close all the gates to switch the collector off. If your system is fitted with a strong blower that allows you to collect from several machines at one time, you can mount separate toggle switches for machines that don't have blast gates.

Wireless remote control

A very convenient collector control that's extremely easy to install uses wireless remote-control technology. Simple systems such as the X-10 (from Radio Shack) or the Long Ranger (see Sources of Supply on pp. 194-195) work by using a battery-powered radio-frequency remote sender to transmit a signal to a receiver module. Unlike when using infrared television remote controls, you don't have to be in sight of the receiver module to activate it. All the remotes I've tried have a long enough range for even the biggest shop. The module, designed to plug into a wall receptacle, has a relay in it that switches electricity on or off to the blower motor.

Remote-control modules are designed to handle only so much electrical current, so there's a limit to the size of the motor they'll work with. Further, most remote modules are 110 volts. You can switch a dust collector with a 220-volt blower on and off using Long Ranger's 220-volt module, or you can use a regular 110-volt X-10 remote-control module. Run the X-10's output to the coil of a contactor. The contactor must have a 110-volt coil and two contacts to connect/disconnect power to both hot leads to the 220-volt motor.

To keep your remote handy, try clipping it to your shop apron or work coveralls. If you don't wear special work duds, you might try attaching your remote to the end of the pull chain on a Janitor's key

Controlling a central collector with an electronic remote control allows you to turn the collector on and off from anywhere in the shop. Keep the small remote handy by attaching it to the chain on a Janitor's-style key reel clipped to your belt.

reel (which hooks on a belt or waistband), as shown in the photo at left. Using a reel also helps prevent the remote from being dropped, which at best diminishes reliability.

Automatic dust collector control switches

What could be slicker than switching your central collector on and off automatically? Like the smaller-capacity models designed to work with portable power tools and shop vacuums (see pp. 85-86), automatic control switches sense current from machines connected to them. When the machine is turned on or off, the automatic switch turns the dust collector on or off as well. The big advantage of these systems is that you don't have to remember to switch the collector on and off; just turn on the machine (and open a blast gate, as necessary) and you're in business.

There are several different brands of automatic control switches on the market, which differ in the way they connect to your shop's wiring. The R.F. St. Louis Associates DC2400 is wired directly into the circuits that feed your machinery. A built-in delay switches the blower on just after the machine. This feature is very important (especially if your shop has poor current-handling capacity), because the current load of both collector and machine motors starting simultaneously is likely to overload the wiring and trip the circuit breakers. The DC2400 can discriminate circuits that feed tools and machines not on the collection system, and not switch the collector on when those tools are operated. It also works with circuits running 110-volt and 220-volt machines, although you need to install one unit per number of machines that you run simultaneously.

The Teckaid automatic switch, shown in the photo on the facing page, uses a special sensor that mounts inside your shop's breaker box. A hot wire from each circuit that powers machines served by dust collection is simply routed through the coil of the sensor; it is not direct-wired to the auto switch itself. The sensor detects current when a machine is switched on or off and sends a signal to the unit's main circuit board and contactor, which are both housed in a metal box mounted near the breaker box.

Even if you use an electronic switching system as the primary control for your dust collection system, it's a good idea to install a simple backup system (such as regular electrical switches, described on p. 162). Electronic devices are much more complex—and therefore, more subject to failure—than simpler switching schemes, which will keep your collector up and running if the gremlins invade your high-tech controller.

The Teckaid automatic switch uses a small pickup (the light-colored object in the lower right corner of the breaker panel) that can sense flowing current. When a machine is switched on, the sensor sends a signal to the main unit (housed in the box next to the breaker box) to turn the dust collector on.

CHAPTER 9

Collection Hoods and Other Devices

Just because you've installed a perfectly designed ductwork system fed by a gargantuan dust collector, there's no guarantee that your shop will stay clean—you've got to get the dust into the system in the first place. Effective dust collection begins with good collection hoods that provide ample airflow and direct it to capture the maximum amount of particles at their source. Woodworking machines with well-engineered ports are easy to connect to a collection system; other sources of woodshop sawdust aren't as easy to handle. Older machines and portable power tools, such as orbital sanders and routers, often don't have built-in collection ports or, if they do, they are poorly designed or too small for good collection performance. Even hand operations, such as shaping a chair's arms with a rasp or smoothing a panel with a sanding block, can raise significant amounts of dust that are a problem to capture.

But there are solutions for all these situations: well-designed custom hoods that ensure efficient collection from stationary machinery; shop-built devices for capturing dust produced by portable power tools that lack built-in collection; and sanding tables, booths and hoods that arrest fine dust generated by hand sanding before it escapes into the air. The time taken to implement these solutions is but a fraction of the time it takes to install your central dust collection system. But when you consider how much better your system will operate with them, it's certainly time well spent.

Fitting each machine on a central collection system with a well-designed dust hood is the first step to efficient capture of chips and sawdust. The built-in chip chute on a jointer can be used as an effective hood by enclosing it and fitting it with a port for attaching a flexible hose.

Hoods for stationary machines

Many stationary machines already have built-in dust collection ports (sometimes called "outlet collars"); all you have to do is attach a flexible hose from your branch duct, and you're in business. Unfortunately, the ports found on most light-duty and home-shop machines are designed to accept 2½-in. diameter vacuum hoses. These small ports severely limit the air volume that's needed for effective collection from these tools (see the chart on pp. 136-137). For much better performance, it's best to adapt such ports to accept a 3-in. or 4-in. hose. If the port is in a sheet-metal panel or housing, you can use a nibbler tool (available from a hardware store or electronics supply house) to enlarge the opening. A flange-type pipe fitting (called an angle ring or starter ring) can then be screwed or pop-riveted in place (see the photo below). If fitting an angle ring is inconvenient or impossible, the next best thing to do is to fit a reducer as close to the tool as possible; the reducer steps the size of the hose or duct down to suit the port. Using a reducer is preferable to running a smaller-diameter branch duct to the tool, which would result in reduced airflow with much higher friction losses.

Newer machines that don't come with built-in dust ports often have optional hoods that you can buy from the manufacturer (for example, Delta offers an extensive line of hoods for their machines). However,

An angle-ring fitting pop-riveted over a hole cut into a flat metal surface, such as the lower blade enclosure on this bandsaw, provides a dust collection port and a convenient hose mount.

if you have an older machine that doesn't have a hood (or you can't modify a machine's existing hood to suit your needs), you'll have to design and build a custom hood. In many cases you don't need to start completely from scratch: There are many different sheet-metal HVAC components and heating-pipe fittings, such as vent-stack roof flashing, reducers, tapers and transition fittings (rectangular-to-round), that can be adapted with a little trimming and bending to serve as dust collection hoods on a wide variety of woodworking machines. Even plastic sewer-pipe fittings can be used in making custom hoods—just be sure to run a bridge wire to ground the machine to the branch duct that's serving it (see the section on grounding ducts on pp. 154-156).

Making a custom hood

Unfortunately, machines with unenclosed bases (such as older table saws) and machines that have working parts that require clearance or access for adjustment (such as bandsaws) can be hard to fit using standard hoods and fittings. In such cases, you must build a custom hood from scratch, using thin sheet metal, aluminum or plywood. But before you start building, it's a good idea to make a trial hood from corrugated cardboard or foamcore board (available from an art-supply store) fastened together with masking tape; the tape allows you to disassemble components and recut them as necessary. (You can also use tape to secure the hood to the end of a flexible hose for testing.)

To optimize airflow into the collection system, a hood should enclose the area around the cutting tool and keep chips from escaping. But be careful not to overdo it. It's a common mistake to make a custom-built hood so airtight that it starves the air flowing into the collection system; you can't capture and convey chips when you've cut your air velocity and volume down significantly. The idea is to let air flow into the hood at locations that best encourage the capture of chips and dust. For example, in the drawing on p. 172, allowing air to enter the front edge of the hood (past the infeed roller and cutterhead) encourages airflow to capture chips thrown up by the cutterhead and move them toward the hood's outlet. If you're uncertain whether a hood is starving a branch of full airflow, check the velocity and compute volume using a manometer (see pp. 156-157).

Larger chips and shavings produced by machines such as planers and spindle shapers can take a tremendous amount of airflow to capture. These large bits of wood weigh enough to develop a surprising amount of momentum (which you already know if you've been hit in the face by chips hurled by a whirring blade or cutter). Unless the

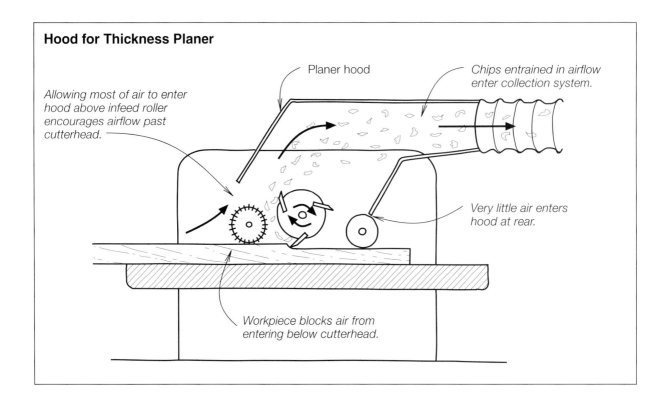

Hood for Thickness Planer

Planer hood

Chips entrained in airflow enter collection system.

Allowing most of air to enter hood above infeed roller encourages airflow past cutterhead.

Very little air enters hood at rear.

Workpiece blocks air from entering below cutterhead.

chips are thrown directly into the hood, it's very difficult for even a powerful stream of air to capture them. Therefore, whenever possible, take advantage of the propellant force with which chips are hurled. Carefully observe the direction in which they are thrown (better yet, have a shopmate cut a scrap workpiece while you just watch). Then try to design and position your hood to deflect or direct chips so they travel with the flow of air into the collection system.

Before testing your trial hood, take a minute to clean up the area around the machine. Start the collector, take a few cuts and see how much dust ends up on the machine or the floor; the amount of dust should give you a pretty good idea of how well your hood is performing. Before final approval, make sure that the hood isn't mounted too close to any moving parts (blades, bits, etc.) and that it doesn't interfere with adjustments, such as blade tilt and elevation.

Building the hood When you've come up with a hood design that seems to work well, you can use the cardboard or foamcore pieces as a pattern to make a permanent hood from sheet metal, Masonite or thin plywood. Because it's easy to work with, I like to use aluminum roof flashing (available from a hardware or building supply store) and pop-rivet the parts together (see the discussion of pop riveting on p. 150). An easy way to add a round port for connecting a duct or flex hose is to use an angle ring or a universal mounting strip (also called a "catcher strip"; see Sources of Supply on pp. 194-195). This sheet-metal strip, which has a 4-in., 5-in. or 6-in. round outlet, can be screwed or pop-riveted to any shopmade hood. Alternatively, you can take just about any round sheet-metal fitting (such as an elbow or a connector) and make it into a flex-hose connector by making short ($\frac{1}{2}$-in. to $\frac{3}{4}$-in.) slits into the end about $\frac{3}{4}$ in. apart, and then bending the resulting strips so that they bend out. Slip the fitting through a hole in your custom hood and pop-rivet the strips to the hood. Use silicone caulk or duct tape to seal up any gaps that leak air. The flex hose from the ductwork can be attached to this fitting—or any other duct port—with one or two adjustable hose clamps.

On tools that require access to cutterheads, blades or bits for change-overs or adjustments (planers, bandsaws, shapers), it's best to make the hood easily detachable (see the photo on p. 181). On machines where the hood is mounted out of the way, you can attach it permanently with pop rivets or even glue (silicone caulk is great, since it's both an adhesive and a sealer).

Adding a second pickup

With many machines, dust collection from a single port or hood just isn't enough to capture and convey all the dust and chips the tool produces. Some machines, such as stroke sanders or multiple-drum thicknessing sanders, may need additional ports or hoods simply because dust must be picked up at different locations on the machine. Other machines, such as radial-arm saws, bandsaws and table saws, may benefit from a second pickup (at the blade housing or above the table) to enhance collection performance.

The trick to connecting more than one pickup to the branch duct that serves a machine is to balance the airflow from the two sources. If you don't, you'll end up with one pickup getting the lion's share of the airflow and the other pickup doing practically nothing. The secret to well-balanced airflow is to make sure that the volume of air coming from the two pickups is about equal to (or slightly less than) the volume of air traveling through the branch duct (see the table on p. 174). For example, a radial-arm saw with a 4-in. duct conveying 350 cfm

AIR VOLUME RELATIVE TO HOSE/DUCT DIAMETER

Hose/duct diameter	Cfm at 4,000 fpm
1½ in.	50 cfm
2 in.	85 cfm
2½ in.	135 cfm
3 in.	195 cfm
4 in.	350 cfm
5 in.	545 cfm
6 in.	785 cfm
7 in.	1070 cfm
8 in.	1400 cfm

from the main hood and a 2½-in. hose adding about 135 cfm from the blade-guard pickup needs a 5-in. branch duct that will deliver 545 cfm (at 4,000 fpm). The hose from the second pickup should join the branch at a 45° tee-on-taper, as shown in the drawing on the facing page. You have to remember that small-diameter hoses (under 2½ in.) are going to draw only 50 cfm to 135 cfm at best, so in situations where an existing branch duct is not large enough to serve two pickups, it's better just to eliminate the second pickup and concentrate collection at the main hood. Large horizontal or stroke sanders should have two hoods (one at each end roller) and should be connected to the main branch with hoses fed from a wye branch. Fitting a blast gate on both legs of the wye will allow you to regulate the air flowing to each pickup, so you can balance it for best performance.

Balancing Airflow on Machines with Two Dust Pickups

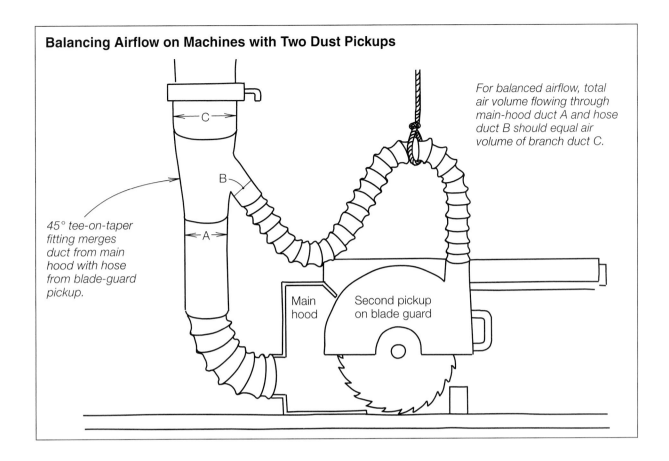

For balanced airflow, total air volume flowing through main-hood duct A and hose duct B should equal air volume of branch duct C.

45° tee-on-taper fitting merges duct from main hood with hose from blade-guard pickup.

Main hood

Second pickup on blade guard

Hoods for common woodshop machines

In the next few pages I offer some design suggestions for dust collection hoods to serve most of the machines commonly found in woodshops.

Table saw Many of the larger table saws (Delta Unisaw, Powermatic 66, etc.) have an enclosed base with a built-in 4-in. or 5-in. dust port and cleanout door. Connecting to one of these saws can do a pretty good job, provided that the system moves an adequate volume of air (350 cfm to 500 cfm is recommended). On open-based saws, such as most contractor-type saws, no dust hookup is provided and you must make a custom hood. Many woodworkers choose simply to enclose the base of such saws by mounting panels of sheet metal, Masonite or thin plywood to the sides and bottom of the saw, and install a port on the underside. The difficulty with this arrangement is sealing the back of the saw, where the motor assembly protrudes and moves when tilted for bevel cuts.

A better approach is to build a hood that partially surrounds the blade, so that sawdust is captured as close to the source as possible. This arrangement not only reduces the amount of chips that is recut by the blade (thus dulling teeth more quickly), but also captures dust before it can clog the saw's adjustment mechanisms. The challenge is to shroud the blade without interfering with the blade-raising and -tilting mechanisms. I built the sheet-metal hood, shown in the photo below, for my Delta 10-in. Bench Top saw and attached it to the trunnion itself, so it tilts with the mechanism when setting the blade for bevel cuts. The bottom of the hood has a 4-in. angle-ring fitting, which provides connection for a flexible hose. A curved slot in one side of the hood provides clearance for the saw arbor so the blade can be raised and lowered. The width of the guard allows clearance for blade changes and the use of a dado set or molding head.

When a saw's chip collection is poor (especially during heavy cuts, as when using a dado blade), many woodworkers will seal up as many points of air entry on the hood or saw cabinet as possible, even covering up the curved bevel tilt slot on the front with a magnetic strip or tape. Unfortunately, sealing up the saw often has the reverse effect of what's desirable: Airflow can become so constricted that collection almost ceases. Very little air gets through the blade slot in the throat plate—even less when you use a close-fitting plate and the workpiece covers up any remaining clearance between the slot and the blade. To

A shop-built sheet-metal hood fastened to the trunnion assembly provides effective dust collection for a table saw that doesn't have an enclosed base. The hood tilts with the trunnion, for bevel cuts.

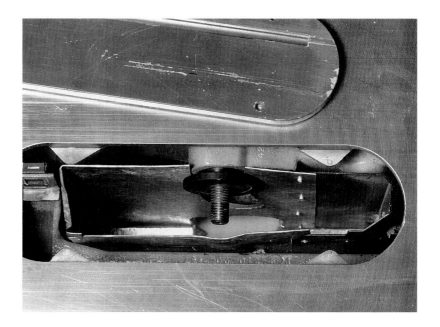

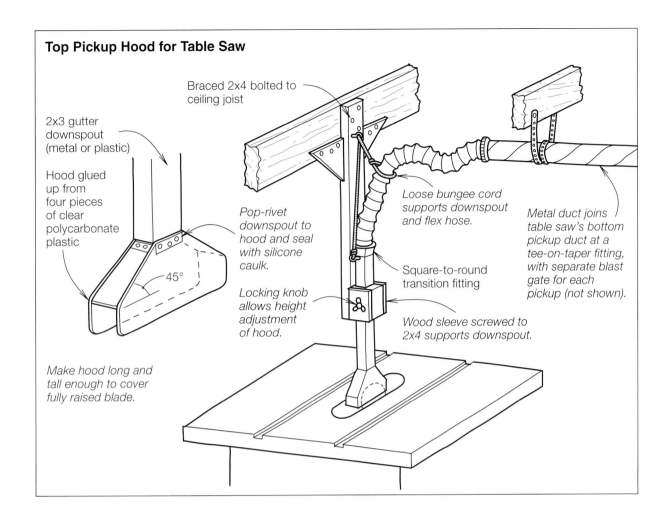

Top Pickup Hood for Table Saw

Braced 2x4 bolted to ceiling joist

2x3 gutter downspout (metal or plastic)

Hood glued up from four pieces of clear polycarbonate plastic

Pop-rivet downspout to hood and seal with silicone caulk.

45°

Locking knob allows height adjustment of hood.

Loose bungee cord supports downspout and flex hose.

Metal duct joins table saw's bottom pickup duct at a tee-on-taper fitting, with separate blast gate for each pickup (not shown).

Square-to-round transition fitting

Wood sleeve screwed to 2x4 supports downspout.

Make hood long and tall enough to cover fully raised blade.

avoid air starvation, leave an air gap between the hood and the table. On my hood, I left a slit to the left of the blade open, to allow air to enter the hood and maintain good air volume.

Even with a pretty strong airflow through the lower hood, a table-saw blade is likely to spew a plume of dust out the top of the table. An easy way to reduce the amount of chips thrown up behind the blade is to seal up any open space at the back end of the throat-plate slot with a piece of duct tape. A more effective method is to install a top pickup (though this won't work if you use a power feeder). Some aftermarket guards, such as the Excalibur Overarm Bladecover, come with a built-in pick-up hose; on other guards, such as the Biesemeyer BladeGuard, the hose is optional. You can also build your own combination blade guard/top pickup, as shown in the drawing above. It uses a short length of rectangular gutter downspout connected to a length of 2½-in. or 3-in. flex hose. The ceiling-mounted guard/top pickup raises or lowers to adjust to the thickness of the work. It also removes easily to allow cutting of tenons or finger joints. The top pickup should also have its own blast gate, so you can shut it off when you use the saw without the guard. As discussed on p. 174, the ducts from the top pickup and bottom hood should converge at a 45° tee-on-taper for better airflow to both pickups.

Radial-arm saw and miter saw The most effective hood arrangement for a radial-arm saw is a hood mounted directly behind the blade, which is where the majority of chips are thrown during crosscutting. A tall, narrow sheet-metal or thin-plywood hood with side shrouds that extend to just behind the fence is best. On saws that have a dust-ported blade guard, it's customary to add a second pickup by running a 1½-in. to 2-in. dia. flexible hose from the port to a 45° tee-on-taper just above the hood (see the photo below). This setup improves collec-

Running a flexible hose from a tee-on-taper fitting on the end of the branch duct to the ported blade guard on a radial-arm saw can improve dust pickup.

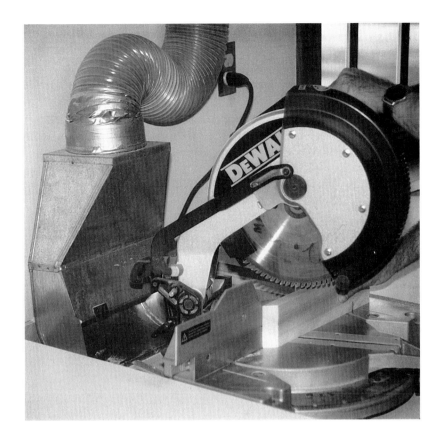

A sheet-metal venturi-box hood located behind the pivoting arm of a bench-mounted miter saw collects chips thrown back by the blade.

tion when the saw head is all the way out on the radial arm at the end of a cut (farthest from the main hood) and when the arm is adjusted left or right for a miter cut. Using a correctly sized tee-on-taper fitting ensures that the flow will be balanced (see the drawing on p. 175). The hose should be long enough to reach out to the farthest point on the arm; use a long bungee cord to suspend the hose and keep it from fouling.

Most miter saws ("chop boxes") and sliding-compound miter saws already have a built-in port for a dust bag, but these ports (typically 1¼ in. dia.) are more suitable for collection by a shop vacuum than a central collection system. It's difficult to add a collection hood to a saw and still keep it portable (I know of only one portable saw, the AEG SKS 300, that has a built-in 4-in. port). But if your miter saw is mounted permanently (or semi-permanently) to a benchtop, you can add a boxlike main hood directly behind the saw's line of cut, similar to the main hood used with a radial-arm saw. To improve the chip capture strength of this kind of hood, you can build a sheet-metal venturi box like the one shown in the photo above. The pinched waist of this box creates the venturi effect, increasing the speed of air at the constriction and the effective pull of the vacuum from the central collector.

Jointer The jointer is one of the easier machines to fit with dust collection. Closed-base jointers usually have a built-in chip chute that can be enclosed and fitted with a simple rectangular-to-round HVAC hood (pop-riveted directly over the end of the chute opening). Most other jointers I've seen have an opening directly under the cutterhead, which makes it easy to mount a hood to pull chips from underneath (see the photo on p. 169). A rectangular-to-round hood (which should be as wide as the opening below the cutterhead) can be screwed to the underside of the jointer's body casting or over a cutout in the base the jointer itself is mounted to.

When a hood is sealed too tightly against the base of the jointer, the collection system's high-speed airflow passes directly through the whirring cutterhead; it can sound as though you have an F-14 taxiing through your shop! To reduce the noise level, simply remount the hood to draw air in from the sides of the cutterhead, or add slots or holes in the hood, which should reduce the amount of air whizzing through the cutterhead without adversely affecting good chip collection.

Thickness planer Many of the newer small planers come with a dust port either built into the housing or on a separate hood offered as an optional bolt-on accessory. Unfortunately, most small (10-in. and 12-in.) planers come with dust hoods that have undersized ports, clearly designed to be connected to a shop vacuum, not a central collection system. For decent performance, I suggest you enlarge these ports to 4 in., although this may prove to be more of a hassle than simply constructing an entirely new hood.

Building a hood for most new planers (or older models) usually isn't too much trouble. An effective hood can be adapted from an existing HVAC hood, or built from scratch from sheet metal or plywood. (I've even seen one very serviceable hood that was built from corrugated cardboard glued and taped together, then coated with polyurethane finish!) One important consideration is to make the hood easy to remove, in order to facilitate quick blade inspections and changes (see the photo on the facing page).

Because the planer produces a considerable volume of large-sized chips and shavings (which require lots of air to capture and convey), it's especially important to make sure that you don't starve the hood of air. Don't bother sealing up the underside of the planer (in the area of the feed rollers and cutterhead); wide boards sent through the planer usually do this anyway. When in doubt, check the air velocity and volume (as described on pp. 156-157). If you need to incorporate extra air entry slots to increase air volume through the hood, try to locate them on the side of the hood opposite the hose port to encourage the flow of air past the cutterhead (see p. 171).

A sheet-metal hood on the thickness planer fitted around the cutterhead is a must for clean planing operations. Mounting the hood with easily accessible screws or bolts makes for quick removal for faster blade changes.

Bandsaw The ideal location for the main dust pickup on a bandsaw is directly below the point where the blade passes through the table. Unfortunately, the blade guides, table trunnions and wheel housings get in the way of installing a hood there. Also, you need to make the hood removable so that you can adjust the guides or tilt the table without a lot of fuss. I built a small hood for my 15-in. General bandsaw by adding a three-sided, ¼-in. plywood box to a 3-in. PVC downspout adapter (a rectangular-to-round fitting). A 3-in. flex hose fastens over the fitting's round end. I cut away one side of the fitting's rectangular part and hot-glued the plywood sides in place, so that they enclose the entire area around the lower blade guides (see the photo at right on p. 182). The back end of the hood is left open, so that air is drawn past the blade for better sawdust removal. To increase airflow into the hood, you can drill half a dozen or so ¼-in. holes through the small throat-plate insert that fits into the table around the blade (not all saws have these).

Enclosing the area directly under the blade is the most effective way to capture dust from a bandsaw. This hood on the author's bandsaw removes quickly for adjustment and blade changes.

Collecting fine dust from arbor-mounted wheels and drums is efficient and versatile using a dust nozzle mounted to a freestanding base.

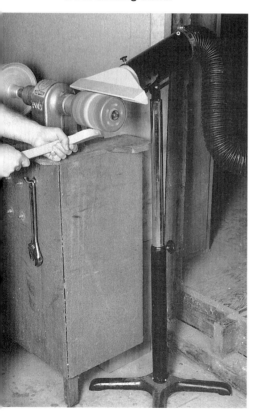

If you use wide, skip-toothed blades with deep gullets (popular for resawing), you're likely to get an accumulation of dust and chips in the saw's lower wheel housing. Adding a second pickup in the form of a dust port in the lower part of the sealed wheel housing should take care of the problem (provided your system has a large enough branch duct to handle the airflow from the dual pickup; see pp. 174-175). Many saws have thin sheet metal doors, which are easy to cut a hole into using a drill and a hand nibbling tool; you can then pop-rivet an angle ring over the hole (as shown in the photo on p. 170). Connecting this port to a tee-on-taper via a flexible hose allows the door to be opened easily.

Stationary sanders Hood designs and setups for stationary sanders are as varied as the sanders themselves. Drum- and wide-belt-type thicknessing sanders usually come with built-in ports, because thorough dust removal is very important for these machines to operate without their abrasives clogging and burning the wood. Some machines, such as the single- and dual-drum sanders by Performax, come with two equal-sized dust ports for more thorough collection along their wide drums. For best performance, run two flexible hoses to these ports from a wye fitting on the end of the branch. For balanced pickup, make both hoses the same length, or crush the leg of the wye feeding the shorter hose to restrict its airflow slightly to match the higher-friction loss in the longer hose.

Disc sanders and combination disc/vertical-belt sanders also usually come with built-in ports, although on less expensive DIY units these ports are undersized. If you find the need to add a different or additional hood on these machines, design it to surround part of the disc or drive roller and locate the port nearest the point where dust is thrown by the sander. Arbor-mounted flap sanding wheels, grinding wheels or pneumatic sanding drums can be enclosed by a hood; alternatively, for working flexibility, a dust nozzle attached to a separate stand can be positioned close to the wheel or drum to catch the dust as it's thrown off (see the photo at left on the facing page).

Horizontal belt sanders typically come with a single ported hood at the "head" (covering the drive roller). Large horizontal belt and stroke sanders often have a second hood at the "tail" end (covering the idler roller). The second pickup is useful, since dust is more likely to be thrown from the belt as it passes around a roller (centrifugal force throws the particles off as they round the corner). Size the duct fittings and hoses to direct 75% of the air to the head and 25% to the tail pickup. If your sander doesn't have a tail hood, you'll catch more dust by adding a second pickup underneath the table. This narrow hood captures dust from the gap between the table and the belt. I made the one shown in the photo below from a 3-in. HVAC taper fitting. The

Dust collection from a horizontal belt sander can be improved by augmenting the machine's stock head hood with a second pickup hood underneath the belt. The narrow hood is mounted to suck dust from the gap between the table and the belt.

long open edge of the hood is only ¼ in. wide, to allow positioning it between the table and the belt. To allow the sander's table to be tilted, the hood is removable, mounted with a pair of screws to the lower inside edge of the table. If you use your sander's tail roller for sanding concave curves, use a dust nozzle (see the photo on p. 182) to catch dust as it comes off the roller.

Stripper jets for belt sanders

One of the difficulties in capturing fine dust from a sanding belt is that the dust doesn't always release readily from the abrasive; static electricity can charge particles and temporarily bond them to the belt. The result is excessive loading of the abrasive, which can burn the wood and reduce the life of the belt. An effective way to get dust off the abrasive is to employ a "push-pull" system: A jet of air blows particles off (the push), so that the collection system can suck them up (the pull).

A stripper jet, such as the one shown in the drawing at right, consists of a series of thin tubes (enough to cover the width of the belt) that blow jets of compressed air against the surface of the spinning belt. The tubes are mounted on a head, which is placed just outside the sander's main hood, with the tubes angled to blow air against the direction of the belt and toward the hood.

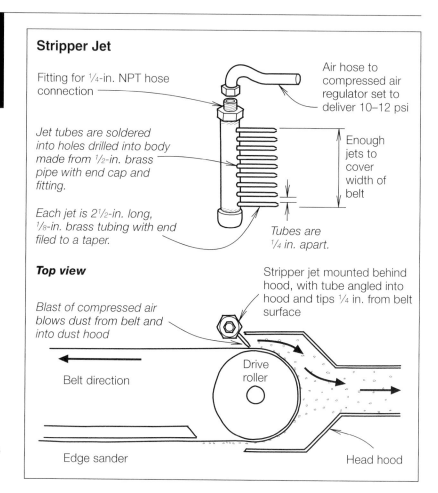

Stripper Jet

Fitting for ¼-in. NPT hose connection

Air hose to compressed air regulator set to deliver 10–12 psi

Jet tubes are soldered into holes drilled into body made from ½-in. brass pipe with end cap and fitting.

Enough jets to cover width of belt

Each jet is 2½-in. long, ⅛-in. brass tubing with end filed to a taper.

Tubes are ¼ in. apart.

Top view

Stripper jet mounted behind hood, with tube angled into hood and tips ¼ in. from belt surface

Blast of compressed air blows dust from belt and into dust hood

Belt direction

Drive roller

Edge sander

Head hood

While few such heads are in use in small shops (and industrial stripper jets are expensive), a simple jet shouldn't be too hard to make, and the technique certainly seems worth experi-menting with. I'm currently experimenting with using stripper jets to improve dust and chip collection from bitted and bladed machines, such as the shaper and table saw.

Shaper and router table Because of the wide range of cutters they handle—from small veining bits to gigantic raised-panel cutters—shapers and router tables are some of the more difficult machines to collect sawdust from effectively. Most stock shaper and router-table fences incorporate a hood and/or dust port on the back side of the fence, directly behind the cutterhead. But a single rear-mounted hood has a hard time containing large chips that are thrown radially by a large cutter. Adding a second pickup is usually not practical, since it will interfere with lumber handling (as well as prevent mounting a power feeder).

One way to improve large-chip capture is to deflect chips so that they can be captured by the fence hood, and yet not seal off the flow of air around the cutter/workpiece (which starves the system of air and reduces collection efficiency). One way to do this is to mount featherboards around the cutter opening in the fence (see the photo below). Air flows between the fingers, while the featherboard also serves to hold the workpiece down during the cut—and to keep your fingers out of harm's way. If featherboards won't work, use a chip deflector made from an old wallpaper brush or a cheap, wide paintbrush, mounted so that it will cover the largest gap between the workpiece, the cutter and the fence.

A pair of polyethylene plastic featherboards attached to the fence and table on a router table deflect chips into the dust port opening and serve to guide the workpiece.

Most router-powered joinery machines (such as the JDS Multirouter or the Wirth machine) don't have built-in dust ports, which makes collection difficult. One arrangement is to enclose the entire router inside a hood made from a length of 8-in. or 10-in. dia. pipe with a reducer on the end (see the photo below). Use tin snips to trim the hood to clear the router's handles or protruding parts of the joinery machine. You might also have to enlarge the throat opening on the machine or drill holes through it, to allow more air to flow into the hood.

Wood lathe As with other dust collection situations, the best way to deal with shavings and dust created on a wood lathe is to pick them up as close as possible to the point where they are first created. Wood-turner and air-handling specialist Peter Fedrigon uses a simple nozzle

Capturing chips produced by a router-powered joinery machine can be accomplished by enclosing the entire router inside a hood made from HVAC pipe and a reducer fitting. Slots cut into the hood provide clearance for handles, cords and other protrusions.

Chips are captured as they come off the turning tool with a simple nozzle-style hood, made from an HVAC elbow. To allow rapid repositioning, a bungee cord holds the hood to the tool rest or lathe bed.

on the end of a flex hose (see the photo above). The nozzle is positioned directly underneath the tool rest, to catch shavings as they come off the turning (or dust when power-sanding a turning). Secured with a bungee cord, the hood is easy to reposition or remove to vacuum shavings out of the inside of closed vessels, such as deep bowls and vases.

If you plan to turn materials that are either toxic (such as asbestos-laden soapstone or fossilized ivory) or that commonly cause allergic reactions, as exotic rain-forest species often do, you might work best using a dust box, such as the one shown in the drawing on p. 188. This special ventilation hood completely encloses a small bowl or other turning chucked in the lathe.

Built from plywood like a five-sided box, the hood is mounted to the lathe bed beneath the tool-rest post. It has a slotted hole for the chuck and two slotted ports that provide access for turning tools. A clear polycarbonate plastic top provides a good view of the work and is

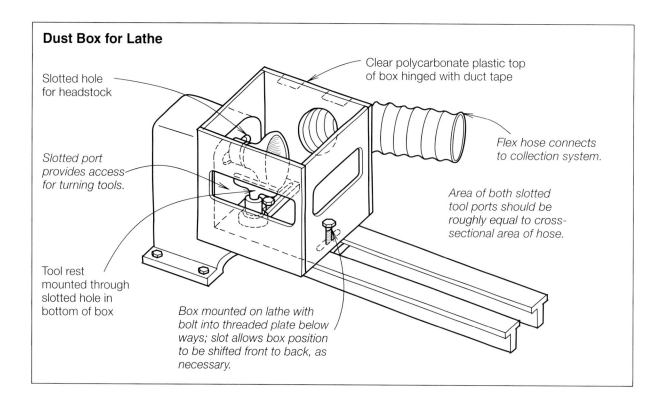

Dust Box for Lathe

Slotted hole for headstock

Slotted port provides access for turning tools.

Tool rest mounted through slotted hole in bottom of box

Box mounted on lathe with bolt into threaded plate below ways; slot allows box position to be shifted front to back, as necessary.

Clear polycarbonate plastic top of box hinged with duct tape

Flex hose connects to collection system.

Area of both slotted tool ports should be roughly equal to cross-sectional area of hose.

hinged for access to the work and for tool-rest adjustments. A flexible hose connects at the rear of the hood, and draws air through the slotted turning-tool ports, which are sized roughly to equal the cross-sectional area of the hose.

Drill press Because such a wide variety of bits and setups are used with a drill press (or a vertical mill-drill), in most cases it's best not to create a permanent hood for this tool. The most versatile arrangement is a flexible hose with a small nozzle or flanged hood (similar to the one shown in the photo on p. 187) that can be positioned wherever required for a particular operation. Mounting the nozzle on the end of a long gooseneck (available from a lamp shop) allows you to position the nozzle wherever it's needed. By making the hose easily detachable from the hood, you can use the hose to clean up around the drill press after the job is done.

Capturing sawdust from portable tools

As with stationary machines, the best means of collection from portable power tools that have built-in dust ports (such as belt sanders and plate joiners) is to connect them to primary collection. But because the ports on these tools are so small—typically between ¾ in. and

1¼ in. dia.—running a single tool's skinny hose off a 3-in. or 4-in. dia. branch line is quite a bit of overkill. If you have several portable tools you'd like to have hooked up all the time, you could add a small manifold to the end of a branch and connect hoses for all the tools (see the drawing on p. 97). The total cross-sectional area of these hoses should roughly equal the cross-sectional area of the branch line. But for more casual use with a tool or two at a time, it usually makes more sense to collect dust from portable tools with a shop vacuum (see pp. 84-86).

Collecting sawdust from tools that lack built-in collection ports, such as most routers, laminate trimmers and electric drills, is a problem. With its high speed and large bits that hurl chips in every direction, the router is particularly troublesome. You can improve capture of a router's chip output by making a custom subbase that has a built-in collection hood and hose port (although this method works only for edge-shaping and kerf-cutting operations). The hood, shown in the drawing below, can be sawn from a single block of 3-in. thick wood with a 2¼-in. hole bored into it, glued and screwed to a ¼-in. Masonite subbase plate. An ⅛-in. Masonite bottom cover directs more suction around the bit. The hood takes a standard 2½-in. shop-vacuum hose that connects to a 3-in. branch duct, or to your portable vacuum.

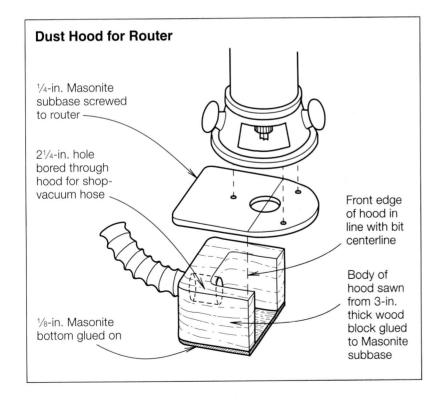

Dust Hood for Router

¼-in. Masonite subbase screwed to router

2¼-in. hole bored through hood for shop-vacuum hose

⅛-in. Masonite bottom glued on

Front edge of hood in line with bit centerline

Body of hood sawn from 3-in. thick wood block glued to Masonite subbase

Rotary tools such as right-angle grinders and die grinders don't lend themselves to fitted custom hoods—the hoods tend to get in the way. But you can catch most of the chips these tools produce by using either a portable dust nozzle or a flanged hood. A portable nozzle, such as the one shown in the photo at left on p. 182, mounts on a stand that allows adjustment for height and position. A portable flanged hood, such as the one shown in the photo on p. 193, can be set on top of a workbench, on the floor or on the workpiece itself. A 3-in. or 4-in. flexible hose connects either device to your central collection system (a convenient hookup is at one of the clean-up stations I recommend you install in your shop; see p. 132). To get the best chip capture from a portable nozzle or flanged hood, try to position the workpiece as close as possible to the air intake. Also, work with the tool so that the dust plume thrown off the cutting or abrasive tool travels toward the air intake.

Adding dust collection to jigs

Often you'll get better dust collection performance by building a hood directly into a jig or fixture used with a machine or portable power tool. For example, I have a biscuit-joinery jig that I use on a router table that has a small housing directly behind the kerf-cutting bit. The housing provides a place to mount a flexible hose and attach a clear Lexan chip deflector, both for safety and for better dust capture. For more ideas on adding dust collection to jigs, see Chapter 8 of my book *Woodshop Jigs & Fixtures* (The Taunton Press, 1994.)

Capturing fine sanding dust

Very fine wood dust particles generated during sanding operations are much easier to capture than sawdust and larger chips. (They're easier to capture because they stay aloft longer—the "drop rate" of a 5-micron particle is 6 ft. per 30 min., whereas a 100-micron particle drops at 16 in. per second!) A stream of collection air need only be moving at the relatively slow speed of between 200 fpm and 500 fpm to capture fine dust particles. You can take advantage of this fact to collect a great amount of the sanding dust created by portable power tools that lack or have poor built-in dust collection, or to capture the dust created by hand sanding. The high volume of air generated by even a small central collection system is enough to collect sanding dust near its source (before it has a chance to waft away into the furthest reaches of your shop) when connected to a sanding table, booth or portable dust hood.

A 4-in. flexible hose connects Penn State's benchtop sanding table to a central dust collection system. The downdrafting air pulls fine dust created by hand or machine sanding down through a porous padded mat and perforated top, away from the woodworker.

Downdraft sanding table

Essentially just a hollow box with a slotted or perforated top connected to a source of vacuum, a downdraft sanding table pulls dust down and away from parts that are sanded on top of it. Large commercial sanding tables are available that connect to a central collection system or have their own built-in fans and filters. For the small shop, you can purchase an inexpensive unit, such as Penn State's benchtop sanding table shown in the photo above.

You can also build your own sanding table, such as the one shown in the drawing on p. 192. This slat-topped table operates optimally with 750 cfm of air and can be used on a benchtop or mounted on its own stand. You can make the top any size, as long as you maintain at least 200 cfm of air per square foot of table area (cover any unused part of the top to improve collection). The baffles on three sides of the table not only help to contain dust thrown out by portable power tools, such as random-orbit sanders and belt sanders, but also help contain the flow of air to keep fine particles from escaping. By adding larger

Sanding Table

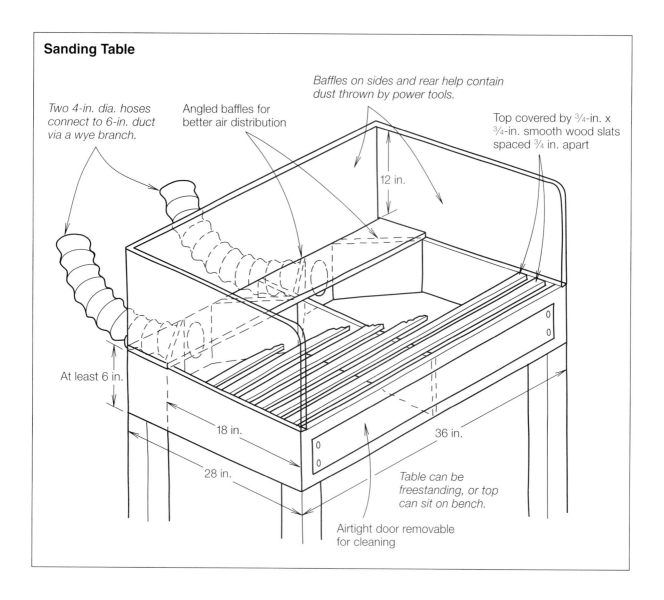

Two 4-in. dia. hoses connect to 6-in. duct via a wye branch.

Angled baffles for better air distribution

Baffles on sides and rear help contain dust thrown by power tools.

Top covered by ¾-in. x ¾-in. smooth wood slats spaced ¾ in. apart

12 in.

At least 6 in.

18 in.

28 in.

36 in.

Table can be freestanding, or top can sit on bench.

Airtight door removable for cleaning

baffles and a top, you can create a small sanding booth that will increase the speed of the airflow coming into the open side, to contain and capture dust even more efficiently.

Sanding tables are terrific for sanding small parts, because air flowing around the parts pulls dust down and away from you. They don't do so well though when you are sanding large flat boards or panels. Dust tends to stay on the horizontal surface because the air flowing into the table mainly draws in dust nearest the edges of the surface. Sanding tables are also limited in that you can't sand large assembled casework or furniture on top of them. In these cases, it's better to use a sander with built-in collection (see pp. 84-86), or use a portable flanged hood.

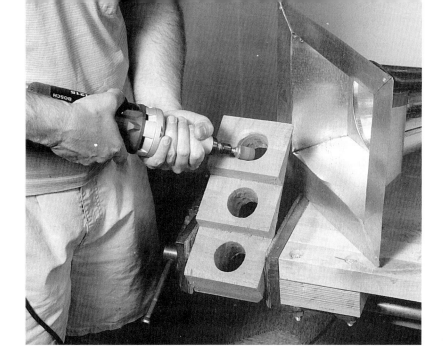

Dust and chips created by free-hand sanding or grinding operations can be captured if you work close to a flanged hood. The hood here was made from a 4-in. roof jack.

Portable flanged hoods

A quick and versatile way to bring fine-dust collection to a benchtop or other work area is with a portable hood: Any kind of round or rectangular sheet-metal or plywood hood will work, as long as it draws at least 250 cfm. You'll get the best performance by adding a flange at least 2 in. wide to the outside edge of the hood. The flange reduces the air drawn from behind the duct, thus reducing entry loss (the energy it takes for air to enter an opening) and increasing pickup efficiency. You can buy a ready-made flanged hood or make one yourself: I made the hood shown in the photo above from a 4-in. roof jack (used for flashing a vent pipe that comes through a roof) that I cut, bent and pop-riveted to shape.

The most important thing to remember when using a portable flanged hood is to set it as close as possible to the source of dust. The farther that dust particles are from the intake, the less likely they'll be captured. Air velocity decreases in proportion to the square of the distance to the hood opening. In practical terms, this means that to maintain a capture velocity of 200 fpm (the minimum air speed for catching fine dust) when sanding a workpiece 2 ft. from the hood intake will require 16 times the cfm that it takes at only 6 in.! On the benchtop, place the hood directly in front of where you're working. If you're using a belt sander or rotary grinder, position the hood in the path of dust thrown by the tool. When sanding a freestanding carcase or furniture piece, attach the hood to a stand (as with the dust nozzle, discussed on p. 183) and position it as close as possible to the area you're sanding. Remember, the more effort you take to capture dust as it is created, the less dust will end up in the air, and in your lungs.

SOURCES OF SUPPLY

The following source listings are intended to help you locate many special and hard-to-find items used for dust control and collection that are discussed throughout the book. I've also included addresses and phone numbers for numerous mail-order suppliers, dealers and manufacturers of dust control and collection machinery and components. These listings are by no means complete. They were compiled in Spring 1996 and are subject to change.

*I*tems cited in the text

Air-filtration device (AFD) kits
Eagle America, WoodsmithShop

Angle ring (starter ring)
Air Handling Systems

Blower inlet plate (replacement)
Oneida Air Systems

Contactors (relays for remote collector switching)
W.W. Grainger

Crimping tool (for ductwork)
Woodworker's Supply

Dust preseparator canister lid
Grizzly Imports, Penn State Industries, Trend-lines, Woodworker's Supply

Electronic dust collector switches
Doughty Electronic Systems, Oneida Air Systems, Penn State Industries, Radio Shack (contact your local store), R.F. St. Louis Associates (manufacturer), Teckaid (manufacturer), Woodcraft, Woodworker's Supply

Fan wheel (cast aluminum, replacement)
Oneida Air Systems

Filter bags, filter media
CS&S Filtration, Midwesco Filter Resources, Oneida Air Systems, P & S Filtration, Snow Filtration

Filter bags (replacement, for single-stage collectors)
Oneida Air Systems

Filters (replacement, for AFDs)
W.W. Grainger

Flexible hose
Air Handling Systems, Dayco (manufacturer), Oneida Air Systems

HEPA-rated disposable masks
Lab Safety Supply, Racal Health & Safety (manufacturer)

HVAC pipe and fittings
Arrowsmith & Lang-Borne, Oneida Air Systems, Woodworker's Supply

Lateral saddle-tap tee fitting
Air Handling Systems, Murphy-Rodgers

Magnehelic gauges, manometers, Pitot tubes
Oneida Air Systems, W.W. Grainger

Mask case
Lab Safety Supply

Plenum box, shaker box (sheet metal)
Oneida Air Systems

Quick-disconnect fittings (for portable collectors)
Air Handling Systems

Remote-control dust collector switches
Oneida Air Systems, Penn State Industries (Long Ranger switches), Radio Shack (contact your local store), Woodcraft (Long Ranger switches)

Respirator disinfectant
Lab Safety Supply

Respirator test kit
Lab Safety Supply

Shop-vacuum muffler
Beam Industries

Smoke stick
Lab Safety Supply

Squirrel-cage blowers
W.W. Grainger

Timers (for AFDs)
Total Shop (manufacturer), W.W. Grainger

Universal mounting strip (catcher strip)
Murphy-Rodgers, Woodworker's Supply

*D*ust control and collection components

Air-filtration devices (AFDs)
Aercology (manufacturer), Air Cleaning Specialists (manufacturer), Airflow Systems (manufacturer), Hartville Tool, JDS (manufacturer), Penn State Industries, Total Shop (manufacturer), Trend-lines, Woodcraft

Central dust collectors, blowers and cyclones
Cincinnati Fan & Ventilator, Delta Machinery, Dust Boy, Electra-Bekum USA, Grizzly Imports, Holz Machinery, Jet Equipment and Tools, Lobo Power Tools, Makita USA, Murphy-Rodgers, Oneida Air Systems, Penn State Industries, Rees-Memphis, Shopsmith, Sunhill Machinery, Torit Division (Donaldson Co.), Trend-lines (Reliant), Wilke Machinery (Bridge-wood), Woodcraft, Woodmaster Tools, Woodworker's Supply (Woodtek)

Ductwork, pipe fittings and accessories
Air Handling Systems, Arrowsmith & Lang-Borne, Murphy-Rodgers, Oneida Air Systems, Penn State Industries, Trend-lines, Woodworker's Supply

Dust masks, respirators and air helmets
Airstream, Lab Safety Supply, Racal Health & Safety (manufacturer), 3M (manufacturer)

Shop vacuums and accessories
Bosch Power Tools, Delta Machinery, Eureka, Fein Power Tools, Jet Equipment and Tools, Makita USA, Milwaukee Electric Tool, Porter-Cable, Royal Dirt Devil, Ryobi America, Sears (contact your local store), Shop-Vac, Wap Cleaning Systems

*S*uppliers and manufacturers

Aercology (manufacturer)
Custom Drive
Old Saybrook, CT 06475
(203) 399-7941

Air Cleaning Specialists (manufacturer)
180 El Camino Real
Millbrae, CA 94030
(800) 633-4007

Airflow Systems (manufacturer)
PO Box 743366
Dallas, TX 75374
(214) 272-3003

Air Handling Systems
5 Lunar Drive
Woodbridge, CT 06525
(800) 367-3828
(203) 389-9595

Airstream
Highway 54 South
PO Box 975
Elbow Lake, MN 56531
(800) 328-1792

Arrowsmith & Lang-Borne
PO Box 126
Lumberport, WV 26386
(304) 584-4246

Beam Industries
1700 W. Second St.
Webster City, IA 50595
(515) 832-4620

Bosch Power Tools
100 Bosch Blvd.
New Bern, NC 28562-6997
(800) 334-5730 (customer service)

Cincinnati Fan & Ventilator
7697 Snider Road
Mason, OH 45040
(513) 573-0612

CS&S Filtration
2901 Long St.
PO Box 2400
Chattanooga, TN 37409
(423) 756-7067

Dayco (manufacturer)
1 Prestige Place
PO Box 1004
Dayton, OH 45401
(513) 226-4665

Delta Machinery
Machinery Division/Dust collection
246 Alpha Drive
Pittsburgh, PA 15238
(412) 963-2400

Doughty Electronic Systems
23 Arnold Drive
Texarkana, AR 75502
(501) 772-5849

Dust Boy
10002 North Hogan Rd.
Aurora, IN 47001
(800) 232-3878

Eagle America
PO Box 1099
Chardon, OH 44024
(800) 872-2511

Electra-Bekum USA
401-403 Kennedy Blvd.
Somerdale, NJ 08083
(800) 223-8600
(609) 784-8600

Eureka
2003 108th St.
Suite 301
Dallas, TX 75050
(800) 282-2886 (customer service)

Fein Power Tools
3019 West Carson St.
Pittsburgh, PA 15204
(412) 331-2325

Grizzly Imports
PO Box 2069
Bellingham, WA 98227
(800) 523-4777 (east)
(800) 541-5537 (west)

Hartville Tool
940 W. Maple St.
Hartville, OH 44632
(800) 345-2396

Holz Machinery
45 Halladay St.
Jersey City, NY 07304
(201) 433-3800

JDS (manufacturer)
800 Dutch Square Blvd. Suite 200
Columbia, SC 29210
(800) 382-2637

Jet Equipment and Tools
PO Box 1477
Tacoma, WA 98401
(800) 274-6848

Lab Safety Supply
PO Box 1368
Janesville, WI 53547
(800) 356-0783
(800) 356-2501 (safety/technical
information)

Lobo Power Tools
9034 Bermudez St.
Pico Rivera, CA 90660
(213) 949-3747

Makita USA
12950 E. Aldondra Blvd.
Cerritos, CA 95701
(714) 522-8088

Midwesco Filter Resources
400 Battaile Drive
Winchester, VA 22601
(800) 336-7300

Milwaukee Electric Tool
13135 West Lisbon Road
Brookfield, WI 53005
(414) 781-3600

Murphy-Rodgers
2301 Belgrave Ave.
Huntington Park, CA 90225
(213) 587-4118

Oneida Air Systems
1005 West Fayette St.
Syracuse, NY 13204
(315) 476-5151

P & S Filtration
4563 Jordan Rd.
Skaneateles Falls, NY 13153
(315) 685-3466

Penn State Industries
2850 Comly Rd.
Philadelphia, PA 19154
(800) 377-7297

Porter-Cable
P.O. Box 2468
Jackson, TN 38304-2468
(901) 668-8600
(519) 836-2840 (Canada)

**Racal Health & Safety
(manufacturer)**
7305 Executive Way
Frederick, MD 21701-8368
(800) 682-9500
(301) 695-8200

Rees-Memphis
2426 Channel Ave.
PO Box 13225
Memphis, TN 38113
(901) 774-8830

**R.F. St. Louis Associates
(manufacturer)**
12 Cove Rd.
Branchville, NJ 07826
(800) 526-0602

Royal Dirt Devil
650 Alpha Drive
Cleveland, OH 44143
(800) 321-1134

Ryobi America
5201 Pearman Dairy Rd.
P.O. Box 1207
Anderson, SC 29622
(800) 323-4615

Shopsmith
3931 Image Drive
Dayton, OH 45414
(800) 543-7586

Shop-Vac
2323 Reach Rd.
Williamsport, PA 17701
(717) 326-0502

Snow Filtration
4902-T Spring Grove Ave.
Cincinnati, OH 45232
(513) 777-6200

Sunhill Machinery
500 Andover Park East
Seattle, WA 98188
(206) 575-4131

Teckaid (manufacturer)
157 Via Bellaria
Palm Beach, FL 33480
(407) 844-6578

**3M Corporation (OH&ES
Division)**
3M Center, Bldg. 260-3A-07
St. Paul, MN 55144-1000
(800) 364-3577 (product
information)

Torit Division (Donaldson Co.)
PO Box 1299
Minneapolis, MN 55440
(800) 365-1331

Total Shop (manufacturer)
PO Box 25429
Greenville, SC 29616
(800) 845-9356

Trend-lines
135 American Legion Hwy.
Revere, MA 02151
(617) 853-0900
(800) 767-9999 (orders)
(800) 877-7899 (customer service)

Wap Cleaning Systems
170 E. Freedom Ave.
Anaheim, CA 92801
(800) 237-2368

Wilke Machinery
3230 Susquehanna Trail, North
York, PA 17402
(717) 764-5000
(800) 235-2100

Woodcraft
210 Wood County Industrial Park
PO Box 1686
Parkersburg, WV 26102
(800) 225-1153

Woodmaster Tools
2908 Oak St.
Kansas City, MO 64108
(816) 756-2195
(800) 821-6651

WoodsmithShop
2200 Grand Ave.
Des Moines, IA 50312
(800) 444-7002

**Woodworker's Supply
(Woodtek collectors)**
5604 Alameda Place, NE
Albuquerque, NM 87113
(800) 645-9292

**W.W. Grainger (wholesale
distributor)**
333 Knightsbridge Parkway
Lincolnshire, IL 60069
(708) 913-7400 (technical support)

INDEX

Editor: PETER CHAPMAN

Production Editor: DIANE SINITSKY

Layout Artist: LYNNE PHILLIPS

Illustrator: ORIGINAL DRAWINGS BY LORANT NAGYSZALANCZY,
COMPUTER-RENDERED BY SCOTT BRICHER

Photographer: SANDOR NAGYSZALANCZY

Typeface: GARAMOND

Printer: QUEBECOR PRINTING/HAWKINS, NEW CANTON, TENNESSEE